The Nature of an Ancient Maya City

CAE

CARIBBEAN ARCHAEOLOGY AND ETHNOHISTORY

L. Antonio Curet, Series Editor

The Nature of an Ancient Maya City

Resources, Interaction, and Power at Blue Creek, Belize

Thomas H. Guderjan

THE UNIVERSITY OF ALABAMA PRESS

Tuscaloosa

Typeface: Minion

∞

The paper on which this book is printed meets the minimum requirements of American National Standard for Information Sciences-Permanence of Paper for Printed Library Materials, ANSI Z39.48-1984.

Library of Congress Cataloging-in-Publication Data

Guderjan, Thomas H.
The nature of an ancient Maya city : resources, interaction, and power at Blue Creek, Belize / Thomas H. Guderjan.
p. cm. — (Caribbean archaeology and ethnohistory)
Includes bibliographical references and index.
ISBN-13: 978-0-8173-1565-8 (cloth : alk. paper)
ISBN-10: 0-8173-1565-9 (alk. paper)
ISBN-13: 978-0-8173-5426-8 (pbk. : alk. paper)
ISBN-10: 0-8173-5426-3 (alk. paper)
1. Blue Creek Ruin (Belize) 2. Mayas—Urban residence—Hondo River Region (Guatemala, Mexico, and Belize) 3. Mayas—Hondo River Region (Guatemala, Mexico, and Belize)—Antiquities. 4. Maya architecture—Hondo River Region (Guatemala, Mexico, and Belize) 5. Excavations (Archaeology)—Hondo River Region (Guatemala, Mexico, and Belize) 6. Hondo River Region (Guatemala, Mexico, and Belize) I. Title.
F1435.1.B6G83 2007
972.82′1—dc22

2007015863

Contents

Illustrations

Figures

Tables

Acknowledgments

This book is only a partial outcome of many years of fieldwork, and there are vastly too many people who deserve thanks for their efforts at Blue Creek for me to scratch the surface. Since 1992, more than a thousand students and volunteers have participated in our program. Project staff members alone number in the dozens. However, there are some very special people who have contributed to this work.

The Maya Research Program board members have worked behind the scenes, never getting the credit they deserve for all of their efforts. Past and present MRP board members who have made special contributions include Dr. Grace Bascopé, Bill Collins, Kim Cox, Merri-jo Hillaker, Gene Hogan, Marion Lee, George Marra, Father Charles Miller, Keith Peacock, Jerry Reed, Ambassador Eugene Scassa, and Dee Smith.

Staff members who have led fieldwork and completed major reports or graduate work on the project include Dr. Jeff Baker, Dr. Jason Barrett, David Driver, Jerry Ek, Antoine Giacometti, Dr. Helen Haines, Colleen Hanratty, Bob Lichtenstein, Colleen Popson, and Tim Preston. Other colleagues who have aided our work include Mark Aldenderfer, Tim Beach, Sheryl Luzzadder-Beach, Steve Bozarth, David Freidel, Jim Garber, David Glassman, Nikolai Grube, Laura Kosakowsky, Gene Lené, Holly Moyes, Kent Reilly, Bob Ricklis, and Norbert Stanchley. Luis Jaime Castillo provided a safe haven in Chepen, Peru, where a large part of this volume was written.

Funding for this project has been provided by the following organizations: The Ahau Foundation (to Jon Lohse and Laura Kosakowsky), American Philosophical Society (to Steve Bozarth), The Arnold Foundation, The Denver Foundation, Estate of Mamie Lambert, Foundation for the Advancement of Mesoamerican Studies, Goldsbury Foundation, Mallory Investments, National Geographic Society (to Tim and Sheryl Beach), National Science Foundation (to Jeff Baker), San Antonio Area Foundation, Sigma Xi (to Jeff Baker), Texas Christian University (Research and Creative Activities Fund), and a number of individuals who prefer to be anonymous.

Many thanks go to the project staff members who contributed to the illustrations in this volume. They include Marc Wolfe (Figure 1.4), Mike Lindeman (Figure 1.5), Jason Barrett (Figure 1.6), Bill Collins (Figures 2.4, 2.7, 2.8, 2.10, 2.13, 4.5, and 4.6), Jo Mincher (Figure 2.11), Helen Haines (Figure 2.12), Bob Lichtenstein (Figure 2.15), Joe Brown (Figure 3.6), Colleen Hanratty (Figures 4.3 and 4.4), Bill

Bowman (Figure 6.1), and Lori Diel (Figure 4.7). Kustom Graphics, Fort Worth, Texas, produced Figures 1.1, 2.1, 2.3, 2.5, 2.6, 2.9, 2.14, 3.1, 3.2, 3.4, 3.5, 3.6, 3.7, 4.1, 4.4, and 5.1. Sheridan Productions of Fort Worth produced Figures 2.12 and 4.7.

This project would not be possible without the active support and enthusiasm of the contemporary community of Blue Creek (thanks, Marge!) and the Institute of Archaeology of the National Institute of Culture and History of Belize. We owe much to both of these groups of people. Special thanks go to Marion Lee, Alex Pastrana, John Ruff, Bill and Connie Welker, and my wife, Colleen Hanratty.

The Nature of an Ancient Maya City

1 Introduction

The primary purpose of this book is to examine the spatial and structural organization of the ancient Maya city of Blue Creek in northwestern Belize. These are archaeologically observable variables that directly reflect the nature of power, legitimacy, and authority. Other questions of importance include, What were the economic resources of the city? Who controlled them? How did the persons in power interact with each other and with other cities? While there is debate about whether ancient Maya communities were cities or not, I take the position that we cannot impose models of urbanism developed elsewhere onto the Maya.[1] Instead, to understand Maya cities, it is necessary to create models of them in their own terms. In other words, the semantic wall created by the "cities or not" debate does little to enhance our understanding of ancient Maya life. Whether we call them "cities" is less important than whether we can understand what Maya life was about.

Another goal of this volume is to introduce the reader to the archaeology of Blue Creek, a Maya community that existed for two millennia. Over time, it became an economic and political center of some 15–20 thousand people. Since 1992, Blue Creek has been the focus of a multidisciplinary, multinational research effort. This research has created new insights into the Blue Creek Maya and the ancient Maya in general. However, many new questions have been raised and remain unanswered. This is, of course, the nature of archaeological research and all scientific inquiry. Therefore, I hope that Blue Creek as a case study provides the reader with a better understanding of what we know and what we do not about this fascinating part of humanity's past.

Finally, this is a case study of the complexity of large-scale archaeological research. How archaeologists come to know about the past is often an obtuse process, unlike that in most sciences. Further, understanding this process has become a justifiable obsession of many scholars in the field. Some of our best-known scholars are not known for their "great discoveries" but for their contributions to our methodologies.[2] Most fieldworkers are like myself—we focus on understanding the past but are still deeply concerned with the approaches taken to research. Typically, we express this concern in a research design written prior to undertaking fieldwork. As years go by, especially in large-scale field projects, research designs tend to change and grow with our knowledge about our subject. So, this book is also an appraisal of more than a decade of research design change and growth as each year's fieldwork caused our perceptions to change.[3]

Most books on archaeological projects are written after the completion of the fieldwork. In this case, that is not so. The Blue Creek project is designed to incorporate 20 years or more of intensive study of a single part of the Maya area in northwestern Belize. I directed the project for its first decade (1992–2001) and Jon Lohse succeeded me from 2002 to 2005. During these years the project took a regional approach, leaving most additional work at Blue Creek to me when I returned in 2006. During my second directorship, my colleagues and I will be addressing very different questions than we did in the first decade. This book documents some of the first decade of fieldwork and brings its disparate parts together into one integrated whole.

While doing these things, I make the assumption that the reader already has a familiarity with the subject. It is not within the scope of this book to introduce a new reader to the fundamentals of Maya archaeology. At the same time, I did not attempt to write this book at a level only understandable to scholars who specialize in Maya studies; that role is for articles in scholarly journals. So, I hope to walk the line between these two positions in a way that will make our work understandable to the nonprofessional and meaningful to the professional.

The Role of Research Designs

Going about the business of archaeology requires much more than just going out and digging. Where one excavates is a function of what one wants to know. Part of the creative process is to ask a question of the archaeological record, then to determine how to best collect data to address the question. Research designs are simply another way of stating the purposes of fieldwork. Research designs keep us focused on our goals and explain the process of understanding the past that we intend to use. Then, research designs give us baselines to compare what we did with what we intended to do. In the case of the Blue Creek project, our research design has been a constantly dynamic document that changed with what we learned and with what we realized we could learn from the site. However, as the project evolved there came to be a single central theme to our research.

The Blue Creek project was designed with the intent that it would be an integrated study of the dynamic structure and functional interrelationships among the parts of a single Maya city. Just what was a Maya city? How did its constituent parts interact? How did it change through time? We have been only partly successful at answering these questions. While this is an inherent part of archaeological research, I am constantly impressed with the level of success in understanding Blue Creek that we have achieved.

Like all other people, archaeologists bring the baggage of their own background when initiating any field research. This can be seen as an individual's intellectual capital that has accumulated over years of being a student, researcher, teacher, or whatever the individual's professional and personal background may be. Our theoretical interests, those of our mentors, and our own experiences shape our research. So, knowing something of my background may be useful for the reader as it may help explain some of the rationale for how the Blue Creek project developed.

While in graduate school at Southern Methodist University, planning doctoral work on Paleo-Indians in the southern United States, I was diverted for a semester by David Freidel to assist in the final season of fieldwork at the site of Cerros. Cerros lies on Corozal Bay on the Caribbean coast of Belize and was a Late Preclassic period trade port. While at Cerros, I was involved in conversations regarding how ancient Maya trade could be studied on Ambergris Caye.[4] Ambergris Caye is actually a peninsula that protects Chetumal and Corozal bays from the open Caribbean. Not long afterward, I discarded my plans regarding the Paleo-Indians and initiated a research project on Ambergris. My colleagues Jim Garber and David Glassman at Southwest Texas State University (now Texas State University) and Herman Smith at the Corpus Christi (Texas) Museum and I spent three summers (1986–1988) excavating small sites on Ambergris Caye, learning about patterns of Classic period Maya coastal trade.

After that experience, having become a Mayanist by a circuitous route, I wanted to gain experience working with the large-scale centers of the interior rather than have my experience just be limited to the small-scale sites of the coast. That opportunity presented itself when Barry Bowen, a Belizean businessman, offered the opportunity to visit his "farm," which actually consisted of nearly a million acres of forested land. As our relationship developed, I received a Fulbright Fellowship to map and study the many Maya centers on the property and spent most of 1990 undertaking this survey.[5] By then, the property had been divided into several sections, including Barry's Gallon Jug Ranch, Yalbac Ranch, the Programme for Belize's Río Bravo Conservation Area, and a large tract purchased by Coca-Cola. I worked in these areas and the area north of the Río Bravo Conservation Area owned by the somewhat isolated Mennonite community of Blue Creek.

By the end of 1990, I had experience on the coast and surveying large sites in the forest, but I now wanted to study a single site intensively. While many of the other sites in the area were larger than Blue Creek and more romantically situated in the forests of northwestern Belize, Blue Creek offered many distinctive advantages. First, it was accessible. Blue Creek is only a few miles from the main, though unpaved, road to Orange Walk Town and Belize City. Further, the contemporary community of Blue Creek provided access to housing and two small stores. The Maya site of Blue Creek has the advantage of having attributes of much larger sites, such as a ballcourt and large pyramids. However, it is not so large as to present the massive excavation jobs that very large sites would. Finally, it is located at the headwaters of the Río Hondo, which drains into Chetumal Bay, connecting it to places where I had previously worked: Cerros and Ambergris Caye. I was excited by the prospect that trade and commerce, which I believed provided an economic glue interconnecting Maya polities, could also be studied at Blue Creek. So, in 1992, the Blue Creek project began.

Initially, the research design for the Blue Creek project was quite simplistic—and naive. Blue Creek is located at the top of the Bravo Escarpment, overlooking the headwaters of the Río Hondo (Figure 1.1). This location is literally on the edge of the Petén physiographic district where it meets the Belize coastal plain. The ethnohistorian Ralph Roys had mapped the locations of Maya languages during colonial times, and his division between the Yucatec- and Chol-speaking areas followed the Bravo Escarpment, running precisely through Blue Creek. Further, there are distinctive differences in the architecture and artifacts of the Classic period between the Petén and the coastal plain. So, I saw Blue Creek as a perfect location to study the interaction between these two physiographic and cultural zones. Additionally, Blue Creek's location at the terminus of the riverine-coastal trade system offered a fruitful research setting. Further, while I was unsure of whether it was true, I postulated the "straw dog" hypothesis that Blue Creek was a satellite or daughter site of the larger center of La Milpa, approximately 20 kilometers to the west. I saw Blue Creek as La Milpa's access to neighboring polities and the riverine trade routes. While this point has clearly been demonstrated to be incorrect, it was a mechanism for framing our efforts. Most amazingly to me today, I believed that I would spend three field seasons at Blue Creek, then move to its eastern neighbor, Kakabish, in order to compare the architecture and artifactual material with that of Blue Creek. At this early time, our efforts focused only on the research domain of understanding monumental architecture and the information that could be gained from it regarding ancient political organization.

For the most part, the first several seasons were devoted to excavations in Blue Creek's central precinct or core area. However, by 1996, we located the first ditched agricultural fields at Blue Creek and also realized that the ease of access to the "settlement zone" meant that survey and excavations outside of the central precinct could be easily conducted. Consequently, our research goals expanded as well.

Overview of Blue Creek

The vision of a Maya site that comes to most people's minds usually has tall, graceful pyramids rising out of the tropical rain forest. To an extent, this vision is true. The monumental center or site core of a Maya site does, indeed, have such buildings. However, a Maya center, whether it is Blue Creek or Tikal, is much more than that. The surrounding areas were once complex communities consisting of a

Figure 1.1. Location of Blue Creek and other sites mentioned in the text within the Maya region.

variety of structurally and functionally different components. Blue Creek's monumental core area is not very different from the first vision in most people's minds. The site core sits on top of the Bravo Escarpment, rising 100–150 meters above the lowlands of the adjacent coastal plain. It was the central place for discrete communities above and below the escarpment. This setting is similar to that of Palenque, overlooking the Tabasco lowlands.

Blue Creek's setting was important to its residents and is important to our ability

Figure 1.2. View of Bravo Escarpment from the east. Plaza A is located at the highest area on the left and Structure 9 is the highest point in the center of the photograph.

to understand its larger regional role. We have named the Maya site of Blue Creek after the local Mennonite community of Blue Creek, which itself was named for its location adjacent to the Río Azul, which forms the contemporary border between Mexico and Belize. However, much of the Río Azul is a seasonal stream that generally flows only during the rainy season. Not only is it otherwise dry, but it is also difficult to even detect in some locations. The dominant landscape feature in the Blue Creek area is the Bravo Escarpment, rising approximately a hundred meters above the relatively flat coastal zone of Belize (Figures 1.2 and 1.3). At the base of the escarpment, the elevation is 20–40 meters above sea level. Above the escarpment, the terrain is marked by karstic hills, 40–60 meters high, with elevations in the range of 180–200 meters above sea level. The escarpment runs generally south to north, then abruptly turns to the east-northeast and continues along the Belize-Mexico border. The Río Azul descends the escarpment in a deep canyon. In this canyon it is fed by numerous springs and becomes a permanent stream known as the Río Hondo. The Río Hondo follows the base of the escarpment for about four kilometers, then joins the Río Bravo. Downstream from this location to the mouth at Chetumal Bay, the river is easily navigable throughout the year. Blue Creek's location at the headwaters of the Río Hondo has been likened to the first cataract of the Nile.[6] Despite maps showing the river continuing upstream, upstream canoe traffic was not possible and the site of Blue Creek certainly was central to the termini of both the Río Hondo and the Río Bravo.

Figure 1.3. The Río Hondo as it flows eastward along the base of the Bravo Escarpment. North of the river is Mexico and south of the river is Belize.

Further, canoe travel on the river was blocked by a dock and dam complex in the canyon. This complex feature not only necessitated a portage but also apparently functioned as a water divergence and a fish weir and possibly was used for on- and off-loading goods.[7]

Blue Creek's site core or public district consists of two large plazas, Plaza A and Plaza B, each with a number of associated buildings (Figure 1.4). Plaza A covers an area of about 100 × 125 meters and is surrounded by six buildings, Structures 1–6. Structure 1, on the plaza's north side, is the largest at Blue Creek and is more than 12 meters tall. Behind and north of Structure 1 is a large platform with a ballcourt on it. Plaza B and the buildings arranged around it are about two hundred meters northwest of Plaza A.

Plaza A is a typical arrangement for a Maya site but Plaza B is very atypical and reflects a regional expression of site planning and organization. Plaza B, covering about 35 hundred square meters, is also much smaller than Plaza A. On the north and south sides, it is flanked by residential compounds. On the west side, it is bounded by a long, narrow building, and the plaza is open to the east. The two flanking residences, the Structure 13 Courtyard and the Structure 19 Courtyard, were the most central in the site and were probably the residences of some of Blue Creek's rulers. The Plaza B area then extends north and south along a ridge system and terminates at both ends with high pyramids, Structures 9 and 24.

The buildings in the public sector reflect Blue Creek's peak of political and eco-

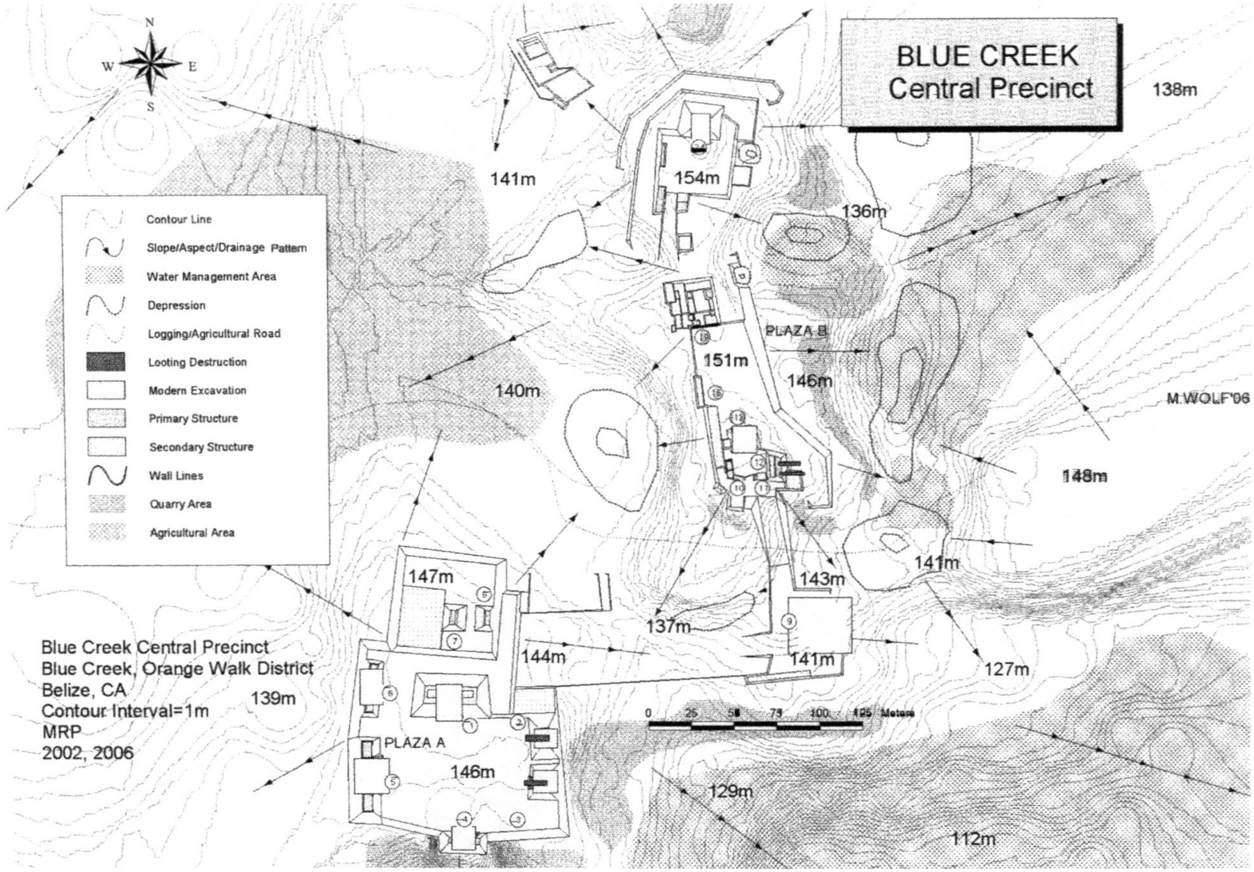

Figure 1.4. The central precinct of Blue Creek, showing topography and drainage (one-meter contour interval).

nomic power and authority. The first of these were constructed at about A.D. 100 or so. For the next four hundred years, construction projects continued at a rapid pace. I mark A.D. 500 as a pivotal point in Blue Creek's life for reasons that will become clear later. However, A.D. 500 was by no means the end of monumental construction at the site. During the early part of the Late Classic period, perhaps until A.D. 700, both Plaza A and Plaza B saw large-scale renovations of existing buildings and even construction of new buildings. While there was no decline in construction, there was a shift in its nature after A.D. 500.

Surrounding the public sector are bounded residential groups that were themselves surrounded by agricultural lands. Each of these groups or residential components had its own character but shared some commonalities with the others. I estimate that elites who lived in the core area of Blue Creek ruled over an area of approximately 100–150 square kilometers and something in the range of 15–20 thousand residents. However, one of the sticky methodological problems of archaeology in the southern Maya lowlands is deciding where one site begins and another ends—or, as the problem applies to this case, how big was Blue Creek? In my years of work in northwestern Belize and in my colleagues' experience throughout the region, it has become clear that Classic Maya habitation covered the region like a blanket. Population densities were extremely high during the Classic period, with estimates ranging up to 20 million persons for the Maya region and several, if not many, cities of more than 100 thousand persons.[8]

This "blanket" of population was more of a quilt, with hundreds of administrative centers like Blue Creek scattered across the landscape. We can translate the question of "how big was Blue Creek?" into the spatial issue of "how much area did any given center control?" In many areas, this is difficult to answer because of pragmatic issues. Any surveyor who, like myself, has not noticed large buildings next to a path for two weeks while mapping other large buildings understands this. The forest hides a great deal.

At Blue Creek, though, much of the forest has been cleared for agriculture and the remaining forested areas are well known to the local people and us. We know that Blue Creek is the only administrative center for a number of kilometers in each direction. Further, in all directions there are easily defined geographic boundaries that would impede passage and administrative control. For example, to the east lies the Río Bravo and the expansive Booth's Swamp. On the far side is the neighboring site of Kakabish. To the north is the 100-meter-deep gorge formed by the Río Azul as it descends the Bravo Escarpment. Beyond the canyon, the nearest neighbor is the site of Chocoha. To the west is a large *bajo*, the Dumbbell Bajo, which covers about 40 square kilometers. Finally, to the south is another deep gorge cut into the Bravo Escarpment, probably an ancient course of the Río Azul. Within this area of approximately 125 square kilometers, the only administrative center is at Blue Creek.

Consequently, when I speak of Blue Creek, I refer to everything within this zone and believe that all such settlements were under the administration of the single site center. While the nature of this administration's authority is a later topic in this book, the site's role as a political and economic central place is not disputable. Since the nature of this administration is still quite vague, the 125 square kilometers of Blue Creek is best referred to as a "polity." This means, simply, that it was a clearly defined political unit of ambiguous nature. It can also be termed a "city" because the nature of Maya urbanism is, unlike other situations, a low-density form of urbanism. Also, I will later turn to the details of what we know about several of the residential components or communities of Blue Creek. For now, though, it is enough to say that we know of about a dozen such communities (Figure 1.5). Each has its own distinctive character and is geographically confined. They range from clusters of housemounds that once were substructures for pole and thatch homes upwards in complexity and energetics to those with grand masonry compounds. One "low-energy" community is Chan Cahal, situated on a low rise below the escarpment and surrounded by ditched agricultural fields. Chan Cahal would have been a hot, buggy settlement probably inhabited by workers in those fields. The people of Chan Cahal were apparently farming those lowlands for a millennium before the construction of the first monumental architecture at Blue Creek. At the other end of the range, there are communities above the escarpment, such as Kín Tan, which have little apparent relationship to the mundane aspects of life such as farming. Instead, the residents of Kín Tan seem to have been politically and economically important and did not settle these high, breezy hilltops until Blue Creek was becoming a complex society in the Late Preclassic period.

There are other, nonresidential, components of Blue Creek as well. Within the bounds of Blue Creek are several types of large-scale agricultural systems. Several of the residential components, such as Chan Cahal, are directly associated with these agricultural resources. Aside from the large-scale systems, there are also specialized ecological niches, which clearly provided equally special agricultural potential.

Time at Blue Creek: Ceramic Chronology

Archaeologists have long discussed Maya civilization in terms of Preclassic, Classic, and Postclassic periods, each generally with Early, Middle, and Late aspects. However, there are numerous variations on this theme. Some variations seem silly while others are expressions of real and important insights into the dynamics of the Maya world. Also, archaeologists generally develop a local sequence for each site, particularly those with major excavations such as Blue Creek. Such chronologies are developed through study of ceramics and the subtle temporal changes involved in them. In this volume, I will use a mixture of general terms for ease of understanding and terms that have been developed at Blue Creek for clarity of specific meanings and implications. For convenience, I will use Gregorian calendar dates

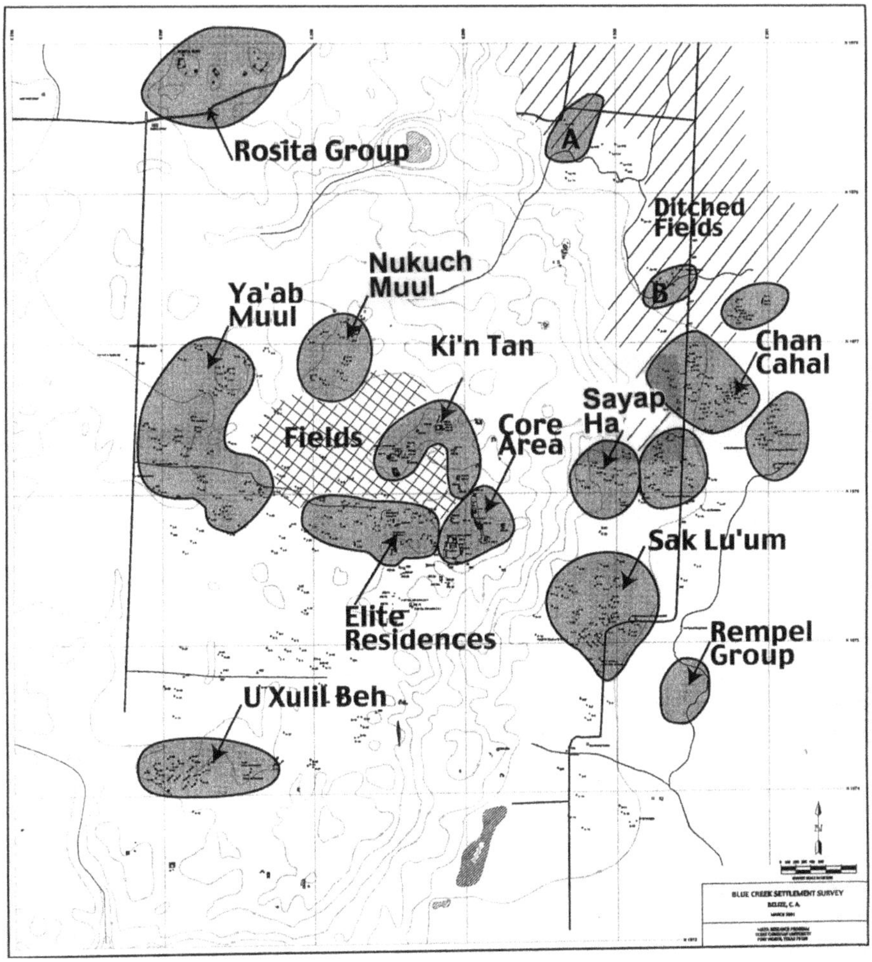

Figure 1.5. Central precinct and Kín Tan (10-meter contour interval).

rather than the general archaeological convention of years before present (B.P.) or reference to the Maya calendar.

A chronology of ceramic complexes has been developed for Blue Creek on the basis of stylistic attributes of pottery (Table 1.1).[9] These complexes are composed of distinctive sets of types of ceramics, such as "Sierra Red Type; Sierra Variety." As pottery and styles change through time, they can be equated with temporal periods. So, we can refer to the Linda Vista ceramic complex at Blue Creek as the "Linda Vista period," which is the local manifestation of what is more broadly known as the Terminal Late Preclassic period. The dates that we ascribe to these periods result from a series of sources including radiocarbon dates from Blue Creek and elsewhere and the known dates of related ceramic complexes elsewhere. The tem-

Table 1.1. Blue Creek ceramic complexes

Temporal Period	Estimated Beginning Date	Blue Creek Ceramic Complex
Postclassic	A.D. 1000	???
Terminal Classic	A.D. 830–850	Río Bravo
Late Classic II	A.D. 750	Dos Bocas
Late Classic I	A.D. 600	Aguas Turbias
Early Classic	A.D. 250	Río Hondo
Terminal Late Preclassic	A.D. 100–150	Linda Vista
Late Preclassic	350 B.C.	Tres Leguas
Middle Preclassic	650 B.C.	San Felipe
Early Middle Preclassic	1000–800 B.C.	Cool Shade

poral aspects of these complexes are constantly being revised and fine tuned. It is thus important to understand that these dates are estimated and always subject to minor change.

Cool Shade Ceramic Complex, Early Middle Preclassic Period (1000/800–650 B.C.)

The first evidence of occupation at Blue Creek dates to about 900 B.C. and is found in small middens or garbage deposits that underlie a few of the housemounds below the escarpment at Chan Cahal. This early period is generally associated with low populations and farming in such low-lying locations along rivers and in similar spots. Nowhere in the Maya world do we see complex society yet in place at this time. However, we see growing evidence for interaction between these Maya villagers and the complex Olmec society of the Veracruz coast.[10]

San Felipe Ceramic Complex, Middle Preclassic Period (650–350 B.C.)

This period is still very poorly known at Blue Creek, with only a few more deposits known than have been found for the preceding Cool Shade complex. However, it is likely that broader environments were being exploited as some of these deposits were found at the top of the escarpment deeply buried under plazas and monumental architecture. Elsewhere by this time we see complex villages form throughout the Maya region and the rise of the earliest known Maya city, Nakbé, in the state of Petén in Guatemala.

Tres Leguas Ceramic Complex, Late Preclassic Period (350 B.C.–A.D. 100)

The population of Blue Creek grew rapidly in the Late Preclassic and almost every location at the site is occupied. Only one residential component has been identified that was not yet occupied. This coincides with rising populations throughout the Maya lowlands. Large cities were coming into existence. In particular, El Mirador became the dominant power in the geopolitics of the southern lowlands. The concept of complex society was also spreading. Cerros was rapidly built on the northern Belize coast and many other sites began to exhibit the initial phases of their planned public architecture and probably had completed the transformation from the fundamentally egalitarian communities of the Middle Preclassic to hierarchically tiered, stratified kingdoms.

Linda Vista Ceramic Complex, Terminal Late Preclassic Period (A.D. 100/150–250)

During this period, most of the sites in northwestern Belize and throughout the region saw the construction of large-scale public architecture. The ceramics of the period are similar to many that follow and they are often difficult to separate from each other. Earlier ceramic analysts believed that a series of stylistic attributes abruptly fell out of use at the end of the Preclassic period, but, rather, they often persisted for hundreds of years more. The consequence of this was to incorrectly date occupations to this period when they were in fact more recent.[11] Additionally, the presence of Usulatan-related ceramics in the Belize Valley led other analysts to conclude that this period saw the influx of new peoples from elsewhere. This now also is seen as erroneous.

During this period, the first monumental architecture was built at Blue Creek, as was the case at most other sites in northwestern Belize and elsewhere. The essential footprint of the public district was established and there is a clear continuity between this period and the Classic.

Río Hondo Ceramic Complex, Early Classic Period (A.D. 250–600)

It was during the Early Classic period that much of the monumental construction occurred at Blue Creek. Unlike most sites where the Early Classic is either nonexistent or buried under later construction, Blue Creek offers an opportunity to better understand the Early Classic patterns. While scholars have often viewed the Early Classic as a stable period in terms of both interpolity interaction and population, it was probably not stable in either area.

Aguas Turbias Ceramic Complex, Late Classic I Period (A.D. 600–750), and Dos Bocas Ceramic Complex, Late Classic II Period (A.D. 750–830/850)

In the Late Classic, other sites in the region seem to become politically energized. For example, ballcourts are built at La Milpa, Chan Chich, and Gran Cacao (RB43). Construction of public architecture at La Milpa accelerates considerably. Most scholars also argue for an increased population during the Late Classic as well.

At Blue Creek, however, the onset of the Late Classic saw significant shifts in orientation of the monumental architecture and probably the political scene. Even so, there were continuities in the elite residential sectors of the site, with old lineages building grander and grander residences. The population of Blue Creek seems to have expanded as well. New residential areas were founded in previously unoccupied areas.

Río Bravo Ceramic Complex, Terminal Classic Period (A.D. 830/850–1000)

We see little or no new construction of public or residential architecture at Blue Creek during the Terminal Classic period. Most Río Bravo complex deposits at Blue Creek are associated with the abandonment of the sites and have been interpreted as ritual termination deposits or garbage discarded by the sites' final occupants. The process of abandonment, while not a focus of this volume, is critical to understanding the end of Classic Maya society and is yet a barely understood issue.

Postclassic Period (after A.D. 1000)

Before 2005, there had been almost no Postclassic period remains documented in northwestern Belize. At La Milpa, one or two households were built from the crumbling ruins of the abandoned pyramids.[12] At Blue Creek, we found an ephemeral reoccupation of a small area of the Chan Cahal residential area. A single Postclassic vessel was recovered from a *chultun* during road construction and given to us. Two other Postclassic vessels at Chicago's Field Museum come from somewhere in the area. With such little data, no ceramic complex had been defined for the Postclassic at Blue Creek. However, in 2005 the Blue Creek project investigated the Rempel group, an outlying complex approximately two kilometers southeast of the core area on the Río Bravo. The investigators found a Postclassic occupation of an earlier Classic period group.[13] While the implications of this spectacular discovery are great, they are beyond the scope of this book. These discoveries notwithstanding, it is clear that in the Postclassic, few of the many thousands of people who once lived at Blue Creek remained.

Blue Creek's Role in Regional Geopolitics: The Neighbors

To place Blue Creek into a better context, it is useful to review what we know of the site's nearest neighbors: Chocoha, Bedrock, La Milpa, Kakabish, Indian Creek, Xnoha,[14] Gran Cacao (RB43), and Lamanai (Figure 1.6). These communities, mostly larger than Blue Creek, surrounded the city and defined the role Blue Creek played in the geopolitical context of the region.

Blue Creek's nearest neighbor to the north is an enigmatic site known as Chocoha. A French explorer, Maurice de Perigny, first located Chocoha in the early part of the twentieth century. It was not formally relocated until the summer of 2002, when we went looking for it.[15] It consists of a small, Early Classic architectural complex overlooking fairly expansive agricultural lands. However, after sev-

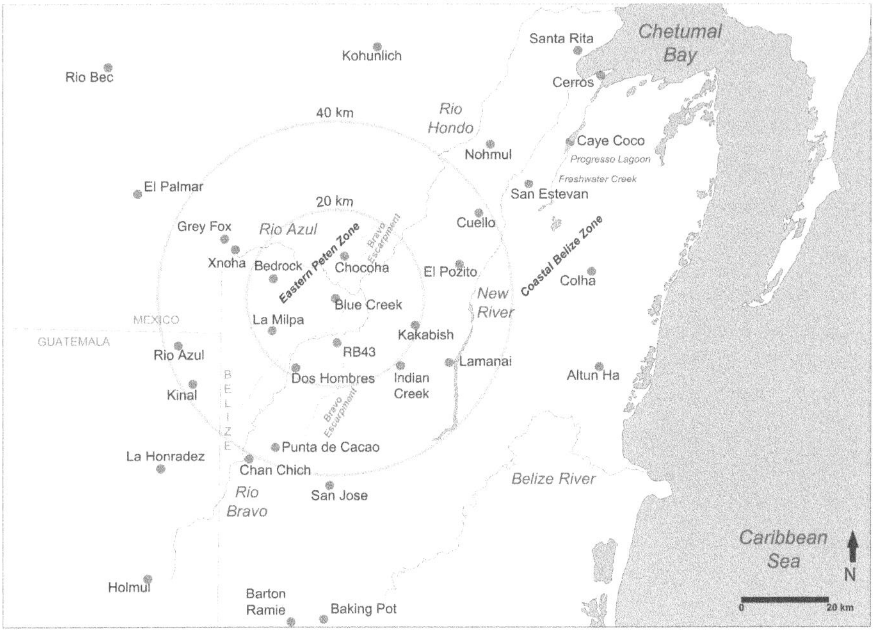

Figure 1.6. Blue Creek and its nearest neighbors.

eral visits and exploring the area, we were left with the odd feeling that we had only seen a small portion of the site, but we had no idea where else to look.

For the purposes of this study, probably the most important aspect of Chocoha is its lack of relationship to the Río Hondo. I had argued for many years that Blue Creek was in control of the headwaters of the Río Hondo and the terminus of the riverine trade system. However, we had not conducted a formal survey of the Mexican side of the river to confirm that another, perhaps larger, site did not exist just across the border in a setting where it, too, would control access to the river. Yet, we constantly heard rumors of two sites, one of them being Chocoha. Since a permit from Mexico was required, I delayed the effort until Jon Lohse had taken over the Blue Creek project and I was free to focus time on the effort. What we found was clear. There is no other site on the Mexican side of the river with access to the river in any sense. That role was Blue Creek's alone. Further, Chocoha is located beyond a range of rugged hills from the river and had absolutely terrible access to the river. The apparently small community was in no way a competitor with Blue Creek for control of riverine trade.

To the west, Bedrock is Blue Creek's nearest neighbor. Bedrock is a relatively small center located on the northern side of the Dumbbell Bajo that consists of a central plaza surrounded by medium-sized public buildings.[16] Early Classic ceramics were found by the farmers who cleared the site and, in 1999, we salvaged a Terminal Classic vaulted chamber about a kilometer from the main plaza. In 2002, test excavations in Bedrock's main plaza confirmed a Late Preclassic to Terminal Classic sequence at the site. So, while I originally thought that Bedrock might be a Late Classic outlier of La Milpa, which is only a few kilometers south of the Dumbbell Bajo, this appears not to be the case. However, I would still not be surprised if Bedrock was a political subjugate of La Milpa that consolidated La Milpa's power over the agricultural resources of the Dumbbell Bajo. Of course, I did say much the same thing about Blue Creek at one time and was quite wrong in that case.

Farther west than Bedrock are two sites, Xnoha and Grey Fox. Xnoha was first located in 1990 and was mapped and partially excavated in 2002–2004.[17] The site consists of one very large plaza and a range of residential architecture. Grey Fox was located in 1998 and a sketch map made, but no member of our project has returned to it. Both of these are smaller than Blue Creek but still substantial and important in the framework of regional geopolitics. However, we yet know little of their roles.

La Milpa, which competes with Lamanai for being the largest center in the region, includes three public plazas with four buildings taller than 20 meters and more than a dozen stelae.[18] Since 1992, excavations at La Milpa have been conducted under the auspices of Boston University and we now know significantly more about the site than my initial mapping. La Milpa rose to power in the Late Preclassic period and underwent an uncertain Early Classic period. While an Early Classic royal tomb was found at La Milpa, Norman Hammond asserts that it had diminished power during that time. In the Late Classic, the site saw renewed vigor in construction projects and an apparent, significant population increase.

Using the locations of other surrounding centers and the topography as a basis for estimation, investigators at La Milpa have argued for a polity with a radius of six kilometers, which is approximately twice the area that I argue was under the control of the Blue Creek polity. However, La Milpa saw much greater amounts of public construction and very likely much higher population levels and density. Moreover, Gair Tourtellot and his various co-authors argue that La Milpa's political structure was integrated by the establishment of minor administrative centers, such as La Milpa East and Say Ka, located at approximately six kilometers from the site core and approximately at the cardinal directions. Beyond this distance, administrative centers such as Blue Creek and Maáx Na that are larger than Say Ka and La Milpa East, but significantly smaller than La Milpa, are seen to be independent centers. Similar arrangements have been argued for other sites such as Tikal, Ek Balam, and Caracol.[19]

La Milpa, though, clearly was a dominant regional power. I believe that much of that power derived from consolidation of authority over a fairly large area in the Late Preclassic and La Milpa's control of significant agricultural resources, perhaps including the lands of the Dumbbell Bajo.

We know little of the nature of most of the sites to the east and south of Blue Creek. Although Indian Creek and Kakabish were mapped by our team and Gran Cacao (RB43) was briefly investigated by the Programme for Belize Archaeological Project, the only excavations done at any of them were test excavations and an excavation into the Late Classic ballcourt at Gran Cacao.[20] Indian Creek consists of at least one large plaza complex, and little or no looting has occurred there. On the other hand, Kakabish is possibly the most looted site in Belize. It consists of two large plazas, surrounded by large, public buildings except where one such building was bulldozed off the main plaza for road access. On the basis of size alone, if Blue Creek was an independent polity, then certainly Kakabish must also have been.

Beyond Kakabish is the site of Lamanai located along the New River Lagoon. A decade of excavations were conducted by the Royal Ontario Museum and there has recently been a renewal of work, first under the Royal Ontario Museum again but then transferred to the Institute of Archaeology of the University College, London.[21] Lamanai, approximately the same size as La Milpa, grew to prominence during the Late Preclassic period with one structure reaching about 30 meters tall at that time. Lamanai continued to thrive through the entire Classic period and well into the Postclassic, seeing the construction of another 30-meter-tall structure at that late date.

It is very likely that Lamanai's strategic location along the New River provided access to the coastal trade system, and the excavators argue that the small site of Marco Gonzalez was actually a port connecting Lamanai to this network. Whether Marco Gonzalez was under Lamanai's direct control or not is uncertain, but the two sites certainly interacted intensively. Further, it was surely Lamanai's strategic location that allowed it to thrive so much later than the rest of the region. A survey along the road from Lamanai to today's San Felipe indicates that there may have been little Postclassic population outside of the central area. So, Postclassic Lamanai should probably be best regarded to have been a depopulating kingdom that retained geopolitical power as a result of its connection to the mercantile system of the Postclassic.

The primary excavations at Lamanai were conducted in the 1970s, when access was quite difficult. Further, Pendergast's excavations focused on the major architecture. Consequently, we have a very rich understanding of Lamanai's central precinct but we know little in terms of population estimates and site structure outside of the core area.

Characterizing Blue Creek

So what was Blue Creek? How can the community be described, in a nutshell, before we go on to a more complete discussion? Or, for another way of putting the question, how can I describe the nature of the site so the reader can make sense of the next several chapters?

First, it was clearly a wealthy Maya city. The large quantity of Late Preclassic and Early Classic jade found at Blue Creek attests to this. Two major factors contributed to the basis of this wealth. Blue Creek controlled some of the best and most expansive agricultural lands in the Maya world. Further, these lands were located adjacent to the terminus of an established river linkage to the coastal trade system. Agriculture was a hugely valuable economic resource for the people of Blue Creek. Its value was enhanced as they had access to markets for agricultural products. And at the same time, they were strategically located to benefit from all sorts of trade going up and down the Río Hondo between the densely populated, central Petén and the Caribbean coast.

Another important aspect is that Blue Creek apparently had a relatively low population density for a Maya city. I will explore this in more detail later but can lay out the essential concept now. A glance at the map of Blue Creek shows that there were large expanses of unoccupied lands within the city itself. That is because, simply enough, these were the rich agricultural lands that supported the Blue Creek economy. So, the city plan was a dispersed mosaic of public areas, residential components, and agricultural lands. Blue Creek never had the population density of many of its neighbors.

Blue Creek was probably an independent kingdom in Linda Vista and Río Hondo (Terminal Late Preclassic and Early Classic) times. A number of lines of evidence support this. For example, in the Terminal Late Preclassic, Linda Vista, period, a major cache of obsidian blades may mark the installation of the first king at Structure 4. Later, in the Early Classic period, Structure 1 was a unique columned building, exhibiting architectural innovation that could be indicative of an independent kingdom. While this alone would be very weak evidence, when it is combined with the *ahau* masks adorning the front of Structure 9-IV, the royal tomb in Structure 1, and the widespread distribution of jade during the Early Classic, especially the A.D. 500 event at Structure 4, the case becomes compelling.

In the Late Classic, things changed at Blue Creek, much more subtly than I once thought, but they certainly did change. The Late Classic saw expansion of the monumental architecture, entrenchment and increased wealth of the community's elites, and expansion of the community into new lands. However, by the end of the Classic period in the Río Bravo period, Blue Creek's life as a political, agricultural, economic, and population center ended. Like many Maya cities, it was abandoned for a millennium.

The rest of this book is an exploration of what happened during nearly a millennium, roughly A.D. 100–850, when Blue Creek was a vibrant, active, and wealthy Maya city.

2 Public Architecture, Ritual, and Temporal Dynamics

In this chapter I summarize the public architecture and related residences in Blue Creek's core area in order to document the temporal dynamics of power and politics as expressed by its builders.[1] The "core area" of a Maya site is the public, "downtown" sector or the central precinct with large, open public plazas flanked by large buildings that functioned as religious and administrative edifices. Expressions of religion, power, and authority were incorporated into the architecture of the public sector. The images of rulers, their lives, and their accomplishments were displayed on monolithic stelae. However, most stelae were not carved. Instead, they were probably plastered and painted, leaving us with little or no specific information today.

Maya monumental architecture can be seen as a symbolic, physical representation of Maya religion, specifically their understanding of creation. The Maya view of the cosmos reflects elements of the creation story told in the Popul Vuh. The creators, Xpiyakok and Xmukane, had already made and destroyed the world three times before the present and fourth creation. The creation was made possible "with the utterance of a word and the appearance of the thing embodied by the word."[2] During the third creation, the Lords of the Underworld killed the uncle and father of the Hero Twins. The men had angered the Xibalbans by playing the ballgame too loudly. So, the Xibalbans killed them and buried them under the ballcourt and hung the father's decapitated head on a tree. The skull then magically impregnated the daughter of one of the Lords. She sought refuge in the world of people and gave birth to the twins, Hunahpu and Xblanke. They eventually went to Xibalba and defeated the murderer of their father and resurrected their father and uncle.

When the creators began again with the fourth creation, they knew that corn and water would make up humanity but did not know where to find corn. They heard of a place full of food named the "Witz Mountain" or "First-True-Mountain" or "Split-Mountain," which rose from the "Primordial Sea." The maize there was molded into the first four humans and the water became their blood.

Almost everything in Maya life is linked to this creation story and symbolic re-creations of the Maya cosmos. Freidel, Schele, and Parker have demonstrated that Classic Maya public architecture is, in fact, a reenactment of the landscape of creation. Maya temples are the symbolic Witz Mountain rising from the plazas, which themselves are symbolically the primordial sea. Further, Kent Reilly has shown that this arrangement dates to the origins of complex society in Mesoamerica. The Olmecs at La Venta originated this symbolic re-creation by making the Witz Mountain a volcano and "painting the Primordial Sea green" with large serpentine mosaics.[3] Mathews and Garber correctly point out that these motifs, particularly the quadripartite directional symbolism, exist at a multiplicity of scales and are seen on single small artifacts as well as at the macro level in site planning.[4]

The plans of public sectors were built on consistent principles that related to the Maya views of directionality and religion. Ashmore has shown that directional symbolism is inherent in these plans.[5] Elaborating on our understanding of such site planning, Houk has shown a continuity of plans in the eastern edge of the Petén.[6] Such similarity among public sectors reflects their regional sociopolitical integration. For example, there is a similarity between the Blue Creek site plan and that of Nohmul farther downstream along the Río Hondo as well as with those of several sites along the Bravo Escarpment. If this is an expression of sociopolitical integration, as Houk argued, it is especially interesting that these sites (except Nohmul) follow the Bravo Escarpment, which Ralph Roys saw as dividing the territories of Yucatecan and Chol speakers in colonial times.[7]

One of the most overlooked aspects of Maya public architecture is in some ways the most obvious—the plazas themselves. These were multifunctional public places where religious, administrative, and civic activities occurred. Plazas were used for markets and trade fairs, much like the system that still remains in Oaxaca today and much like the system partially seen in most Middle American towns today. Clearly plazas were controlled by the ruling elite, who in some manner benefited by their sponsorship.

Casual visitors as well as archaeologists often overlook the energy required to build these huge plazas. When we step into a Maya plaza, the towering pyramids surrounding these open spaces awe us. This natural human reaction obscures the important reality that the construction of the plaza often represents more work than the construction of the buildings on top of them. While plazas are most commonly built upon hilltops and other elevated surfaces, there is no such thing as a large flat surface in the karstic limestone landscape of the Maya lowlands. So, the hilltops had to be truncated while the hillsides had to be raised. At the Late Preclassic site of Cerros, the Maya built large construction pens that they then filled with rubble to raise an area of more than 10 thousand square meters at least three meters.[8] That represents 30 thousand cubic meters of construction. At Blue Creek, we have not investigated the entire area under the main plaza. Even so, we know that there are at least three meters of fill under the east and west sides of the plaza but relatively little under the center of the plaza. A crude and minimal estimate of the volume of fill under the plaza is 50 thousand cubic meters, while the volume of the largest building on the plaza is only 15 thousand cubic meters.

One case example south of the central precinct demonstrates this even better. There is a modern home built on a hilltop that was reshaped by the ancient Maya. At one point, the platform construction is at least five meters thick and we estimate that 15 thousand cubic meters of fill were required for the platform. On top of the platform was only a low (50 centimeter) masonry substructure for a perishable building that incorporated only a maximum of 10 cubic meters of stone. My point here is only that we often underestimate the scale and effort required to build sites such as Blue Creek. There is often as much construction under our feet as in the buildings we see on top of these platforms and plazas.

Ballcourts were another common element in the public sector. While we do not know the specifics of how a ballgame was played, the presence of these alleyways in such central and important areas attests to their importance in Maya ritual life.[9] Playing a ballgame was a ritualized reenactment of the story from the Popul Vuh in which the Hero Twins save the Maya from the Lords of the Underworld. This was symbolically replayed every time a ballgame was played. One of the most striking things about the ballgame, at least to me, is the fundamental difference between it and our modern sports. Archaeologists often argue that the presence of a ballcourt may mark a higher level of political authority, perhaps the presence of an independent kingdom, much like the presence of an NFL stadium in American cities marks status. However, unlike modern high school, collegiate, or professional sports, the Maya ballgame was not for public viewing. For example, at Blue Creek, it *might* have been possible for 20 people to view a game from the court itself and ground level. And, it *might* have been possible for 20 more to view the game from the top of Structure 1. But those numbers are probably too high. So, we must recognize that the Maya ballgame was not a public, spectator sport, despite its obvious importance acknowledged by the important location of the ballcourts.

Another major component of the core areas of Maya cities was the residences of the most elite members of society. Nowhere is this better exemplified than at Palenque, where the palace is located across a plaza from the city's largest monumental building. The palace at Palenque has several open courtyards, three stories of masonry architecture, and a tower that afforded a view of the Tabasco lowlands below the site, and it was built by several generations of rulers. Like Palenque, the core area at Blue Creek has important residences that housed the city's leaders.

The rulers were not the only residents of the core area. While we are uncertain who the other residents were, we know they were there. In the Blue Creek central precinct, there are several residences that may have been occupied by lesser elites or people who served the rulers. It is simply difficult to know. We also probably underestimate their population as many of their residences are very difficult to detect. For example, at Chan Chich, we located the floors of several of these "invisible" houses only when a water-line ditch was dug through the main platform behind the public architecture. This revealed the slightly buried floors of at least three houses.[10] Whether these were residences or storage buildings or functioned in some other way, we cannot be certain.

The public architecture of Blue Creek consists of two areas, the Plaza A complex and the Plaza B complex (Figure 2.1).[11] Plaza A, on the edge of the Bravo Escarpment (Figure 2.2), is dominated by Structure 1, Blue Creek's largest building. Immediately north of Structure 1 is a large platform covering about 25 hundred square meters. On a portion of this platform is the ballcourt (Structures 7 and 8). However, the platform is oversized for the ballcourt and must have accommodated additional functions as well.

Structure 9, defining the south end of the Plaza B complex, lies about 150 meters east of the ballcourt platform. The complex stretches from there about three hundred meters to the north, where it terminates at Structure 24. Centered between the two is Plaza B, flanked by two other important groups, the Structure 19 Courtyard and the Structure 13 Courtyard. In their final Late Classic forms, these were the most important and most centrally located residences at Blue Creek.

Blue Creek exhibits a significantly different architectural and sociopolitical history from that of many other sites. While other sites certainly had as much monumental construction during the Early Classic period, many buildings at Blue Creek were not rebuilt or were minimally rebuilt during the Late Classic period. As a result, Blue Creek's monumental zone provides us with an unusually rich database of Early Classic materials.

Plaza A Complex

Plaza A covers approximately 10 thousand square meters and is surrounded by six structures. This was Blue Creek's major public and sacred space.

Structure 1

The largest building on Plaza A is Structure 1 (Figure 2.3), rising 12.7 meters above the plaza and measuring 46 meters across the base and 26 meters wide.[12] There are six construction phases, Structure 1-I through Structure 1-VI.[13] The earliest, Structures 1-I and 1-II, were low platforms built during the Terminal Late Preclassic period (Linda Vista, A.D. 100/150–250), and Structure 1-III was an Early Classic (Río Hondo, A.D. 250–600) construction. The most important phase was Structure 1-IV, an Early Classic period (Río Hondo) tiered pyramid with a central staircase and a columned superstructure. We are uncertain how tall the building was in its final form, as the columns were truncated in preparation for later construction. However, the superstructure's floor is about 10 meters above the plaza level and remnants of the columns extend at least 2 meters higher and are approximately 1.5 meters in diameter. As they are made of a stone and marl conglomerate, they would not have been able to support a stone roof. There are two rows of columns, with eight

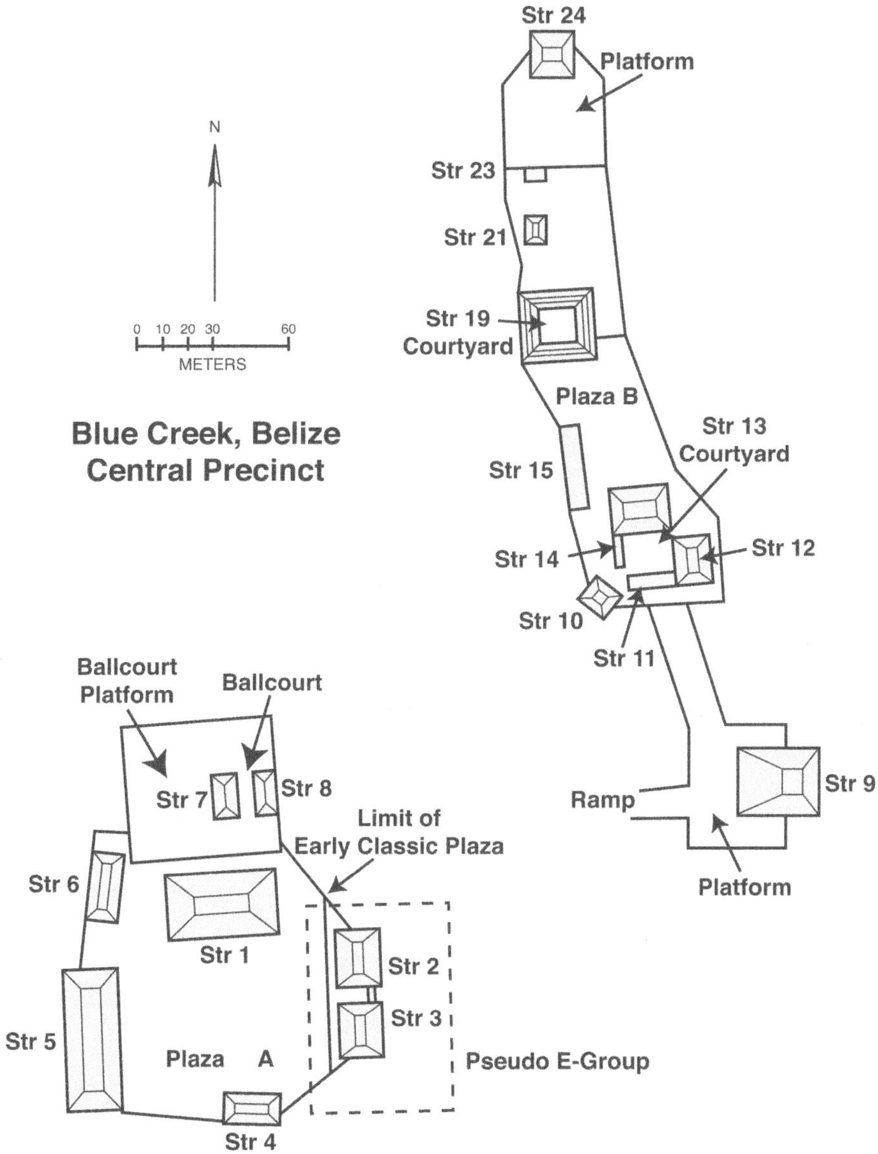

Figure 2.1. Simplified architectural drawing of the central precinct, showing the Late Classic Pseudo-E-group.

in both the front and back rows. This remarkable building is the earliest known columned building in the southern lowlands and only one at Aké in northern Yucatán may be as old.[14]

At some time about A.D. 500 to A.D. 550, the columned superstructure of Structure 1-IV was razed and a new construction, Structure 1-V, was built.[15] The sum-

Figure 2.2. Aerial view of Kín Tan on the hills in the foreground and with the central precinct on the top of the Bravo Escarpment in the middle ground.

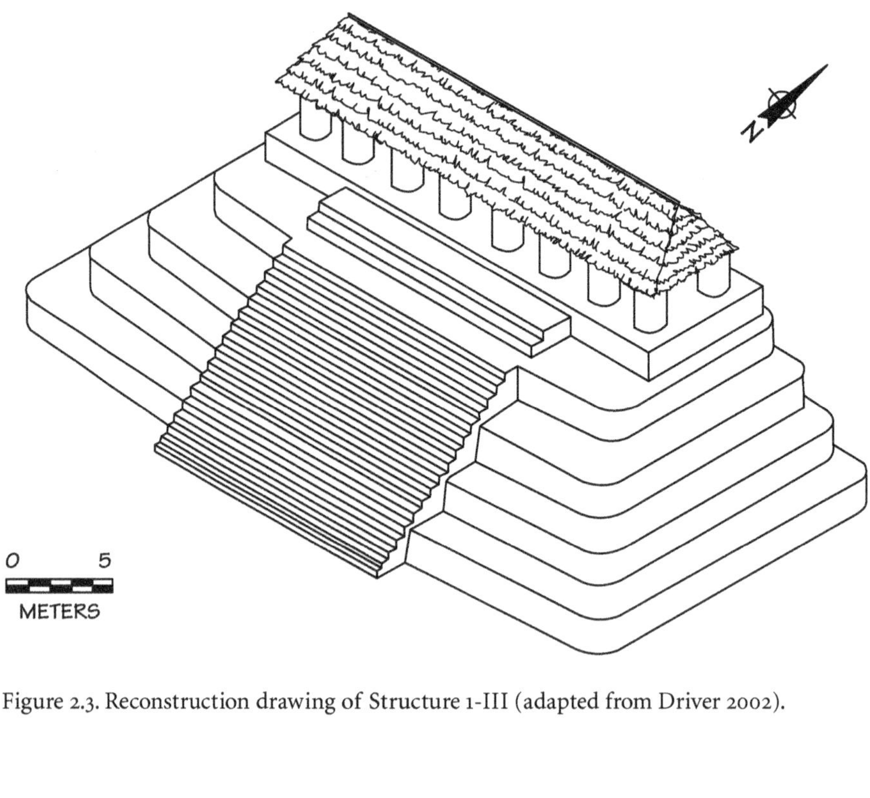

Figure 2.3. Reconstruction drawing of Structure 1-III (adapted from Driver 2002).

Figure 2.4. Vessels from Tomb 4, Structure 1.

mit was elevated about 2 meters and reconfigured into a platform, then more than 12 meters above the plaza level. It is certainly possible that Structure 1-V may have supported a similar columned superstructure if those columns were wooden poles. While this is uncertain, the reason for the construction of Structure 1-V was clearly to accommodate Tomb 4. This was the interment of an important, probably royal, young adult male.[16] The tomb also contained a pair of jade ear spools, three ceramic vessels dating to the end of the Early Classic period, and a possible bloodletting kit composed of two obsidian blades, two bone skewers, and a shell plaque (Figure 2.4).

Two sets of caches, Cache 4 and Cache 6, were associated with the construction of Structure 1-IV. Cache 4 consisted of two sets of small Aguila Orange vessels placed lip-to-lip. Within Cache 4A were a pair of jade plaques with central drill holes, six jade beads, two unworked greenstone fragments, one piece of hematite, a marine shell (*Crepidula aculeta*), and other marine shell fragments, as well as numerous sponge spicules and possible cacao phytoliths.[17] Cache 4B contained fragments of marine shells and shell conglomerates and numerous sponge spicules. Cache 6 also consisted of two sets of Aguila Orange bowls placed lip-to-lip. Cache 6A contained two jade earflares, a smashed jade bead, an unworked greenstone fragment, a polished shell disk, two marine shells, numerous sponge spicules, possible cacao phytoliths, and a platanillo (*Heliconia*) phytolith. Cache 6B included two

Figure 2.5. Conceptual drawing of the relationship between aspects of "lip-to-lip "caches and the Maya cosmos.

jade earflares, a smashed jade bead, four unworked greenstone fragments, a worked shell disk, four marine shells, and a sea urchin spine. No sample adequate for biosilicate analysis was retrieved from Cache 6B. All of the sponges and marine shells were imported to Blue Creek from the Caribbean and associated lagoons, approximately a hundred kilometers downstream via the Río Hondo.

These caches, like others at Blue Creek and in the Maya world, are known as dedicatory caches. They are intentional placements commonly at the base and the centerline of the building during rituals that embedded life and sacredness in that structure. This is symbolically the same location where the base of the first Witz Mountain meets the primordial sea. It is, in fact, the place of the origin of life. Not surprisingly for such an important location in the sacred landscape, this arrangement of highly valued objects from liminal and terrestrial contexts, covered with the dome of the upper vessel, is a representation of the Maya cosmos. The three-part cosmogram consists of the representation of the primordial sea, the earth-based materials connected to the Witz Mountain, and the domed-shaped roof of the sky. In dedicatory caches, sponges and other marine materials such as shell, stingray spines, and coral represent the primordial sea. The earth-based materials include jade and other stone artifacts. Finally, the dome of the sky is represented by the inverted bowl capping the cache (Figure 2.5).[18] This pattern is seen not only in dedicatory caches in monumental architecture but also in caches in elite and non-elite residences as well as in burial contexts throughout Blue Creek in the Late Preclassic and Early Classic periods. The Maya consistently replicated their cosmos in symbolic fashion in all of these contexts.

The final construction, Structure 1-VI, was added in the Late Classic and consists only of a 50-centimeter-tall addition to the central portion of the summit. As we repeatedly see at Blue Creek, the initial construction at Structure 1 was in the Terminal Late Preclassic (Linda Vista) with significant (and in this case, innova-

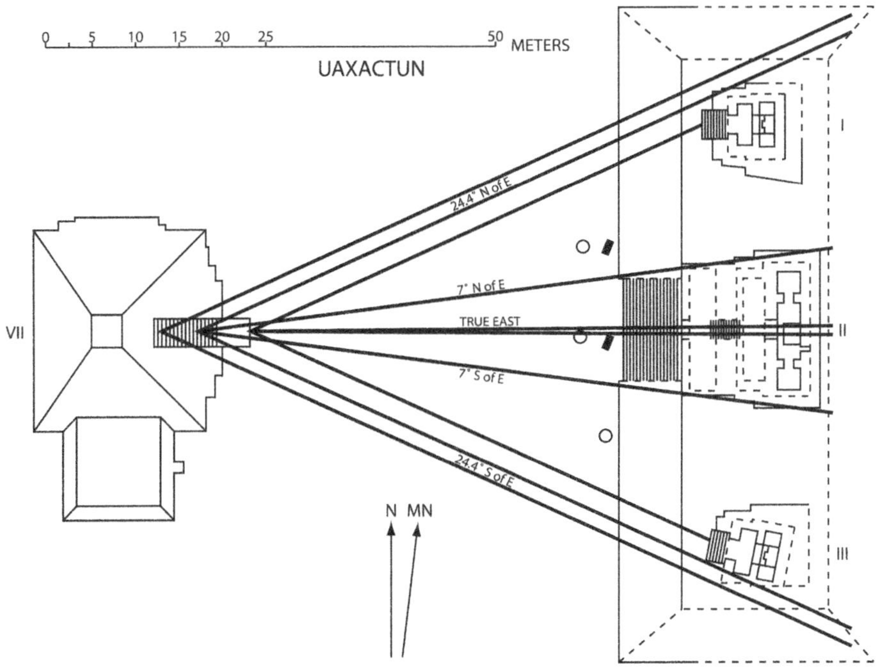

Figure 2.6. The observatory at Group E, Uaxactun (adapted from Ricketson 1928).

tive) construction in the Early Classic period (Río Hondo). However, in the Late Classic (Aguas Turbias, A.D. 600–750), there was only a very modest renovation of the building.

Structures 2 and 3

The pair of pyramids, Structures 2 and 3, that bound the east side of Plaza A form a variant of the E-group solstice observatories of the Petén (Figure 2.1).[19] In the Petén most E-groups follow closely the form of the archetype, Group E at Uaxactun (Figure 2.6) and consist of two buildings oriented north to south and defining the east side of a group of buildings or plaza. On the west side is a third building from which an observer could see the sun rise on the solstices and equinoxes. The eastern Petén variant simply omits the third, western side building and the observer must stand at some point in the plaza for the same effect. In other words, the size of the paired buildings is smaller relative to the open plaza than in the central Petén variant. Such Pseudo-E-groups are known to occur at Blue Creek, San Jose, and Chan Chich. Importantly, the Pseudo-E-groups also postdate the Late Preclassic and Early Classic E-groups. By the Late Classic, when the Blue Creek buildings and other known examples were built, they were not functional observatories. Instead, they had become a part of the architectural complex that was part of the Maya identity. In other words, by building an E-group, the rulers of Blue Creek were asserting their authority in a prescribed symbolic manner. Further, they may have been assuming responsibility to seat the *may,* described by Prudence Rice as a ritual assumption of responsibility for the well-being of the polity.[20]

Excavations were conducted at Structures 2 and 3 in 1998 and 1999. Unfortunately, Structure 3 was so massively looted when we first came to Blue Creek that we elected to backfill the trench to protect the integrity of the remainder of the building. While the building is 7.85 meters tall today, it certainly exceeded 8 meters tall prior to the looting. Excavations revealed that there was only one major construction episode in the early part of the Late Classic (Aguas Turbias). Unfortunately, the scale of the looting in this building makes it impossible to understand its architecture as well as we would like. However, we do know that Structure 3 has a broad, central staircase, approximately 8 meters wide, rising at least 5 meters up the facade of the building and including at least 12 steps. At the base of this staircase is an unusual feature, a vaulted shrine chamber extending 80 centimeters from the staircase. At some later date, an addition was constructed, bringing the staircase forward to the front of the chamber.

However, the chamber appears to have been open to the front, as the scatter pattern of Terminal Classic (Río Bravo, A.D. 830/850–1000) sherds that were deposited later indicates.[21] The shrine consisted of a small arched room, extending 0.8 meters out from the staircase. It was 3.0 meters wide and at least 2.5 meters tall. It had a low door about 0.8 meter wide and about 1 meter tall. The interior chamber was 1.6 meters deep by 1.15 meters wide. The chamber had a well-preserved plaster floor and plastered walls. Set into the floor was a limestone boulder or what is sometimes called a pseudo-stela rising about 60 centimeters from the floor. This is known as a hearthstone shrine, similar to one found at Tonina.[22]

Under the floor was a dedicatory cache, Cache 45, consisting of a large, lidded effigy vessel (Figure 2.7) depicting a deity that may be G1 of the Palenque Triad. However, Driver and Wanyerka identify this deity as Kinich Ahau, the sun god. They also note that the burial of the sun god in this location may "emulate and mark" the sun's descent into the underworld on the winter solstice. This makes a great deal of sense, given that Structure 3 would, in fact, be the building of the E-group that would be used to observe the winter solstice.

The contents of Cache 45 represent another clear example of the re-creation of the primordial sea and the Maya cosmos. The vessel contained 24 pieces of jade and greenstone, marine shells (including *Spondylus*), stingray spines and fish vertebrae, and, judging from the analysis of biosilicates, a massive amount of marine sponges.

Structure 4

Structure 4 is a relatively small building, only six meters tall, that defines the south end of Plaza A.[23] There are three major construction phases, Structure 4-I being the

Figure 2.7. Anthropomorphic vessel from Cache 45, Structure 3.

earliest. As best we can tell, Structure 4-I is a low, Terminal Late Preclassic (Linda Vista) platform. When constructed, a dedicatory cache, Cache 21, was placed under the plaster floor, just in front of the building along the medial axis. Cache 21 is dated and calibrated to 1870 ± 50 B.P. (Beta-82949; Linda Vista complex) and consisted of 7 chert bifaces, 5 pieces of coral, 10 shells (mostly riverine bivalves), 17 jade artifacts, and 458 pieces of obsidian. The obsidian included 425 blades and 27 cores, all from El Chayal. These materials were found bundled together as though they had been wrapped in a cloth, a fragment of which was recovered, but identification is not certain.

As at many sites, Cerros, for example, this period appears to have been when the royal lineage was instated.[24] The first instatement of a royal lineage may also have occurred at Blue Creek. Cache 21 may be the material remains of a massive bloodletting ceremony related to the dedication of this building and, perhaps, the installation of Blue Creek's first king. I can envision a ceremony during which hundreds of people used the obsidian blades for bloodletting and in which the bloodletting tools were then buried in Cache 21, at the symbolic location of creation. Such a ritual would be the validation of a ruler's blood lineage and establish his authority and rule.

Structure 4-II was built on top of Structure 4-I and was a significant expansion of the building. This was a small pyramid, about four meters tall, built in the Early Classic period (Río Hondo). We are uncertain about the form of the superstructure, as only the remains of an interior wall were found. Apparently, much of the superstructure was razed in preparation for constructing Structure 4-III.

Several important features were found on the plaza associated with Structure 4-II. The first was the remains of a retaining wall projecting into the plaza from the building about five meters. The wall then turned east 90 degrees to parallel the building for 11.6 meters, finally turning north, away from the building, for another two meters. Within the confines of the retaining wall structure, we found a small altar composed of several cut stones that were once plastered together and a stela platform from which the stela had been removed. This feature differs from stela shrines found at Tikal and Xunantunich in that this feature does not open to the front of the associated building.

The most striking features of Structure 4-II, however, are related to the "shaft caches." At some time in the Early Classic (Río Hondo) but probably close to A.D. 350, based on the dates from Tikal of similar ceramics, a section of Structure 4-II was excavated to enable the Blue Creek Maya to build a stone-lined shaft. A large area was removed from the front and summit of Structure 4-II. Then the shaft was built and fill replaced around it. Radiocarbon dates from this material suggest that Structure 4-I was impacted as well and material from that building recycled into the newly modified Structure 4-II. The shaft was then capped with a bannerstone, a large circular limestone disk with a hole in the center 50 centimeters in diameter that was the opening of the shaft. An uncarved stela was laid on top of the edge of the bannerstone. This stela had probably been removed from the platform in front of the building.

At the time of shaft construction, Cache 12 was placed below the bottom of the shaft. Cache 12 consisted of the placement of a four-pointed chert eccentric with a central hole and a small Hewlett Bank Unslipped miniature vessel. Also, at the time of construction, a series of other caches were placed around the shaft. The common pattern was the stacking or nesting of Aguila Orange bowls within the fill surrounding the shaft.[25] Seven caches (11, 13, 14, 16, 17, 18, and 19) consisted of such placements of multiple vessels and, while no count of total vessels has been made, at least two hundred are represented in these caches.

Surrounding the shaft near its upper opening were four caches, Caches 8, 15, 24, and 25, arranged in the cardinal directions. Caches 15 and 25 consisted of Aguila Orange vessels with no additional artifacts. Cache 8 consisted of an Early Classic, zoomorphic Caldero Buff Polychrome vessel with the body of an infant or neonate interred within the vessel. Cache 24 consisted of another such vessel depicting an owl (Figure 2.8).

The shaft was open and empty for perhaps a century prior to the shaft-filling event. Though the construction date of the shaft is somewhat vague, we know that

Figure 2.8. Early Classic Caldero Buff Polychrome zoomorphic vessel from Structure 4.

it was filled in a dramatic ritual at approximately A.D. 500. We obtained two corrected radiocarbon dates from the interior fill of the shaft. One from the upper portion of the shaft dated to 1440 ± 110 B.P. (Beta-75432) or A.D. 510 and another from the lower portion dated to 1450 ± 100 B.P. (Beta-75433) or A.D. 500.

Seven caches were found within and below the shaft that relate to this filling event (Figure 2.9). Cache 46 was found below the shaft in the area of the Cache 12 chert eccentric and included 426 jade artifacts and 16 non-jade artifacts.[26] These artifacts, or at least the vast majority of them, came to be in Cache 46 by being dropped into the stone-lined shaft, probably during the major filling event. In addition, Cache 46 included four Candelerio Appliquéd ring stands. These are approximately 15–20 centimeters high and the same in diameter. Each is clearly a depiction of a ceiba tree done in the same manner as is done by Lacandon Maya people today (Figure 2.10). Cache 46 also contained one restorable Aguila Orange bowl that probably sat on top of one of the ring bases. While these ceramics have been assigned to Cache 46, sherds from many of them were also found in Cache 9A, indicating that they were broken before being deposited in the shaft and that the shaft filling was a single event, rather than a protracted process. Four additional Candelerio Appliquéd ring stands were found in Cache 9A.

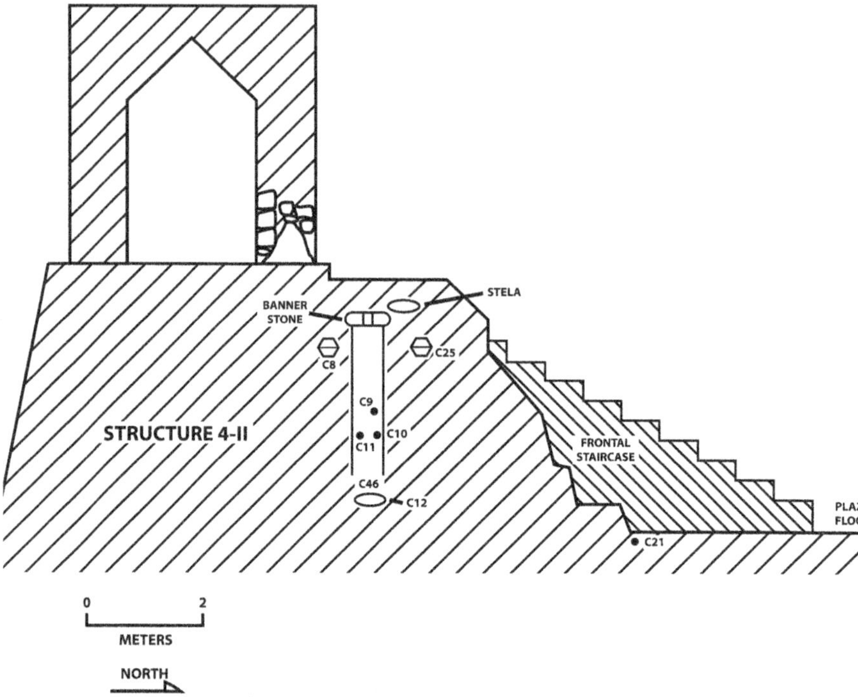

Figure 2.9. Schematic profile of Structure 4-II showing location of shaft and caches.

Figure 2.10. Example of Candelerio Appliquéd ring stands from Structure 4.

Cache 11 includes all 42 jade artifacts found within the shaft below Caches 9B and 9C. While no non-jade or ceramic artifacts are assigned to this cache, sherds from several of the Candelerio Appliquéd vessels assigned to Cache 46 derive from this deposit. Included in the deposit was an anthropomorphic, tubular jade bead, 7.2 centimeters long.

Cache 10 was placed within the shaft below Caches 9A and 9B. This consisted of two bowls placed lip-to-lip containing one jade bead and approximately a hundred mollusks. A marl "cap" was placed in the shaft, separating Caches 10 and 11 from the materials subsequently placed in the shaft. On this marl cap were two lip-to-lip placements of small Aguila Orange bowls, Caches 9B and 9C.

Cache 9B contained 341 jade artifacts and 21 non-jade artifacts within two Aguila Orange bowls. Notable among these were 33 earflares, 4 anthropomorphic pendants, and 5 zoomorphic pendants (Figure 2.11). One of the jade pendants (BC505) is an Olmecoid bib-and-helmet face and another (BC513) depicts a monkey's face. Cache 9C contained four jade artifacts within two Aguila Orange bowls. One jade artifact is a large anthropomorphic bead and another is a unique bib-head pendant. The other two artifacts are sub-spherical jade beads.

Above these caches were numerous other materials designated Cache 9A. Cache 9A included 91 jade artifacts and 17 non-jade artifacts. This included a "jade profile pendant" and a large earflare 9.5 centimeters in diameter. Also included were four Candelerio Appliquéd ring stands and a human phalange.

Large amounts of charcoal and partially carbonized wood were found throughout the shaft fill. Clearly, burning wood was dropped into the shaft and extinguished as the shaft filled. Equally important, the majority of the artifacts in Cache 9A were broken and smashed in the same manner that Garber notes for termination rituals at Cerros.[27] Finally, the filled shaft, covered by the bannerstone and stela, was buried under a plaster floor at the summit of Structure 4-II.

The shaft, the four-pointed eccentric in Cache 12, and the four surrounding caches (8, 15, 24, and 25) represent the tree of life, connecting the primordial sea through the Witz Mountain to the sky. Not only is this a symbolic cosmogram, but it also marks Structure 4 as an *axis mundi* upon which the world is symbolically centered.

While the meaning of the shaft is understandable, the meaning of the ritual filling of the shaft is much more vague. However, it does demarcate a major change in the trajectory of Blue Creek's history. The Early Classic at Blue Creek is identified with probable political independence and dynamic construction of monumental architecture and is expressed in the ceramic record with influence from the Petén and in the display of wealth and power in the ability to accumulate elite goods. The Late Classic, though, is quite different. After the massive caching event in Structure 4, few large-scale constructions, Structures 2, 3, and 9 being major exceptions, are seen in Blue Creek's public district. However, as we will see, the community's population continued to grow and large-scale expansion of elite residences oc-

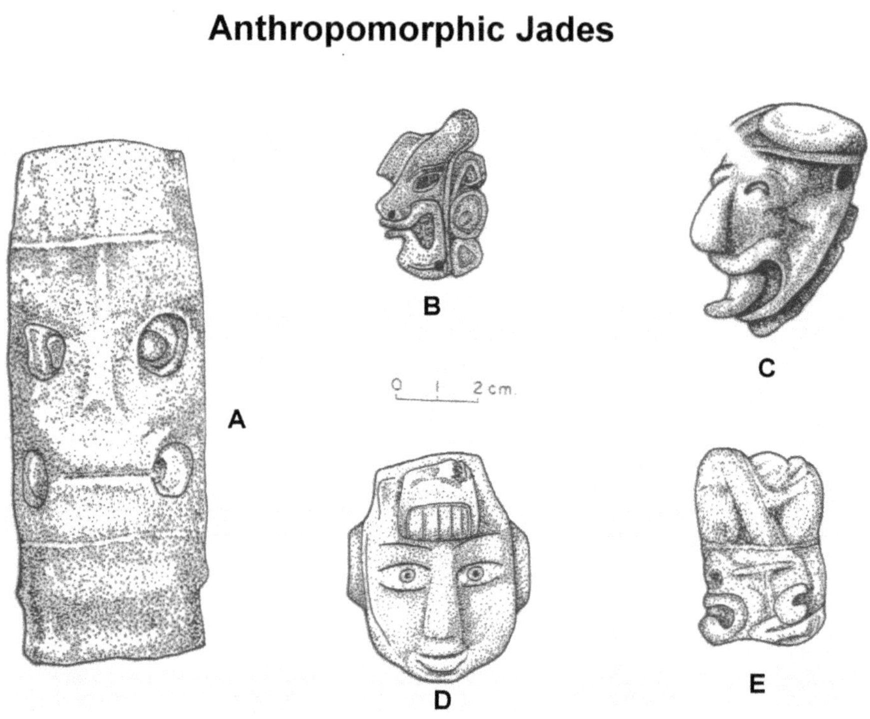

Figure 2.11. Anthropomorphic beads and pendants: a, large anthropomorphic bead (BC671); b, God K pendant (BC729); c, bib-head pendant with extended tongue (BC674); d, bib-head, Olmecoid (BC505) (a–d from Structure 4); e, acrobat pendant from Structure 34, Tomb 7 (BC6753).

curred. Whatever the nature of the caching event, it occurred during a time of fundamental change in the nature of Blue Creek.

The specific nature of the ritual event associated with the caching may never be known. In earlier discussions, I suggested that the event was associated with the termination of a royal blood lineage, perhaps the same one that had been initiated at the same building four centuries before.[28] I further suggested that the jade in the deposit was probably not solely from Blue Creek and the deposit included royal jewels of neighboring rulers who made a pilgrimage to Blue Creek in a communal rite of passage. However, I can no longer support this pilgrimage interpretation. It was based upon disbelief that a community the size of Blue Creek could possess so much jade. Several years later, large quantities of jade have been found throughout the Blue Creek community in Late Preclassic and Early Classic contexts and the Structure 4 caches are no longer so anomalous. In support of the lineage termination view, it can be pointed out that the shaft and its contents are structurally similar to tomb shafts dug into buildings and then filled. It is certainly an elegant argument that the royal lineage was first initiated at Structure 4 at about

A.D. 100, then terminated at the same place four hundred years later. Unfortunately, it may not be true.

Another plausible argument was developed by Kent Reilly and myself. In this view, the shaft may have held a pole with a banner such as those taken into battle by kings. The filling of the shaft was then done to enhance the sacredness of the royal space and to make preparations for warfare. Most likely, such a war would have been with a neighboring polity and Blue Creek did not appear to prevail. This scenario would explain the changing nature of public construction after this date and the possible disuse of the ballcourt in the Late Classic period. If Blue Creek fell under the hegemony of a neighboring kingdom, then we would have an explanation for the fact that in all other respects, Blue Creek thrived during the Late Classic.

Structure 5

Structure 5 is a building 52 meters long and relatively narrow, only 16–18 meters at the base, rising about 6 meters above the plaza floor and defining the west side of Plaza A.[29] We expected to find a series of complex construction events, and we were surprised to find only two.

While there may be remnants of smaller buildings under Structure 5-I that we have not encountered, despite two major trenching efforts, we do know that Structure 5-I was built in the Early Classic period in, by and large, the final form of the building. This is the large, long substructure of the final form, with rounded corners and two tiers and a nine-step central staircase. We do not know the form of the superstructure, as it was razed for the construction of Structure 5-II. Structure 5-II consists of a single vaulted room, with Structure 5-I as the substructure. The interior of the room was about 45 meters long and about 2.5 meters wide. It had a central doorway flanked by three more on either side and there were doorways at the end of the building for a total of nine entrances. All of these opened onto a walkway around the building overlooking the Main Plaza. As the vaulted roof of Structure 5-II has collapsed, we can assume that its original height was in the range of seven meters above the plaza level with the summit floor about five meters above the plaza level. Again, we do not have a clear date for the construction of Structure 5-II, but we also assume it to have occurred in the Early Classic.

Dale Pastrana argues that this is a viewing gallery from which nobles could observe activities in the plaza. While determination of building function in public areas is a difficult topic, her point is certainly important. First, the building provides full view of all activities on the plaza and an individual can move from point to point in order to see activities from differing perspectives. Second, this building would provide extraordinary views of sunrises (and sunsets from the back side) and any ritual activity associated with the solstices and equinoxes as well as Structures 2 and 3. Further, while a small dedicatory cache was found at the summit of Structure 5-I, it was one of the least elaborate at Blue Creek. I believe that Structure 5 was not associated with the same sense of sacredness that other buildings were. Instead, as Pastrana says, it served as a viewing gallery where nobles could see the truly sacred activities on the east side and central portion of the Main Plaza.

Structure 6

This building is also located along the west side of the Main Plaza and faces the west side of Structure 1 about five meters away.[30] It is about half the size of Structure 5 and was 28 meters long, 10.6 meters wide, and 2.7 meters high. During the 1970s, the southern end of the building was bulldozed away. While there were several small remodelings of Structure 6, it had only one major, Early Classic, construction episode. The building consisted of a single-room superstructure, with apparently only a single two-meter-wide doorway. The back wall had completely fallen away from the building, but still there were inadequate materials to conclude that Structure 6 had a vaulted roof. Instead, it seems to have been a partially stone-walled superstructure with a perishable roof. This superstructure was atop a substructure that was slightly more than 2.5 meters high, with a central staircase providing access.

The Ballcourt

The ballcourt consists of Structures 7 and 8 and rests on top of a very large platform built during the Early Classic (Río Hondo). Several points regarding the ballcourt are important, the first being its very existence. Some have argued that the presence of a ballcourt is direct evidence that the center had a royal presence. While this may not be true, there is a strong correlation between the presence of ballcourts and the presence of royal elites or nobility.[31] Further, there is clearly a power-based connection between the ritual playing out of Maya creation through the ballgame and those who would be able to commission formal ballcourts. Like most southern lowland ballcourts, this one is positioned between the two public plazas, possibly with the game functioning as a mediating force involving factions of leadership.

Beyond the presence and general location of the ballcourt at Blue Creek, its puzzling setting atop an oversized platform must also be addressed. At other sites, Chan Chich, for example, a large platform space located outside of the public plaza may have been used for artisans' workshops. The Chan Chich platform was at least used as a dump for lithic debitage from workshop activities.[32] Whether the activities actually occurred at the location of the debitage dump is difficult to determine. So, in pursuit of such possibilities at the Blue Creek ballcourt platform, we conducted a test-pitting operation on the platform looking for similar deposits, but without success. Currently, the function of the non-ballcourt part of the ballcourt platform remains unknown.

There were significant quantities of lithic debris on top of Structure 8 and the ballcourt alley itself as a final deposition. It seems very unlikely that the ballcourt could have been used again after this dumping event. However, we do not know whether this was a postoccupational deposit or a termination ritual deposit or even when it occurred. The presence of these materials, though, raises the possibility that the ballcourt was nonfunctional in the Late Classic period. If so, this is a further reflection of significant changes after A.D. 600.

Plaza B Complex

Structure 9

The Temple of the Masks, Structure 9, is one of Blue Creek's most important buildings.[33] Built atop a large, ramped dance platform, it rises more than 11 meters above the platform. At the escarpment's edge, it presents an impressive view to visitors coming from the east and it defines the southern end of the Plaza B complex. Structure 9 had been severely looted, with a massive trench dug into the east side and other large trenches in the north and south sides. Consequently, we have lost some important information, notably in the destruction of two tombs. However, several profitable years of excavation were invested in the building.

Relatively little is known of the first three construction phases, as they were only found in the profile of a deep looters' trench. Structure 9-I, the original version of the building, is tentatively dated to the Terminal Late Preclassic period (Linda Vista). This was a small pyramid, rising five or six meters above the platform, with a central staircase. Structure 9-II was an expansion of the original building and probably had no permanent superstructure and may have been the location of a termination ritual accompanying its disuse. Structure 9-III rose about 6.5 meters above the platform and again probably had no permanent superstructure.

Structure 9-IV is much better known than the previous buildings and presents a very complex and intriguing situation. Structures 9-III and 9-IV were both quite standard Petén style temples, with a central staircase leading up to a single-room superstructure. Near the top of each staircase was an outset that could be used for overlooking the assembled public in front of the building. The front of the staircase outset on Structure 9-IV was decorated with five panels of medium-relief stucco masks (Figures 2.12 and 2.13). Two panels and part of a third survive. These Early Classic style masks were originally believed to date to the Late Classic period, in part because of the confusing ceramics found in a cache associated with the superstructure. At that time, these masks were seen as an archaizing trait. While this argument was rather elegant, it was completely incorrect and we now recognize that these Early Classic styles were made in the Early Classic period (Río Hondo), probably about A.D. 300–400.

The two preserved masks have bib motifs under their chins, generally an Early Classic trait. The left head has scrolls and a central bracket under the chin strap or bib, a feature that also occurs in Late Preclassic masks in the North Acropolis of Tikal and at Structure 5C-2nd at Cerros. The headdress of the left head is well enough preserved to identify its cartouche, shaped like an Early Classic *ahau* glyph. The volutes above the cartouche can represent smoke or foliation, or they may be

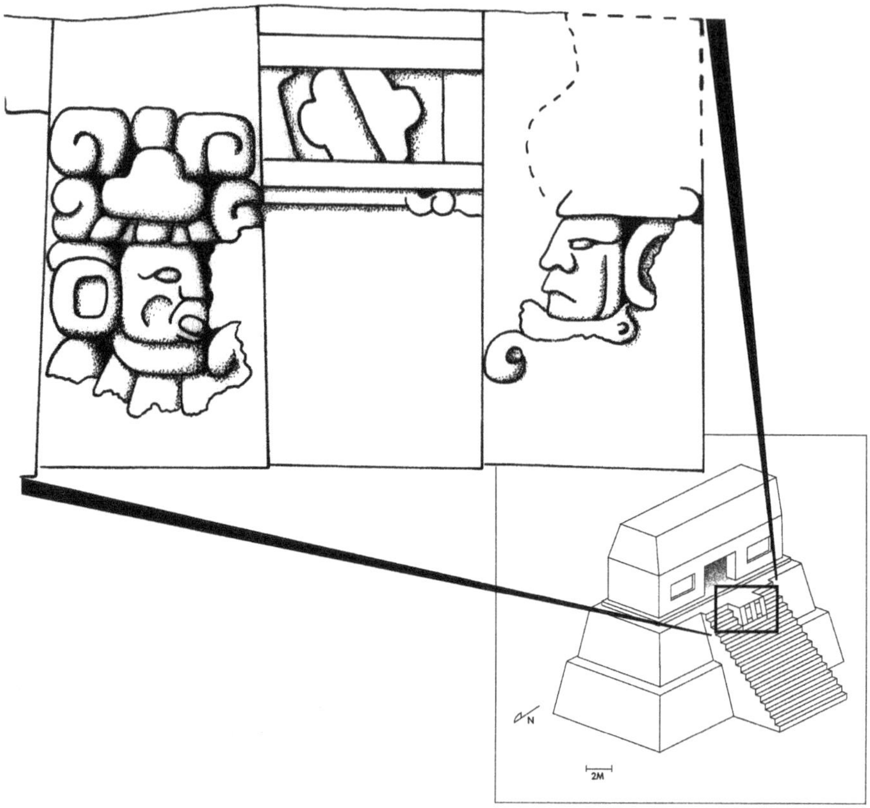

Figure 2.12. Drawing of stucco masks and their location on Structure 9-IV.

the Early Classic form of the syllable *ya* (Thompson's T126). Grube has shown that the simple T533 *ahau* sign, when not used as a day sign, is a logogram for the word *nik,* or "flower." David Stuart also showed that flowers symbolized divine kingship.[34] This *ahau* sign is distinctively early and resembles the *ahau* sign identified on a Middle Preclassic sherd from El Mirador. The volutes are most likely the "smoke" superfix that distinguishes the simple T533 *nik,* "flower," glyph from the glyph "smoking flower" (T535), used as a metaphor for "man's child." The "smoking flower" sign most often appears on the headgear of Early Classic nobles. The head variant of this sign can occur in both human and zoomorphic form. Here, the entire left head can be interpreted as the anthropomorphic head variant.

Between the two remaining heads is an inset panel that once was also stuccoed. Above it is what remains of a sky or earth band. This is an early form of Thompson's T103, generally accepted as having the value *ki,* which probably refers to "heart" or "center." It suggests that the building is not only the geographical

Figure 2.13. Photograph of *ahau* masks on Structure 9-IV.

center of the site but was also seen as the place of the *axis mundi,* the center of the cosmos. The "smoking flower" head represents the god of flowers or simply a personified flower. "Flower houses" were commonly used for counsel and the accession and residences of kings. The best-known "flower house" is House E of the palace at Palenque, which is decorated with polychrome flowers.

Another expression for a *nikteil na* is *popul na* or "mat house." Copan Temple 22a has been interpreted as a *popul na* on the basis of the mat symbols and *na* symbols on its facade. The earliest known *popul na* is Structure H-X from Uaxactun, which was a place where a king interacted with his people and other political leaders. Platforms in front of Structure 10-L 22a at Copan and Structure H-X at Uaxactun have been interpreted as dance platforms, as has the platform in front of this structure at Blue Creek. Dance was an important component of public rituals.

Many scholars have agreed with this general interpretation, which was devised with the assistance of Nikolai Grube. However, not all concur. For example, Karl Taube sees the anthropomorphic heads as the maize god rather than an *ahau.* Further, Kent Reilly and James Garber argue that such bib-heads are, in fact, depictions of the maize god emerging from a bowl as depicted in the Popul Vuh. In addition, in a review of the functions of buildings believed to be Council Houses, Elizabeth

Wagner correctly points out that the Structure 9-IV facade is incomplete and our argument is largely based upon iconography.[35] This leads her to believe that ours is still a speculative argument.

Structure 9-V is a relatively small expansion of Structure 9-IV, incorporating an expansion of the staircase, among other features. However, Structure 9-VI, the very large final construction, represents a complete reconfiguration of the building in the very early part of the Late Classic. The existing superstructure was partially destroyed and a massive frontal and summit expansion buried the previous buildings. Replacing the Petén style masonry superstructure was a new building with a massive frontal staircase and a platform summit. It is certainly conceivable that a perishable superstructure was placed on the summit. However, there was no evidence of its presence. This style is more reminiscent of Belize coastal plain sites such as Lamanai, Kakabish, and Altun Ha than of temple-pyramids of the Petén.

Structure 13 Courtyard

The Structure 13 Courtyard is an elite or royal residence that was originally built as an open, public plaza (Figure 2.14).[36] The first two buildings constructed on the platform were Structures 12 and 13, built in the Early Classic (Río Hondo). At a later date but still in the Early Classic, the platform was expanded and Structure 10 was built. In the early part of the Late Classic period (Aguas Turbias), Structures 11 and 14 were added to enclose space and convert this open plaza into residential space. At about the same time, there was a remodeling and reorientation of Structure 13 so that it faced to the north rather than the south. The functional transformation from public to secular residential space, though, seems to be clear. In the Late Classic, the Structure 13 Courtyard may have functioned similar to much larger acropolis groups such as seen at La Milpa and elsewhere. The shift from public to private space may have occurred at about the same time as the transformational events at Structures 1 and 4. If so, we can develop a strong argument that the nature of rule at Blue Creek fundamentally changed. While the nature of the change may always be ambiguous, there was a new duality, with two major residences in the core area.

Structure 13 is the largest building on the courtyard, at approximately five meters tall. While details of its earlier construction are uncertain, its final construction phase is well known. The north side of Structure 13 faces Plaza B and consists of a multitiered facade with a broad staircase ascending to the front entrance of a masonry superstructure. This superstructure consisted of two large, vaulted rooms, one opening to the north and one opening to the south, and the northern room had a doorway opening onto a terrace that wrapped around the east end of the building and allowed access to a side staircase. The south side of Structure 13 faces the enclosed space of the courtyard. After the courtyard was enclosed by adding Structures 11 and 14, access to the building was gained by a side staircase that led to a midway terrace on the building. Then, access into the building was accomplished by walking across the building to the east end and entering.

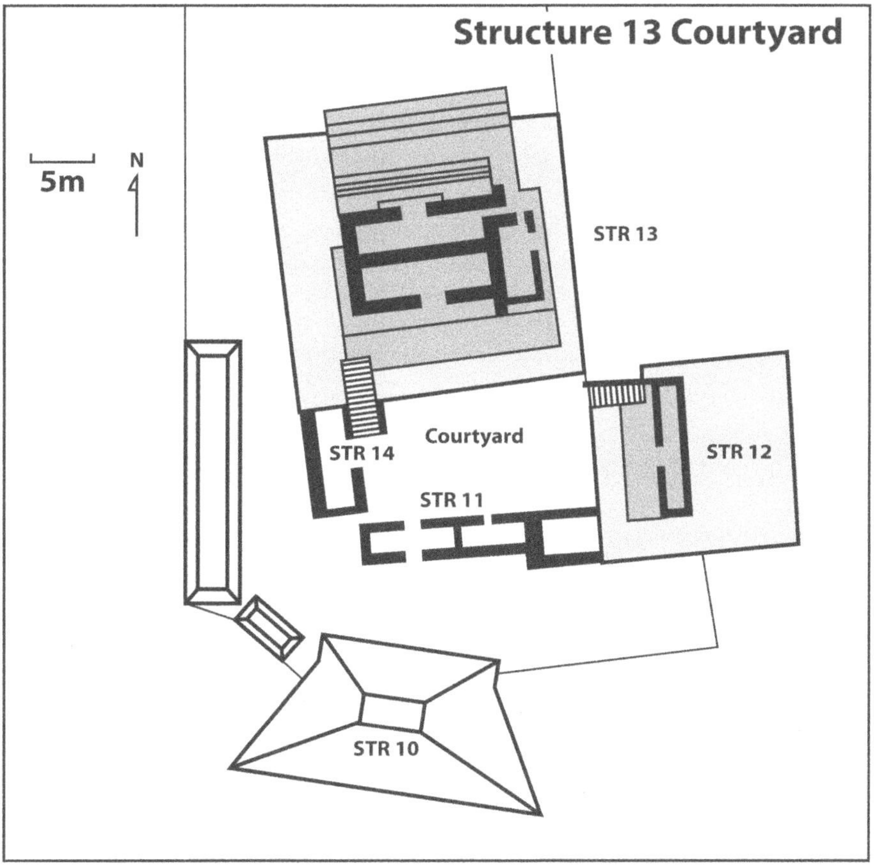

Figure 2.14. Plan view of Structure 13 Courtyard.

Structure 12 was built in four construction episodes. The earliest, Structure 12-I, was a fairly standard form with a central staircase and, possibly, a masonry superstructure. Buried within this was an Early Classic (Río Hondo) dedicatory cache that consisted of two sets of Aguila Orange ceramic vessels placed lip-to-lip and on top of each other. They contained an array of jade, coral, shell, and other artifacts. Analyses of the biosilicates within the vessels indicate that they also contained a number of plants and a large number of sponges following the pattern already discussed.

The final form, Structure 12-IV, mirrored Structure 13. Access was gained by a staircase on the left side of the facade rather than by a central staircase. Then, access continued by walking across the building to the center, then entering a central doorway. While such configurations may exist at other sites, as far as I know this architectural style is limited to these buildings and the Structure 37 Plazuela at Blue Creek.

Structure 11, 20 meters long, was added to Structure 12 to partially separate space. The east half was a vaulted stone room, while the west half was covered with a perishable roof and probably had perishable walls. Similarly, Structure 14 was added to Structure 13 to complete the residential space. Structure 14 consists of a single vaulted room, 8.5 meters long. An entryway between Structures 11 and 14 provided access into the courtyard.

Structure 10

Structure 10 is a medium-sized temple, approximately 4.5 meters tall, that has been very heavily looted, and a great deal of the architectural data has been lost. Excavations indicate that the courtyard platform was greatly expanded to accommodate Structure 10 and the building was erected in a single episode. However, it was clearly done as an expansion of the public plaza in the Early Classic period prior to the conversion of the space into a residence in the early part of the Late Classic period.

In a sense, the Structure 13 Courtyard is analogous to the Acropolis Courtyard at La Milpa. Both are residential complexes with buildings that could have administrative or religious functions and that also overlook activities on a major plaza. However, the Structure 13 Courtyard also represents a transformation of space from the sacred to the secular, probably at the end of the Early Classic period.

Structure 15 and Plaza B

The east side of Plaza B is open and drops precipitously off the ridge. The other sides of this large public space are bounded by Structure 13 on the south, the Structure 19 Courtyard on the north, and Structure 15 on the west. Structure 15 consists of a low platform, 35 meters long, which supported a linear set of vaulted rooms. Built in the Early Classic period over a Late Preclassic platform, it was dedicated with at least one cache, consisting of a pair of Uaxactun Unslipped Ware bowls placed lip-to-lip. The underside of the upper vessel was inscribed with a mat weave design, assumed to depict a royal mat. These vessels contained only organic materials, and preliminary analysis indicates that a wide range of phytoliths as well as abundant sponge spicules exist in this cache.

The Structure 19 Courtyard

The Structure 19 Courtyard is the primary elite or royal residence in the core area.[37] Covering 27 × 22 meters, it consists of a series of rooms, some vaulted and some with masonry roofs, built around two central courtyards (Figure 2.15). In its final form, the complex consisted of at least 14 interconnected rooms and passageways surrounding two private courtyards, covering about 650 square meters with 160 square meters of courtyard space. With construction beginning in the later part of the Early Classic (Río Hondo) and continuing to its final form in the Late Classic (Aguas Turbias), the Structure 19 Courtyard is a true agglutinated complex with

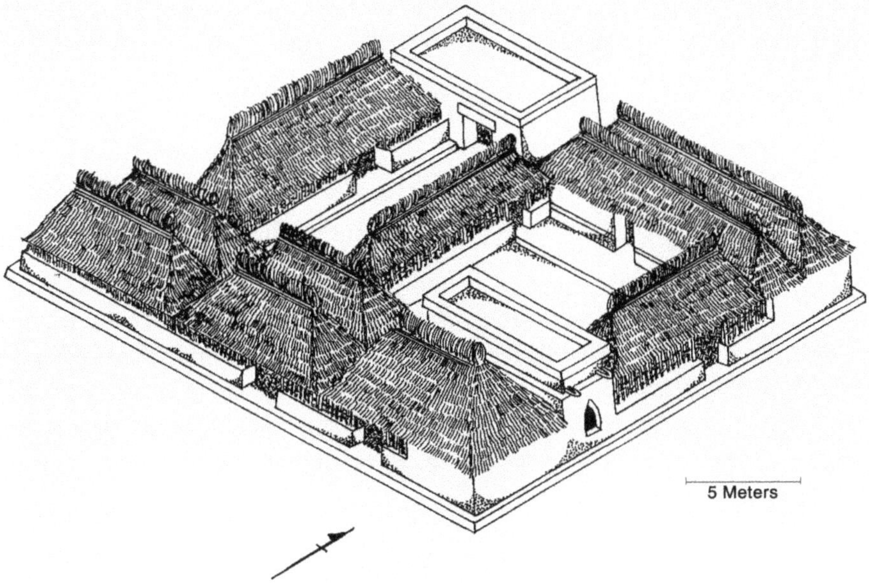

Figure 2.15. Reconstruction drawing of Structure 19 Courtyard.

several construction styles. Some rooms have low masonry walls that supported pole and thatch superstructures while others were vaulted or have beam and mortar roofing. At various times, new walls were added either to create new rooms or to restrict or alter routes of access. The formation of rooms can be seen in several places on the south side of the complex, where the dividing walls that created both Rooms G and E as well as the restricted area in the east end of Room C are visible. An example of restriction and alteration of access routes can be found by examining Courtyard A. Early in the building's history, access from Plaza B was easily obtained by a direct and open route. Later, after a series of structural additions and alterations, access became quite tortuous and convoluted, requiring one to navigate a number of passageways and rooms before entering Courtyard A.

Several points are important regarding the Structure 19 Courtyard. First, its location adjacent to one of the two major plazas at Blue Creek argues for the central importance of its inhabitants. This is strongly supported by its early construction date. Further, in many respects, this is the most elaborate of the site's elite residences. Also, flanking the courtyard to the west and possibly the east are small structures possibly inhabited by servants of the residents. Consequently, it is likely that the Structure 19 Courtyard was the "palace" of the rulers of Blue Creek in the Early Classic. Further, a bench in Room F was used at least four and possibly six or seven times for mortuary purposes. A single corrected radiocarbon date of A.D. 615 ± 60 (DRI 18329) was obtained from this deposit. So, the occupation appears to have been continuous into the Late Classic (Aguas Turbias), probably with a single lineage occupying the structure throughout its history.

Structure 24

Structure 24 defines the northern end of the Plaza B complex. Mary Neivens located the building only after it had been extensively looted, and she named it the "Temple of the Obsidian Warrior" because of the several hundred obsidian flakes she found that had probably come from a looted and destroyed tomb.[38] Later excavations indicated that Structure 24 was built in three episodes in the Early Classic (Río Hondo) period. In 1998, the Structure 24 mound was 9.9 meters tall, although prior to the looting it was probably somewhat taller. The best-preserved portion of the building is Structure 24-II, an Early Classic building with a two-chambered, vaulted superstructure with a doorway at the top of a central staircase. Associated with this phase was a 35-centimeter-deep pit cut through the floor at the base of the stairs. When excavated, this pit was found to have been empty.

Chronological Summary of Events at Blue Creek

The dynamics of public architectural change reflect the dynamics of power and authority. At Blue Creek, these dynamics reveal a pattern that is unlike those of other centers. The following is a chronological summary of the preceding information; the temporal units presented here follow the ceramic complexes established for Blue Creek.

Middle Preclassic Period

At Blue Creek, the enigmatic Middle Preclassic is divided into two periods, the Cool Shade complex (1000/800–650 B.C.) and the San Felipe complex (650–350 B.C.). Middle Preclassic materials have been found in the core area under Plaza A, in middens under the ballcourt, in front of Structure 9, and under the nearby Structure 25 Courtyard. These deposits derive from some sort of nucleated community living on top of the Bravo Escarpment where the public architecture would later be built. While these occupations are not the topic of this volume, there appears to be a population continuum into the Classic period. Further, it is likely that sacred space was being defined that would continue as such for more than a millennium.

Late Preclassic Period

During the early part of the Late Preclassic (Tres Leguas complex) estimated as 350 B.C.–A.D. 100/150, the patterns of the Middle Preclassic largely continued. The occupation where Structure 9 would later be built apparently grew and the occupation of the hilltop where the Structure 25 Courtyard would be built was also significant. Occupation also expanded in various locations in the settlement zone.

Terminal Late Preclassic Period

It was in the latter part of the Late Preclassic (Linda Vista complex), often called the Terminal Late Preclassic or "Protoclassic," that the general "footprint" of the public district was created and the first monumental architecture was built. Construction in Plaza A included Structures 1 and 4 and the formation of the plaza itself. In the Plaza B area, the first monumental construction occurred at Structure 9. Near Structure 24, *chultuns* were converted to tombs in this time. However, construction of monumental and elite residential architecture elsewhere in the Plaza B area had not yet occurred.

The construction of the first monumental architecture at Blue Creek seems to have coincided with the development of kingship at the site and throughout the Maya area. For example, Cache 21 at Structure 4 indicates that the first royal leader of Blue Creek may have been installed at about A.D. 100. Additionally, data from other areas of the site indicate that population increased dramatically as most of the residential areas became established. It also appears, though direct chronological evidence is still sparse, that the first ditched agricultural fields may have been constructed and used and that Blue Creek was beginning to realize its agricultural potential.

These changes brought tremendous wealth to Blue Creek. On an outlying hilltop, Tomb 5 was constructed to inter three individuals with 28 Tres Leguas complex vessels and more than a hundred pieces of jade.[39] This wealthy tomb was apparently not that of a member of the Blue Creek royalty, judging by the distance to the public core area of the site. However, the principal interred person did have very high status and probably oversaw agricultural and riverine trade operations. Whatever the individual's role, Tomb 5 speaks loudly about the wealth and complexity of Blue Creek at the time.

Early Classic Period

During the Early Classic period (Río Hondo complex), Blue Creek continued to grow and thrive economically. In Plaza A, major construction projects occurred at Structures 1, 4, 5, and 6. Behind Structure 1, the ballcourt was also built. One stela certainly stood in front of Structure 4 and another was probably in place at this time in front of Structure 6. Large-scale construction occurred in the Plaza B area at Structures 9 and 10, the Structure 13 Courtyard, the Structure 19 Courtyard, and Structure 24.

The masks on the facade of Structure 9-IV reinforce the idea that Blue Creek was an independent city with its own ruling lineage. The presence of the ballcourt also reinforces this assertion. Further, the construction of the innovative columned building, Structure 1-IV, indicates that Blue Creek was participating in the forefront of regional ideology. Blue Creek's access to jade was at its height at this time as well. Large quantities of jade are found in dedicatory caches and burials in monumental architecture as well as elite and non-elite residences. Residential communities around the core area, for example, exhibit a surprisingly high quantity of jade artifacts, especially given their apparent very low social status.

Also in the Early Classic Period there is widespread use of sponges in dedicatory caches in monumental, elite residential, and non-elite residential settings. Not only do these caches represent symbolic reenactments of the cosmos, but also they represent a shared view of the universe across all social strata. During the Early Classic period, Blue Creek was thriving economically and politically and was an integrated system of residential areas, somehow tethered to the core area.

However, the situation changed at about A.D. 500. The caching event in Structure 4 was an enormous and ostentatious display of wealth that marked a turning point in Blue Creek's history. Whether it was related to warfare, a lineage ending, or attempts to rejuvenate leadership or simply was a massive dedicatory cache, Blue Creek was never to be the same. Soon afterwards, the elegant, graceful columned Structure 1-IV was razed, perhaps for the tomb of Blue Creek's last king. The Structure 13 Courtyard was transformed from sacred to secular space to create a residence for a newly powerful member of the community.

Late Classic

During the Late Classic period (Aguas Turbias complex, A.D. 600–750, and Dos Bocas complex, A.D. 750–830/850), the public buildings of the core area were maintained and in some cases modified. While minor modifications were made to several buildings, significant expansion in the early part of the Late Classic, the Aguas Turbias phase, occurred at Structures 2, 3, and 9. In particular, the construction of the Pseudo-E-group, Structures 2 and 3, marked a continuity of ideas from across the region and, perhaps, increased regional integration.

As I will show in the following chapters, the elite residences outside of the monumental center of the city were greatly expanded with many medium-scale construction events. The community was thriving economically, but jade is no longer found in the Blue Creek record. This is certainly a characteristic of the broader regional pattern of a decline in the presence of jade at Late Classic sites. However, after having disproportionately high access to jade in the Late Preclassic and Early Classic periods, Blue Creek had virtually no access in the Late Classic. This may reflect internal as well as regional dynamics.

Terminal Classic

At the end of the Classic period (Río Bravo complex, A.D. 830/850–1000), Blue Creek's abandonment was marked by large deposits of ceramics and other artifacts in front of Structure 3 and in some elite residences. A debate continues as to whether these are actually ritual deposits related to termination or postoccupational debris.

However, their most important consequence is clear. By about A.D. 900, Blue Creek ceased to exist as a city.

Early Postclassic

Until 2005, the only Early Postclassic material found at or near Blue Creek was a very ephemeral reuse of a building at Chan Cahal, one of the residential components of the site. However, in 2005, the project successfully located an important remnant occupation at the Rempel group, a residential component approximately two kilometers southeast of the site core near the bank of the Río Bravo. This occupation is still being evaluated, but it may represent the last people utilizing the intensive agricultural systems nearby and trading those products down the rivers into the coastal trade system, much as occurred at Lamanai on a smaller scale.

Conclusion

When Mayanists say that a site is "big" or "small," they are generally referring to the size of the buildings in the core area. But, to paraphrase an old saying, it's not the size of your pyramid, it's what you do with it. With two plazas and approximately a dozen buildings, Blue Creek is not huge by Maya standards. I chose to conduct research at Blue Creek because it is large enough to have many of the complexities of truly huge sites without the overwhelming scale that makes excavating larger sites so difficult, not to mention so expensive and labor intensive. Nonetheless, several months of annual fieldwork for a decade were required to assemble this database. The effort, though, has given us a truly detailed understanding of the site core. And despite what we know of the site core, if we had not extended our work into the settlement zone, we would have an extremely skewed and biased view of the city of Blue Creek.

Architectural style is extremely conservative, and shifts in building form and character usually occur very slowly with few radical innovations. Viewed as a series of overlying buildings, the public architecture at Blue Creek offers a database to measure this change. This architectural record provides a dynamic and exceptional understanding of changing attitudes, beliefs, and political organization through time. Blue Creek represents an example of a Maya community with a 15-hundred-year history of dynamic shifts in population, political structure, and economics.

The first known occupants in the Middle Preclassic began to establish residential patterns that would carry into the rest of the sequence. By the early part of the Late Preclassic, it is possible that sacred space had already been defined that would continue to be sacred for the rest of the sequence. In the later part of the Late Preclassic, Blue Creek, like many other communities in the region, began building public architecture as a display of power and authority. Similarly, kingship was becoming the new political structure in the Maya lowlands, and Blue Creek seems to have participated in this development as well. It is very likely that by about A.D. 100, Blue Creek had installed its first king.

Blue Creek thrived for the next four hundred years or so. Numerous construction projects were commissioned, some of which were highly innovative. Blue Creek also became quite wealthy, with disproportionate access to elite goods such as jade. Clearly, the Late Preclassic and Early Classic periods were vibrant times in Blue Creek's history. However, changes seem to have occurred at the end of the Early Classic or early in the Late Classic. Later, Blue Creek's population continued to grow and elite residences were expanded. However, architectural changes seem to indicate that the cities to the east had become more influential than the cities to the west in the Petén. Further, access to exotic goods diminished severely. A realistic appraisal of the causes of these changes at Blue Creek will probably need to wait for equally detailed information from other regional sites. However, it is clear that Blue Creek's political fortunes had changed.

3 The Spatial Arrangement of a Maya City

In the previous chapter, I summarized what we know of Blue Creek's site core. However, like the downtown district of a modern city, Blue Creek's site core housed only a small percentage of the population. Years ago, Mayanists viewed the ancient social system as a naively simplistic dichotomy between elites and commoners. Further, they saw commoners as a homogeneous mass with little input into the society's organization and little to offer us in terms of understanding the past. Nothing could be further from the truth. Today, we have only begun to understand the complexity of the 95 percent or so of the population that lived outside of the site core.[1]

Some aspects of this complexity can be understood by viewing the spatial arrangement of people, their residences, and other activity areas across the landscape.[2] This is a basic tenet of human geography. Unfortunately, it is usually extremely difficult to assess the spatial arrangement of Maya cities as they sprawl through today's forested environment. Consequently, only a few have been well mapped.[3] It is our great fortune to work at a site that had been previously cleared for agriculture and ranching. While the clearing damaged and sometimes destroyed the archaeological materials, it also made the materials more visible. So, while other fieldworkers must cut lines through dense forest, we were able to rapidly map, then (not so rapidly) conduct test excavations across large areas around the site core.

Ancient Maya cities consisted of complex spatial arrangements of functional and structural components. Despite many decades of research, the complexity and variability of these cities are only now becoming clear. In this chapter, I will summarize Blue Creek's spatial arrangement to provide a better understanding of aspects of this complexity. Additionally, the spatial patterning of Blue Creek is contrasted with models of Maya cities to show that such models remain overly simplistic and do not adequately describe the realities of Maya spatial planning.

Blue Creek's location at the headwaters of the Río Hondo offers important strategic resources. Soils at the base of the escarpment are very deep and rich and provide some of the highest agricultural potential in Central America. However, they are associated with high risk factors such as occasional seasonal inundation that can cause complete crop loss. Elevations at the top of the escarpment are in the range of 180–200 meters above sea level. Further, the eastern Petén zone consists of eroded karstic uplands marked by pronounced limestone hills with little or no soil. Separating these hills are expanses of deep, rich soils with high agricultural productivity. While these are not as productive as the soils below the escarpment, they do not have the same high risk of inundation and are used today for mechanized agribusiness. Where these expanses are large, they are termed *bajos*. One, the Dumbbell Bajo that defines the west boundary of the Blue Creek polity, covers approximately 40 square kilometers. I apply the term *bajito* to refer to the much smaller low-lying areas near the escarpment. An example of a bajito is the area between Plaza A and the southern end of Kín Tan (Figure 2.2).

Thus, Blue Creek was strategically located with respect to three important economic resources: the variety of resources availed by the ecotonal zone of the Bravo Escarpment with access to both physiographic zones, the rich agricultural lands above and below the escarpment, and river access to the well-established circum-Yucatecan coastal trade system. This maritime trade system moved exotic, elite, status-reinforcing objects as well as commodities and formed an economic link that bound otherwise independent Maya polities.[4] It also provided an outlet for agricultural goods produced at Blue Creek to enter distant markets. The Río Hondo headwaters area was fully under Blue Creek's control, as the nearest neighboring sites are more than 10 kilometers from the headwaters. As a consequence, Blue Creek, despite its modest size, had inordinately high access to exotic objects such as jade, the most valuable material in the ancient Maya world.

Models of Maya Cities

Scholars are largely in agreement regarding the nature of the core areas of Maya cities. However, the nature of the surrounding settlement zone is anything but clear. This, for the most part, is a function of the focus given to excavations of the monumental architecture. Further, while many studies have focused on the structure and function of households, few have considered how groups of households are arranged across the landscape. Also compounding the issue is the fact that many Maya sites are in high canopy, subtropical forests. Consequently, large-scale surveys and excavations in settlement zones are exceedingly complex and labor intensive to accomplish. Most such efforts follow the pattern of the research at the nearby site of La Milpa, where transect surveys in the cardinal directions were used to extrapolate to the entire settlement zone.[5] While such efforts are useful and the only pragmatic approach in dense forests, transect surveys have limited utility to elucidate information regarding the spatial arrangement of the vast majority of settlement zones. In contrast, the vast majority of the Blue Creek settlement zone has been cleared of forest vegetation and is currently used for ranching and/or agriculture. Consequently, the archaeological visibility at Blue Creek is very high, and large, contiguous areas can be surveyed with relative ease.

Early investigators of Maya sites believed that core areas were "disembodied ceremonial centers" with few people living in them and that most people lived in rural farmsteads practicing slash-and-burn agriculture.[6] It is almost amazing that this view ever existed, given the vast amount of data to the contrary. Today, some archaeologists still take the position that there was no such thing as Maya urbanism, based on the general differences between the nature of central Mexican cities such as Teotihuacan and Tenochtitlan and pre-Hispanic urban centers in Peru such as Huaca de Luna and Chan Chan.[7] However, this is largely a semantic argument that fails to recognize that Maya cities are simply very different from other pre-Hispanic urban cities. Even in our society, population densities and other aspects of urbanism in Fort Worth and San Francisco, for example, are very different. However, both are regarded as cities. Much the same was true of the distinction between Maya and central Mexican cities.

Maya scholars long ago recognized Maya sites as urban centers. In an important article, Joyce Marcus tested several general urban models against spatial aspects of Maya cities: the concentric circle zone model, the sector model, and the multiple nuclei model.[8] The concentric zone model derives from twentieth-century studies of urban growth in the United States and essentially describes a setting in which growth progressively moves outward from a single center (Figure 3.1, left). In this model, functionally similar components are spatially arranged in zones roughly equidistant from the original center. In its original application to American cities, the outer zone is reserved for more affluent, suburban commuters who can afford to live at some distance from their workplaces. Translating this model to contemporary Latin American cities, it is clear that the affluent families live closer to the city center and the most distant communities are actually occupied by recent, generally poor, arrivals. The sector model describes a setting in which original functions located near a city center would continue to expand with growth and these functional sectors would be maintained (Figure 3.1, center). As new functions are created, new sectors are created as well. However, as Marcus notes, concentric circle zone models may be better descriptors of American urbanism while sector models may better describe the spatial distribution of social classes, and cities can display both patterns. Finally, multiple nuclei models describe settings in which multiple centers arise from multiple functional components (Figure 3.1, right). Marcus applies this model to Maya sites that exhibit multiple plazas or public central places.

Wendy Ashmore pioneered another approach to understanding Maya cities. Ashmore argued that public architecture was based on regional templates that incorporated a variety of architectural traits.[9] For example, in the Petén region of Guatemala, a number of sites have palace groups oriented at the south end of the public precinct. In a broader sense, this approach ascribed symbolic elements of cosmology to the design of public architecture, including the use of outlying build-

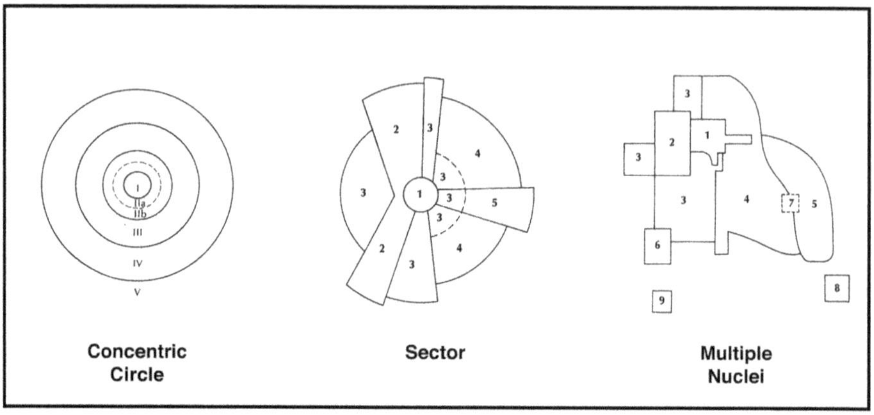

Figure 3.1. Graphic representation of three urban models (redrawn from Marcus 1983).

ings at the cardinal directions that represent the four *bacabs,* mythological sons of Hzamna and Ixchel, who are represented as jaguars holding up the sky. While this approach does offer insight into the design of public architecture, it is still limited in applicability to understanding locational patterns in vernacular architecture. For one thing, formal, public architecture is only a small component of the totality of a Maya city. Such planning principles may exist in the early stages of Maya cities, but the complexity of multiple landscape transformations in really huge cities such as Tikal makes their identification difficult.[10]

Despite the growing focus on settlement zones and settlement patterns in the 1970s and 1980s, field research dealing with mapping and understanding spatial arrangements of sites remains limited. Instead, regional analysis of broad macro-patterns with sites as nodes and examinations of residential elements of Maya cities have been the more common modes of research.[11] The principal reason that site-level analysis was not often conducted was that the fieldwork to gather such information was difficult, labor intensive, and expensive. This is no less true today.

The first major survey of a settlement zone was the pioneering work of Dennis Puleston at Tikal in Guatemala.[12] Puleston's work resulted in the large survey area around the center of Tikal and revealed vastly more complexity than had been previously known. Further, the detailed level of the survey located evidence of approximately 60 percent more residential activity than had been previously known. Subsequently, large block surveys have been conducted at a relatively few other lowland sites, such as Edzna, Seibal, and Cerros.[13] In general, these surveys have revealed that Maya cities have a wide range of complexity. Cerros is the simplest of these examples, largely because it grew rapidly in the Late Preclassic and was abandoned by the Early Classic period. The most complex would still be Tikal, with multiple public centers joined by causeways and settlement arranged in an array across the landscape. With regard to Tikal, Scarborough has argued that high-status families or lineages resided in strategic locations for the control of resources such as water.[14]

One important recent effort has been undertaken at the well-known site of Palenque. Palenque is situated, like Blue Creek, overlooking the agricultural lands of the Tabasco Plain, on the much higher and more rugged foothills of the mountainous Chiapas rain forest. Despite decades of research and the general knowledge that there was intensive settlement outside of the well-documented core zone, little was known about the settlement zone of Palenque. Barnhart surveyed blocks along the Palenque escarpment and documented a high population density zone that is reminiscent of the density of non-Maya, central Mexican cities.[15] Despite this exception, it appears that most Maya cities do not have a particularly higher population density near the core area than elsewhere.

A caveat must be added to that last statement, as there is evidence for buildings in core areas, as well as elsewhere, that are less than apparent today. At the site of Chan Chich, 300 meters of trenches for waterlines for a hotel were excavated in the core area, which revealed at least five buried plaster floors, at least three of which were probably substructures for residences. However, there was no surface evidence for any of them. Additionally, excavations in the settlement zone of Nohmul, where there was also no surface evidence of occupation, revealed numerous buried, overlapping house floors.[16] So, while we generally view the residents of site centers as being the elite of a community, it is very likely that there was also an "invisible" group of residents, perhaps there in the service of the ruling elite.

Mapping Ancient Blue Creek

Mapping of Blue Creek began in 1992 with truly antiquated equipment: a plane table and alidade. The 1992 mapping encompassed the core zone, which at that time was under dense secondary vegetation, and the elite residential group now known as Kín Tan.[17] In 1995, mapping was extended to cover approximately 16 square kilometers centered on the core zone. In this area, 407 features were recorded. These were mostly housemounds, the low mounds upon which perishable structures had been built, arranged in somewhat ambiguous clusters, which at the time were still poorly understood. This survey was conducted with use of a total data station and all data from both surveys were superimposed upon a digitized version of the available topographic maps via AutoCAD software.[18]

These surveys were followed in 1996 and 1997 with more targeted surveys designed to expand the database. During the 1997 and 1998 field seasons, a sample of several dozen ancient residences was excavated in order to understand the temporal aspects of the array of features spread over the landscape that the survey efforts had located. At the same time, Lichtenstein recognized that the clusters previously discovered were actually bounded residential groups and named many of them.[19] Other excavation programs enhanced the database from the settlement zone, particularly in the residential components of Kín Tan, Chan Cahal, and Sayap Ha.[20]

Components of the Blue Creek Polity

Three general types of components have been identified at Blue Creek: the core zone of public and monumental architecture, residential components, and nonresidential resource components. In the following sections, a selection of the residential components and their nature will be compared and contrasted. These components are spatially discrete areas, each associated with varying environmental resources and each differently organized internally. Fifteen such residential areas have been identified, ranging from small, rural communities, to elite communities with masonry architecture, to the homes of the nobility in the core area (Figure 1.5). This social, political, and economic variability is associated with variability in agricultural resources and the nature of how each component interacted with the nobility of the core area.

Residential Components above the Bravo Escarpment

Kín Tan

Closely associated with the core area is Kín Tan, an area of elite residential complexes northwest of Plaza B. Kín Tan includes seven patio groups, three courtyards, and one plazuela.[21] Each of these complexes is composed of large-scale masonry structures located on hilltops with commanding views of the surrounding countryside as well as uniquely clear, uninterrupted views of Plaza A (Figures 3.2 and 3.3). A consistent pattern of construction and occupation is seen in these residences and is typified by the Structure 37 Plazuela, which was initially constructed in the Terminal Late Preclassic period (Linda Vista complex, A.D. 100/150–250) or the very early part of the Early Classic period (Río Hondo complex, A.D. 250–600) but which then experienced large-scale expansion during the Late Classic period (Aguas Turbias complex, A.D. 600–750). Further, it appears that each of these residential complexes has its own ritual central place. For example, in the Structure 37 Plazuela, an Early Classic lineage head and shaman was interred in the center of the open courtyard, close to the burial of the earlier lineage founder.[22] Then, a shrine was built over both of their burials. The growing wealth and authority seen in the later burial, that of the Early Classic shaman, is a reflection of his individual and, therefore, his lineage's growing relationship to the nobility living in the core area. It appears that these people's wealth and authority were based on their role in the centralized authority and with the nobility of Blue Creek.

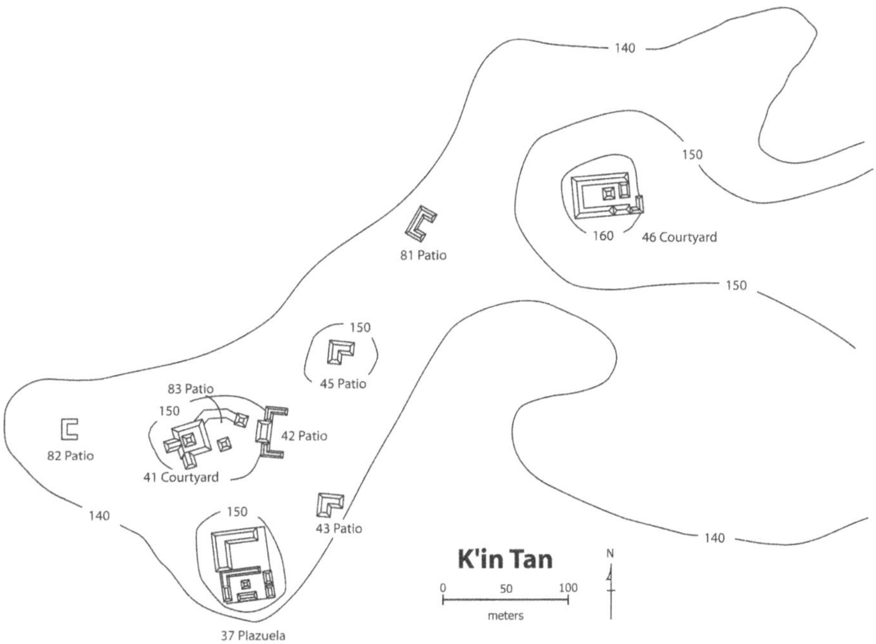

Figure 3.2. Plan view of western portion of Kín Tan showing major residences.

Importantly, Kín Tan is almost completely surrounded (about 320 degrees) by uninhabited flatlands that are so fertile that it is unimaginable that they were not used for dry farming. Clearly Kín Tan held some sort of control over this fertile agricultural resource. However, there are no surrounding secondary residences nor is there evidence of terraces and check dams at Kín Tan. So, the residents of Kín Tan either were the farmers themselves or imported labor from other nearby residential areas.

Nukuch Muul

On top of the Río Bravo escarpment and its back-slope about 1.6 kilometers north-northwest of the core area is the Nukuch Muul residential area.[23] This consists of 41 structures centered on a large plazuela group situated atop a large hill overlooking much of the surrounding area. Nukuch Muul is a significant population cluster that is physically, economically, and socially centered on a single large hilltop plazuela. The residents of the plazuela held a significantly higher social status than those in surrounding homes. What their interrelationships were may not be knowable. They may have been lower-status members of the same lineage or non-lineage members in the service of the plazuela residents. Regardless, it is clear that the plazuela residents held significant authority and their home was the central place for authority in Nukuch Muul.

Figure 3.3. Aerial view of Kín Tan showing Structure 37 Plazuela, Structure 41 Courtyard, Structure 42, and Structure 45 cleared of vegetation (clockwise from lower center).

Interestingly, unlike the situation at Kín Tan, there is much evidence of water control and agricultural terracing on the hill slopes along the west face of the escarpment in this area. This points to a significant distinction between the residents of the two groups. Nukuch Muul was an internally hierarchically tiered community led by a powerful lineage but tied closely to agricultural production in the surrounding flatlands.

Where Nukuch Muul seems to be a vertically integrated community with a range of social strata, all residents of Kín Tan appear to have lived in high-status structures. Further, the Kín Tan residents do not seem to have required the support of a local "service" community nor did they go to any effort to utilize as much of the agricultural potential as possible.

Rosita

The community of Rosita is located on a series of rolling hilltops about 3.5 kilometers northwest of the core area.[24] There are more than 20 visible structures in this group loosely arranged across a series of sculpted and terraced hilltops that rise 20–25 meters above the surrounding bajos. While little excavation has been undertaken at Rosita, the pattern of architecture seems analogous to that of the high-status residences of Kín Tan. Rosita appears to have been an affluent community characterized by substantial architecture and commanding views of the surrounding region. In addition, there is at least one relatively small, nonresidential, pyramidal structure. Material recovered during initial surface collections dates from the Late Preclassic (Tres Leguas, 350 B.C.–A.D. 100/150) through the Late Classic (Dos Bocas complex, A.D. 750–830/850) periods and excavated material date to the Late Classic period. Excavations at one structure confirm that significant amounts of Late Preclassic construction are present.

Rosita's relationship to the core area is entirely different from that of either Kín Tan or Nukuch Muul. Located at the northern portion of the Blue Creek polity, Rosita clearly played an integrative role in that sector. It would be the first large-scale construction encountered by visitors crossing the Río Azul canyon from the north as they entered Blue Creek.

Additionally, the "Rosita Hills" overlook an expansive upland bajito that covers approximately half of a square kilometer. This bajito was an important agricultural resource for the Rosita residents. And, as in the lands surrounding Kín Tan, there was no residential activity in these lands. Today, these are grasslands for cattle and are periodically burned and plowed, giving us almost complete visibility of potential buried remains and equal certainty regarding the lack of habitation.

U Xulil Beh

U Xulil Beh is a small, informally clustered group located 2.5 kilometers southwest of the core area that consists of 22 small, Classic period, housemounds with no monumental architecture or larger residential structures (Figure 3.4).[25] So, the residents of U Xulil Beh seem to have been of relatively low social status. U Xulil Beh is located on a largely flat expanse of land bounded by several large drainages and a series of small hills. While there are a number of large-scale agricultural terraces located at the west end of the group, there is still much less agricultural land available to this community than any other. U Xulil Beh's role in the fabric of "greater Blue Creek" remains unclear. It is anomalous for the lack of central places and the diminutive amount of available agricultural land. Further, it was not occupied until the Early Classic period and, then, significant energy was expended to realize the limited agricultural potential of the community. U Xulil Beh seems to be a later expansion of Blue Creek with agricultural potential for production for its own food purposes but it did not participate in large-scale production as other residential areas did.

Other Residences

There are many other residences and residential components of Blue Creek that are not yet well defined. For example, at the top of the escarpment both north and south of the core are numerous elite residences that overlook the lowlands. The

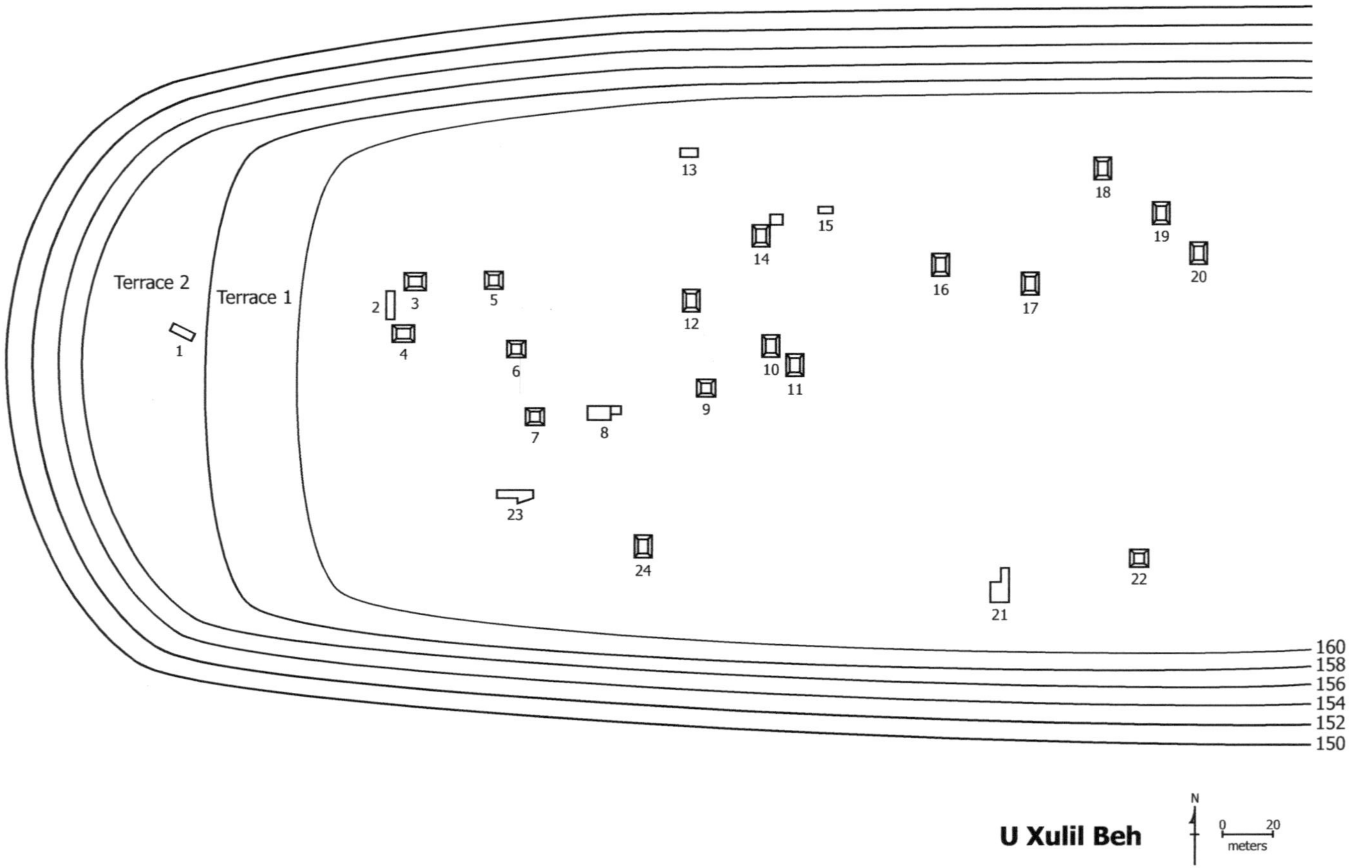

Figure 3.4. Plan view of U Xulil Beh showing locations of housemounds, agricultural terraces, and topography.

Figure 3.5. Schematic plan view of SHB Courtyard.

SHB Courtyard (Figure 3.5) is such a residence, located approximately one kilometer south of the core area. This is a masonry courtyard with a restricted-access entrance on the east side. While the SHB Courtyard was probably built in the Late Classic period, no excavations have been undertaken there.

Another such elite residence is the Structure 28 Plazuela, located only about a hundred meters south of the Main Plaza. This group of four structures is located on a 45-by-70-meter platform. The large size of the platform has led some to believe that this is a third public plaza.[26] However, there are several such large residences located along the top of the escarpment. Regardless of this small disagreement of interpretation, the Structure 28 Plazuela has a construction history that is similar to that of Plaza A. The platform was initially constructed in the Terminal Late Preclassic (Linda Vista complex) and the major architectural construction was completed in the Early Classic. Unlike Plaza A, though, there was little or no Late Classic construction at the Structure 28 Plazuela.

Numerous other elite residences exist at Blue Creek, such as the Quincunx group, scattered unnamed elite residences south of Kín Tan, and the Rempel group. In the Quincunx case, extensive excavations were conducted, but the area around it has not been surveyed. Consequently, it is difficult to link it to the larger view of Blue Creek. In the other cases, we have not yet conducted sufficient investigations to comment beyond their existence.

Residential Components below the Bravo Escarpment

Chan Cahal

Chan Cahal is a non-elite residential community surrounded, in contrast to U Xulil Beh, by extensive ditched agricultural fields (Figure 3.6). Chan Cahal exhibits the longest series of continuous occupations yet encountered at Blue Creek, beginning in the early Middle Preclassic period (Cool Shade complex, 1000/800–650 B.C.) and extending into the Late Classic period (Río Bravo complex, A.D. 830/850–1000). Excavations have shown Chan Cahal to be an informally clustered community of at least 28 small housemounds originally constructed of perishable materials with the exception of one building, Structure U-5.[27]

Structure U-5 is a Late Classic, two-room, masonry building on a subplatform attached to a large platform covering more than two thousand square meters. The exact nature of Structure U-5 is somewhat uncertain. While it was originally thought to be a public shrine or administrative structure, extensive excavations have shown that this structure was in fact an elite residence with possible secondary public functions.

Chan Cahal is surrounded by a huge complex of ditched fields and appears to be the home of at least some of the farmers of these fields. With the exception of Structure U-5, the residences of Chan Cahal represent very long-term habitations, almost certainly predating the construction of the ditched fields. However, once this large-scale production system was in place, the people of Chan Cahal somehow became tied to the royalty of the core area. This linkage is most likely manifest in the construction of Structure U-5. The residents of Structure U-5 were probably the most politically powerful of Chan Cahal and represent the only apparent internal social stratification.

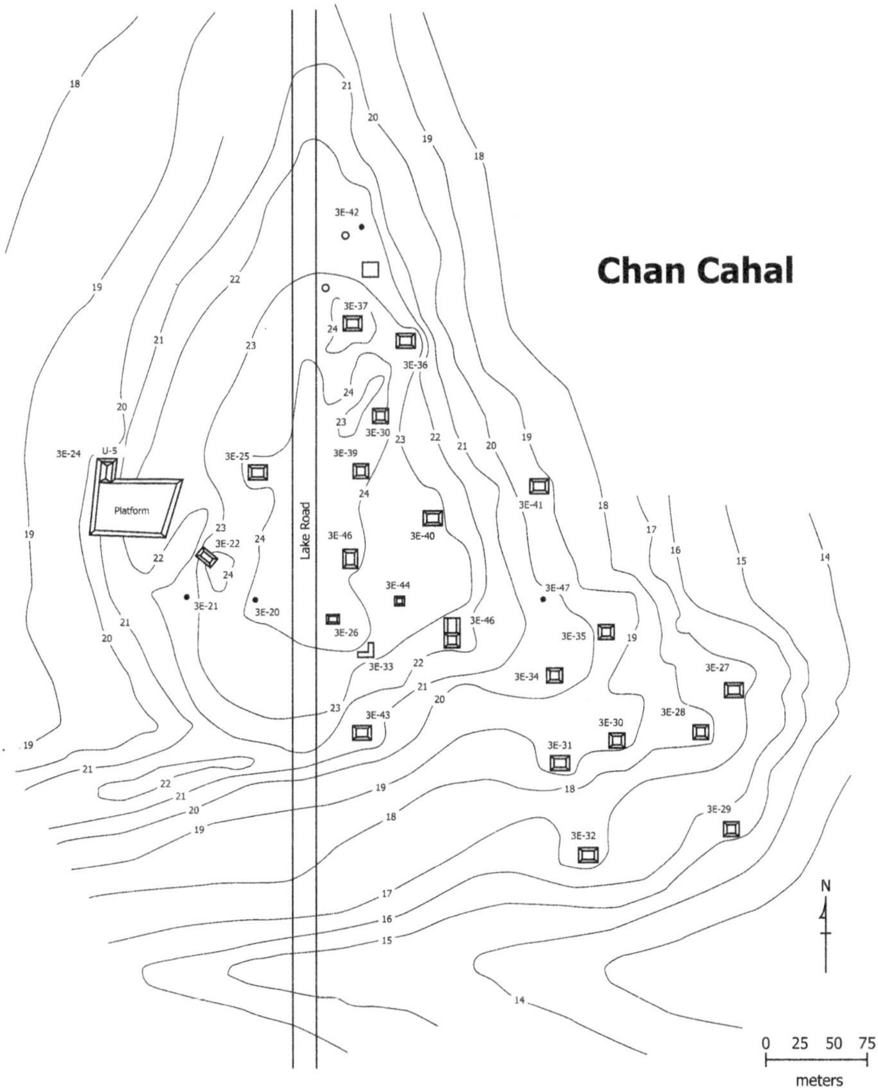

Figure 3.6. Plan view of Chan Cahal showing locations of housemounds, Structure U-5, and topography.

Paradoxically, although Chan Cahal seems to have been inhabited by the least affluent members of Blue Creek society, more than two hundred jade artifacts have been recovered from the area. While these are generally small and made of low-grade materials and workmanship, this is still a remarkable number. The presence of this jade is a reflection of the relationship between the wealthy royalty and those whose work in agricultural fields created wealth for the royalty.

Sayap Ha

Southwest of Chan Cahal and northeast of the core area is Sayap Ha, another informally clustered community of 43 visible structures nestled against the face of the escarpment where freshwater springs emanate (Figure 3.7). The occupation of Sayap Ha dates from at least the Late Preclassic through the Late Classic periods.[28] Our major excavations at Sayap Ha have focused on two large-scale buildings, an Early Classic (Río Hondo complex) vaulted room on a platform and a nearby Early Classic (Río Hondo complex) platform, four meters tall. Other buildings include a small courtyard, several substantial patio groups, and a number of housemounds. Consequently, Sayap Ha differs greatly from nearby Chan Cahal in terms of the structure and physical arrangement of the group, as well as apparently in its temporal aspects.

Authority at Sayap Ha was apparently dramatically different from authority at Kín Tan. At Kín Tan, a lineage was established in the Terminal Late Preclassic period (Linda Vista complex) that grew in wealth and apparent prominence and authority for several centuries. By contrast, burials at Sayap Ha were placed under the floors of occupied houses and had no impact on later configurations of buildings or displays of wealth and authority. In one case, an Early Classic period (Río Hondo complex) male was buried with a set of elite-status goods. Despite his access to such goods, his family did not grow into the sort of long-term lineage with political and economic power as seen at Kín Tan.[29]

Nonresidential, Agricultural Components

For the most part, nonresidential components of Blue Creek are agricultural systems. Although these will be discussed in detail in Chapter 5, a brief introduction is appropriate here. Three large, distinct agricultural systems are present at Blue Creek, including ditched fields in the lowlands below the Bravo Escarpment, dry field agriculture above it, and growing platforms located at the escarpment's base.

Below the escarpment and surrounding Chan Cahal are the ditched field systems. The soils below the escarpment are incredibly deep, rich, and productive. However, they are prone to flooding and seasonal inundation. While I am oversimplifying a very complex topic, the ditches were dug to drain water from low-lying areas so that crops would not be lost to supersaturated soils. Today, the ditches have largely filled with sediments that accumulated since their abandonment. However, they still hold moisture better than the surrounding areas. So, they can be seen easily from low-flying airplanes at some times of the year. For example, at the end of the dry season most of the grasses have become yellow and starved for rain. Grasses growing in the ancient ditches, though, are lush and green; the ditches almost appear as green grouting on a yellow-green tile floor (Figure 3.8).

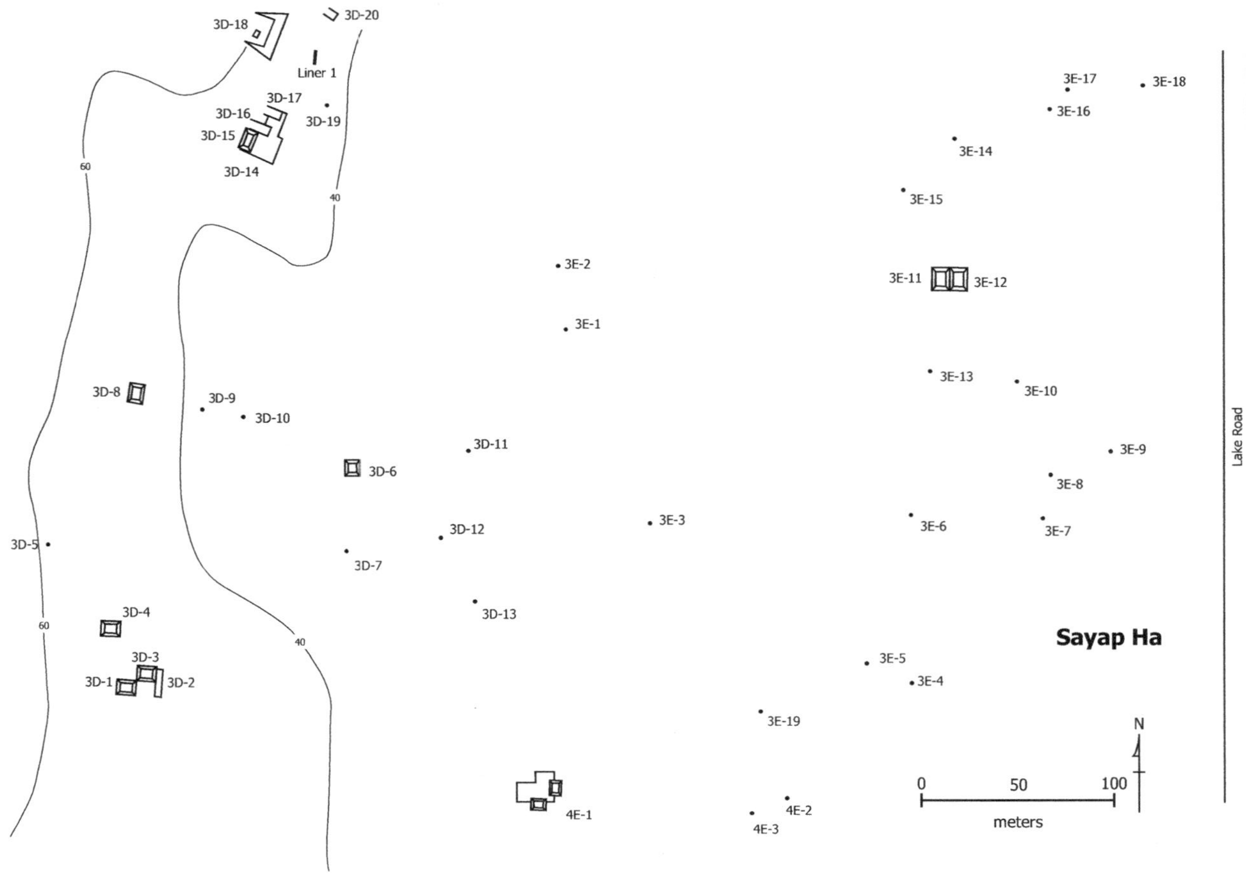

Figure 3.7. Plan view of Sayap Ha showing locations of structures and topography.

Figure 3.8. Aerial photograph showing ancient agricultural canals at the base of the Bravo Escarpment near the Blue Creek airstrip. View is to the south.

Considerable effort has been invested in understanding the nature and complexity of the ditched fields at Blue Creek since their discovery in 1995. Each of the numerous and repeated aerial and ground surveys has revealed more extensive field systems. As many of the fields have been impacted by contemporary agricultural practices, repeated surveys in varying conditions are often required to confirm the location of these ancient ditches.

Nevertheless, we now have at least a minimal estimate of the extent of the ditched field complexes at Blue Creek. Approximately 40 square kilometers of lowlands are located between the Bravo Escarpment and the Río Bravo. Of this land, confirmed ditched fields cover approximately six square kilometers. More likely, the actual amount can be estimated in the range of 12 square kilometers.

So, these ditched agricultural field systems made up a large and economically important asset for the community of Blue Creek. While food for local consumption was no doubt produced, agricultural products for export also were likely produced. With the clear connection to the riverine-coastal trade system, it is likely that export products, including nonfood agricultural products such as cacao, were a major component of the Blue Creek economy.

However, the ditched field systems were not the largest agricultural resource. Above the escarpment are large expanses of highly fertile soils separating hills that were used for residential purposes. The major difference between the soils in these large, highly fertile bajitos and those in the ditched fields is that the upland soils are better drained and not subject to crop loss by seasonal inundation. Direct evidence for the use of these lands for agriculture is sparse. However, the vast energy that was used to construct the ditched fields would have been pointless had these areas not already been under agriculture. Similarly, the platforms and other systems built to increase the productivity of the margins of these highly productive and easily accessible soils would also have been pointless.

Of the 16 square kilometers we have intensively surveyed, approximately 7 square kilometers are of this hill and bajo landscape. Approximately 50 percent of that area is covered by these highly productive soils with no occupation. In the entirety of the Blue Creek polity, this terrain accounts for more than 80 square kilometers. So, extending the estimate to the entire area, Blue Creek incorporated at least 40 square kilometers of such agricultural settings, a truly massive resource. Further, both the 80-square-kilometer and 50-percent estimates were obtained conservatively. A more precise estimate could range considerably higher.

So, while ditched fields are easily identifiable and certainly were an important resource at Blue Creek, the fields that were not ditched were actually more extensive and had lower associated risk. Yet, this was not enough productivity for the people of Blue Creek. Low platforms were constructed at the base of the escarpment and used as growing platforms.[30]

Other features were built across drainages to expand agricultural land and to capture water runoff. Further, the Blue Creek Maya also exploited specialized environmental niches such as *rejolladas,* which will be discussed further in Chapter 5.

Another component of the Blue Creek agricultural production system is the kitchen gardens associated with individual households. Today, such gardens are located within the *solares* or walled compounds surrounding residences in traditional villages such as Yaxunah, Yucatán.[31] Prehistorically, these walled compounds did not exist and kitchen gardens would have been placed just beyond the open area around individual houses. Such kitchen gardens almost certainly existed at Chan Cahal, Sayap Ha, and U Xulil Beh.[32] On the other hand, other residential components, such as Kín Tan, were organized in a manner that precluded such kitchen gardens. However, Kín Tan apparently controlled large tracts of agricultural lands and probably did not need such gardens. Equally so, their presence at Chan Cahal, despite the fact that Chan Cahal was surrounded by ditched fields, indicates that the residents of Chan Cahal did not control the ditched fields but were probably workers in them. A conservative estimate of the impact of kitchen gardens on the overall agricultural productivity of Blue Creek would be in the range of one percent.

Cultural Diversity at Blue Creek

Each discrete component of the Blue Creek polity exhibits extremely diverse characteristics and is unlike all others. They range from communities built of perishable materials with no apparent central place (U Xulil Beh) to Blue Creek's most central place, the core area of monumental structures. They include communities built of perishable buildings with clear central places (Chan Cahal) and communities of labor-intensive masonry structures surrounded or not by secondary quarters (Nukuch Muul and Kín Tan, respectively). Each residential component appears to have housed distinct socioeconomic groups. The residences of the royal elites were in the core area, while Kín Tan was the residence for apparently non-royal elite. Chan Cahal seems to represent residences of some of the least economically advantaged. The residents were most likely the farmers of the ditched field complexes that were probably owned by the royalty. Paradoxically, we have found a large amount of jade artifacts at Chan Cahal, somehow indicating the relationship the residents enjoyed with royalty and reflecting the political economy of the community.

This economic variability is closely tied to the environmental diversity and opportunities present at Blue Creek. Communities below the escarpment (Chan Cahal and Sayap Ha) are clearly tied to the surrounding ditched agricultural field systems. Communities in the uplands are more variable. At one end of the range is U Xulil Beh, which is not tied to any large-scale agricultural resource and had no apparent central place. However, Nukuch Muul and Kín Tan are both surrounded by highly fertile soils, but only surrounding Nukuch Muul's hilltop plazuela are numerous housemounds and agricultural features such as terraces and check dams. None of these exist at Kín Tan. This appears to be the consequence of their differing economic and political settings. In essence, Nukuch Muul was the residence of a powerful lineage that controlled agricultural production around its residence. Therefore, they required complex, though small, agricultural features to maximize production and numerous subsidiary families to conduct agricultural work. On the other hand, the several lineages of Kín Tan were tied more directly to Blue Creek's royalty and political system. Thus, they may have not controlled agricultural production in the same way and may have not needed subsidiary workers.

With the anomalous exception of U Xulil Beh, all known residential components of Blue Creek have clear central places—one structure or area that is out of scale with the rest of the component. Each component had its own sense of centrality and probably its own sense of local centralized authority. At Nukuch Muul and Kín Tan, the largest residential plazuelas were these central places. At Chan Cahal and Sayap Ha, these also seem to be the residences of the most elite members of the group. However, there is a sense that these were the most influential among equals as opposed to being the leaders of Blue Creek as a whole.

What Is a Maya City?

Maya cities exhibit far more complexity than can be understood through the use of the simplistic models that have been previously employed. Certainly, they are not like the compact, densely packed urban areas of prehistoric central Mexico and Peru. However, we do not advance our understanding of the past by belaboring such semantic points. While the concentric circle zone, sector, and multiple nuclei models all offer some insight into the nature of Maya cities, none of these models adequately describe the real complexities involved.

The case example of Blue Creek shows that Maya cities are complex mosaics of structural parts, or components, arrayed across the landscape and functionally interrelated. Maya cities have central places, core zones, which include monumental architecture and public spaces—plazas—which were used for ritual and economic activities. These components include bounded, discrete residential areas. Generally, these residential areas incorporate their own central places or "local" public architecture.

The residences of the ruling lineages were generally housed at or near the core zone. Beyond this commonality, variability is great and probably due to local topography and local resources. Palenque, for example, is located on top of the first foothills of the Chiapas Mountains, overlooking the Tabasco Plain. This is much like the situation at Blue Creek but with much greater elevations and relief. As a consequence, Palenque had a densely packed urban area immediately outside of the core area along the ridge-tops,[33] while Blue Creek had a much more dispersed population and probably a much lower population size.

In the next chapter, I will examine several of the residential components of Blue Creek more closely and will argue that they were tethered to the core area by relationships between members of the ruling lineage and local elite lineages. Again, the data from the residential areas of Kín Tan and Sayap Ha indicate that these relationships were highly variable. Sometimes they were fleeting and not passed to future generations, such as is the case at Sayap Ha. Other times, lineages built upon such relationships and used them to create authority and legitimacy for centuries, such as at Kín Tan.

Also incorporated into the mosaic of Maya cities were natural resources such as agricultural lands that were interspersed with residential components. At Blue Creek, these included large fields for dry agriculture and large labor-intensive complexes of ditched fields, as well as an array of terraces and check dams used throughout the area.[34] While land tenure and ownership systems are unclear, these resources and topography in general are related to the distinct residential components.[35]

The general models for Maya cities outlined by Marcus did not and still do not adequately describe their complexity. Both the concentric circle zone and sector models assume growth to occur outwardly from the center of the city. At Blue Creek, the earliest occupation occurs not only in the core area but also in what would later become residential components. Only one component appears to be a later expansion of the community and this is into resource-poor lands. The concentric zone model predicts that diversity among residential components would be related to distance from the site core, and the sector model predicts that functional units would expand outward from the core area. Again, neither is seen at Blue Creek.

The multiple nuclei model also does not adequately describe the situation of Maya cities. However, it is a better approximation than the others. Again, this model is based upon modern cities with relatively rapid growth during which multiple centers merge together. In the case of Blue Creek, there is clearly one central public sector. However, each residential component has its own "local" public place hierarchically tethered to the core area. While there are multiple nuclei, they do not constitute functionally similar units as would be predicted by the multiple nuclei model.

Consequently, it is clear that Maya cities represent an urban form that is distinctly Maya. Models from the modern Western world as well as models from prehistoric central Mexico and Peru fail to describe the patterns and variability seen in the archaeological record of the Maya. Instead of transplanting such models, we must move toward building new models of cities that apply to the world of the ancient Maya. It is hoped that this volume is a step in that direction.

4 Diversity of Power and Authority in a Maya City

Archaeologists have viewed status and power among the ancient Maya as a function of leadership within lineages.[1] One of the more powerful models is that of the segmentary state, in which lineage heads hold authority over members of their lineage. In this chapter, I argue that such lineages lived in bounded residential components of Blue Creek and that power among them was created and maintained by interaction among leaders of lineages. However, while some lineages rose to positions of multigenerational power, others did not. In essence, I argue that while the Maya state was composed of lineages, heterarchy, or multiple paths to power, existed among these lineages. Further, power was created and reinforced by interaction among lineage heads and the control that lineages had over critical resources.

In the previous chapter, I demonstrated that Blue Creek is composed of bounded, discrete, and distinctive residential components, usually separated by highly productive agricultural lands. More important, each component had its own distinctive organizational and historical dynamics that were probably related to land tenure and resources.[2] However, these dynamics are also related to the structures of power and authority that were established in each component.

In this chapter, I will examine four of these residential components more closely: the elaborate residences of the site core, the elite residences of Kín Tan, and the non-elite residences of Sayap Ha and U Xulil Beh. Each has fundamentally differing organizational principles and internal power structures. How did their political leaders interact and how were they integrated into a single polity? I argue that long-term, multigenerational interaction among the lineages residing in these components reinforced the authority and legitimacy of the rulers in the site core and of the local leaders in each residential component. This approach is steeped in world systems theory, a conceptual framework that archaeologists and others have borrowed and remade into their own from its origins in sociology.

Immanuel Wallerstein first applied his concept of a core-periphery dichotomy to modern world market economics. In essence, he argued that the developed world would always hold economic advantages over the underdeveloped world. Wallerstein argued that the underdeveloped world would supply commodities, such as metals, to the developed world. In turn, the developed world would convert them to value added products, such as automobiles, and sell them back to the underdeveloped world. In Wallerstein's view, the underdeveloped periphery would forever remain unable to catch up to the developed core. Wallerstein went on to define the concept that we live today in an interconnected world system and that the relationships and interactions among the components of the world system define power, authority, and legitimacy within the system.[3]

There is a large leap from Wallerstein's approach to international economics in the industrialized world to analysis of the nonindustrialized, pre-Columbian past. However, Wallerstein's focus on interaction can be extended to other settings. Archaeologists have applied variants of Wallerstein's core-periphery and world systems models to prehistoric cultures in order to model economics and political interaction.[4] In the Maya area, early formulations of Maya economics examined the goods traded among Maya polities. However, William Rathje changed the discussion by using the core-periphery model to argue that interaction between the central Petén Maya and outlying areas created a political economy that led to complex society.[5] Since Rathje's attempts to deal with Maya political economy, a large body of work has developed on both the nature and implications of Maya economic interaction.[6] One approach has been to undertake empirical studies of the mechanics of interregional trade.[7] The second approach has been to focus on the structural relationships within polities that controlled the flow of goods.[8]

Another applicable concept is the idea of human agency as represented in the past. The French philosopher Pierre Bourdieu discussed the notion that human interaction is based on all parties being mobilized into concordance.[9] In other words, a leader cannot simply tell a follower to do something; the follower must have adequate motivation to follow. Archaeologists have transformed this concept into that of "agency," meaning that people create and re-create societies through their actions.[10] The concept of agency focuses our study of the archaeological record on the interactions among individuals. Individuals both compete and collaborate for authority and power. They also use their relationships with each other to manipulate themselves into positions of greater authority, as we have seen in the Big Man systems of New Guinea and in the Kula Rings of the Trobriand Islands. Importantly, though, these systems did not result in multigenerational power.

It has become clear that models focused on exchange and distribution are particularly applicable to understanding social complexity in the ancient Maya.[11] Such models emphasize the materialist position that control of strategic resources leads to social stratification and provides avenues to power and authority within Maya society. It is also clear that ancient Maya society had multiple avenues of acquiring status.[12] Most commonly in the Maya area, such models are based upon the concept that control of resources is based upon first occupancy. Patricia McAnany argues that once the first residents established control over local resources, they and their descendants maintained control and exploited the same resources for purposes of increasing social prestige and authority.[13] This principle helps explain how Maya households seem to be occupied by many generations of the same familial lineage and how some seem to acquire status and authority very early and never lose it whereas others never acquire such status at all.

In the following discussion, I argue that the principles offered by Wallerstein's focus on interaction among components and McAnany's concept of first arrivals' control over resources help explain the diversity seen at Blue Creek. Further, the interaction among components functioned not only to legitimize authority within a given component but also to legitimize the authority of the ruling lineage of the site core.

Residents of the Site Core

There were relatively few residents of the core area, and they were the highest elites of Blue Creek. However, as I discussed earlier, other people of lesser status lived in the vicinity as well. They may have been in some sort of service capacity to the ruling elites and would have lived in residences that are not visible to us.[14]

The two primary residences, though, are the Structure 13 Courtyard and the Structure 19 Courtyard (Figures 2.14 and 2.15). As discussed in Chapter 2, these are very dissimilar residences with very different histories. The Structure 13 Courtyard was originally built as a small public plaza, the "Old Plaza B," flanked by Structures 12 and 13. At some time at the end of the Early Classic period, Structure 13 was reoriented to face what became Plaza B, the platform was expanded, and Structure 10 was built. At about the same time, the "Old Plaza B" was closed to the public by the construction of Structures 11 and 14 and was converted into a residence. Despite the scale of Structures 12 and 13, the Structure 13 Courtyard was a relatively small residence, with an open courtyard space of less than 150 square meters surrounded by only a few vaulted and unvaulted rooms. It was perhaps the residence of only one high-status family.

The other major residence was the Structure 19 Courtyard, located across Plaza B from Structure 13. During the Late Classic period, this was a complex building with at least eight rooms, built on top of an Early Classic platform. It was built around an open court of approximately two hundred square meters, somewhat larger than the Structure 13 Courtyard. Sometime later in the Late Classic, the courtyard was divided to create two smaller courts.

The Structure 19 Courtyard was also almost certainly an important residence in the Early Classic but it is unclear what sort of buildings existed on the platform at that time. If the pattern we see at Kín Tan is also the case here, there were perishable residential structures in use until the end of the Early Classic, when masonry buildings replaced them.

One important feature of the Structure 19 Courtyard is the set of burials in a bench in Room 7. Seven people were interred in the bench in four to six different events. We do not know which of these events our radiocarbon assay of approximately A.D. 555–675 dates.[15] A reasonable guess is that there were burial events before and after this date. If so, then we are likely seeing evidence that the same lineage occupied the Structure 19 Courtyard at the end of the Early Classic period and into the Late Classic period. Interestingly, this is approximately the same time that the Structure 13 Courtyard was converted to residential use and that Structure 15 was built.

There are myriad possible explanations for the shift in form and function of these residences. The change may have accommodated the residence of an externally imposed ruler who maintained the existence of the previous ruling lineage while usurping its authority. A simpler explanation, however, may be that the ruling lineage grew to the size that large residential facilities were needed. At this time, we do not yet know whether either theory is true. An approach that is currently being attempted is to conduct DNA analysis of the elite burials in the core area and elsewhere to determine whether the results better fit the continuous lineage or outsider view of Blue Creek's political leaders.

By the scale of palaces elsewhere, such as at Palenque, these residences are diminutive. However, their complexity and proximity to the monumental architecture indicate that these are homes of the ruling elite of Blue Creek. Whether the residents were kings, local ruling elite, or vassals of another polity is taken up in Chapter 7. For now, it is enough to know that they were the highest-status people at Blue Creek.

Another residence in the core area is the Structure 25 Patio Group. This is a much smaller and less elaborate residence than the courtyards. The earliest occupation of this hilltop dates to the Middle Preclassic period (Cool Shade complex, 1000/800–650 B.C.), but it was in the Terminal Late Preclassic (Linda Vista complex, A.D. 100/150–250) that the hilltop was converted into a formal platform. Then, in the Early Classic period (Río Hondo complex, A.D. 250–600), a set of small buildings was constructed on the platform. The Structure 25 Patio Group is not as central to the public architecture and as elaborate as the other core area residences, so we do not believe that ruling elites lived there. More likely, it was the residence of a lineage that was either in some sort of service to the ruling elite or in some other subsidiary capacity.

The people in the Structure 25 Patio Group controlled a small reservoir at the base of the hill. Like others in the Maya area, this reservoir was probably initially dug as a quarry for construction material. However, its strategic placement at the base of the hill's watershed allowed it to function as a reservoir later with little modification. We excavated the reservoir looking for an outlet where the release of water could be controlled, but none existed. Consequently, we can be quite sure that this reservoir was used for local water consumption rather than for storage for later release to fields or some other such purpose. Perhaps the residents of the Structure 25 Patio Group carried this water to the residents of the nearby Structure 13 and Structure 19 Courtyards.

It is likely that there were other residents of the core area. For example, there are broad terraces below the Structure 13 Courtyard on the east side that may have accommodated service quarters. However, several test excavations were unsuccessful in documenting such residences. Even so, as discussed earlier, they did very likely exist.

Kín Tan

Kín Tan consists of a series of 11 elite residences northwest of the civic-ceremonial core area (Figures 3.2, 3.3). There are seven patio groups (Structures 42, 43, 45, 60, 81, 82, and 83 Patio Groups), three courtyards (Structures 41, 46, and 61 Courtyards), one plazuela (Structure 37 Plazuela), and a civic-ceremonial group (Structure 38). The energy required to construct each of these residences was significant and many of the courtyards and the plazuela are large enough to have housed more than one nuclear family. While there may have been some "invisible" residences housing lower-status people near hilltops that have been lost because of land clearing, the residents of all the known buildings at Kín Tan were high-status members of Blue Creek.

Like nearly all of the residential components at Blue Creek, Kín Tan had a sacred ceremonial center or *axis mundi.* While the core area residents controlled public plazas and soaring pyramids, the residents of Kín Tan's sacred civic-ceremonial center was the much smaller Structure 38. Structure 38 is a six-meter-tall Early Classic pyramid that faces east onto a small bounded plazuela.

The Kín Tan residences are situated on the tops of a string of hills that begin east of Structure 24 at the Structure 60 Patio Group and arch to a terminus at the Structure 37 Plazuela. These hills range from 20 to 40 meters tall and are surrounded by relatively flat, upland *bajitos* that consist of highly productive agricultural soils. These provided an economic basis for Kín Tan's elites and were likely controlled by them in some manner. On the east end, Kín Tan was physically separated from the core area by a 15- to 20-meter-deep drainage that separates it from the Plaza B complex. This drainage becomes less deep toward the south but also separates Plaza A from Plaza B.

Many of the buildings at Kín Tan have been excavated, and we see a clear pattern of occupation and growth.[16] The earliest occupation of these hilltops appears to have been at the Structure 37 Plazuela, where a large Late Preclassic (Tres Leguas complex, 350 B.C.–A.D. 100/150) midden was found. Not long after this occupation, the hilltop was plastered over to create a large platform that was built upon for many centuries.

Throughout Kín Tan, it was common to find burials of important males underneath or within the first construction phase of the main building in each group.

These burials were generally associated with Terminal Late Preclassic ceramics (Linda Vista complex). They often included whole ceramic vessels and jade beads placed with the body in a small crypt. These individuals were early high-status members of their lineages and arguably they are "lineage founders."

The first masonry constructions were commonly low platforms on top of which perishable buildings were constructed in the Early Classic (Río Hondo complex). However, in the Late Classic period (Aguas Turbias complex, A.D. 600–750), most of the groups saw unprecedented construction of complex masonry buildings that buried these low platforms.

As all of these residences commanded extraordinary views, had very restricted access, and required significant investment of energy to construct, I argue that they were the homes of elite members of the society. Further, they were occupied by multigenerational lineages that revered their founders. Consequently, it seems that they held control of the vastly productive agricultural land around them that underpinned their social position and power through multiple generations.

However, it seems equally unlikely that these were royal elites. Their proximity to the core area is somewhat distant, especially in the cases of the most elaborate residences such as the Structure 37 Plazuela and the Structure 46 Courtyard. Nevertheless, they apparently held multigenerational land tenure, conforming to McAnany's "first-arrivals" concept.

The largest and most complex of these residences is the Structure 37 Plazuela, located on top of a 14-meter-high hill about six hundred meters northwest of Plaza A. Intensive excavations by Colleen Hanratty allow us to address the way in which this nonroyal lineage marked and revered its founder and subsequent lineage head.[17] Further, we can see the lineage's fortunes rise with those of the Blue Creek community as a whole and can see this as an extension of the lineage's role in the political life of Blue Creek. This, in turn, offers an interpretive window into the political dynamics of a Maya polity.

In its final form, the Structure 37 Plazuela included seven buildings, Structures 31–37, arranged around two open courtyards or exterior areas (Figure 4.1). The southern exterior space is bounded by Structure 35 to the north and west, Structure 31 to the south, and Structures 33 and 32 to the east. Structure 34 lies in the center of this exterior space. The northern exterior area is enclosed by Structures 35, 36, and 37. These exterior areas share a common platform built on top of the Late Preclassic (Tres Leguas complex) midden deposits and bedrock. Only Structures 34 and 37 were in place prior to the Late Classic period. During the Early Classic period, Structure 37 was a low platform that defined the northern portion of the group. A small shrine, Structure 34, was constructed within what would later become the center of the southern exterior area and capped an Early Classic tomb (Río Hondo complex) and a transitional Terminal Late Preclassic/Early Classic crypt (Linda Vista complex).

The remaining five buildings were constructed during the Late Classic period

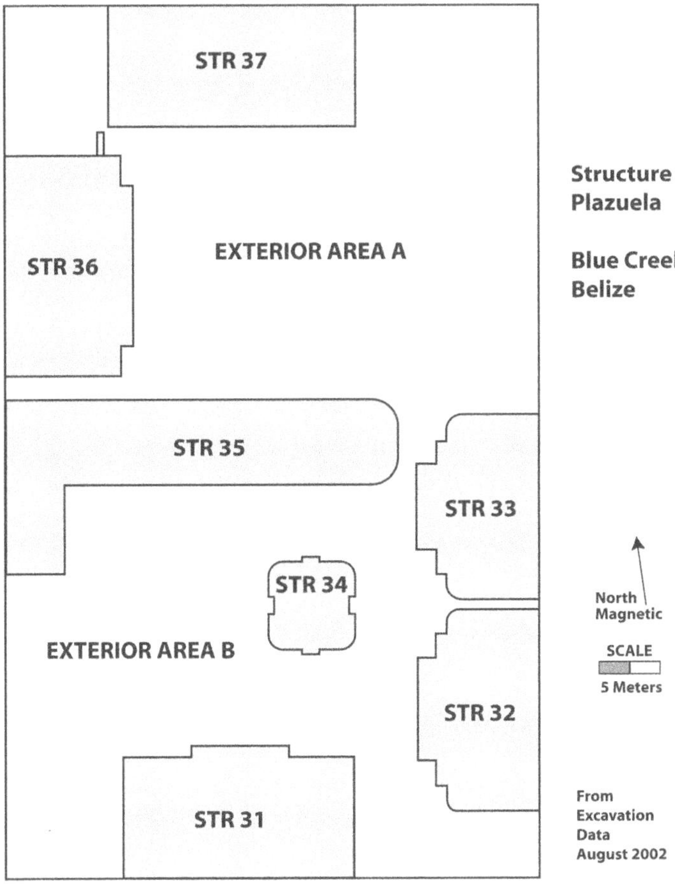

Figure 4.1. Simplified plan view of Structure 37 Plazuela.

(Aguas Turbias complex). Each incorporates a masonry substructure, one to two meters in height, and Structures 31 and 37 also possess masonry superstructures. While it seems likely that earlier perishable structures existed, our excavations have not explored this.

A number of specific events are of interest in understanding the temporal aspects of the Structure 37 Plazuela lineage. The first is the earliest occupation of the hilltop that would become the plazuela. Buried under the floor of the southern exterior area is a significant Late Preclassic (Tres Leguas complex, 350 B.C.–A.D. 100) midden deposit that gives us a reasonable date for this first occupation. Following this, we see the initial construction of the platform and the flooring of the exterior area.

When the platform floor was constructed, a *chultun* was left open in the center of the area. Chultuns are underground chambers with narrow entrances that were

Figure 4.2. Trench through Structure 34 showing Terminal Preclassic plaster floor and locations of Burial 45 (foreground) and Tomb 7 (middle ground).

commonly dug by the Maya near residences and probably used for storage of food and for other functions. Often they were used for burial of relatively important individuals. In this case, the chultun was partially filled and a crypt was constructed in the western part of it for Burial 45 (Figure 4.2). The poorly preserved skeleton was an adult male in a tightly flexed position, lying on his left side and oriented north to south. The only artifact was a red-slipped ceramic pendant. This pendant and ceramic sherds found within the crypt date to the Terminal Late Preclassic period (Linda Vista complex). After the interment, the chultun was plastered over, but the entrance was marked by pecking its outline into the plaster floor. Later yet, but probably not much later, the first version of the shrine, Structure 34, was constructed on top of the burial, publicly marking the individual's importance for future generations.

The crypt's centrality marks the individual as the bearer of the tree of life, and his formal burial in a crypt also marked his importance to his survivors. The marking of his crypt with the first construction phase of Structure 34 reinforces this notion. These points and the fact that he was the first burial anywhere at the plazuela lead to the conclusion that he was the lineage founder who resided in the Structure 37 Plazuela.

Later, in the Early Classic period, a second important burial, Burial 44 in Tomb 7,

Figure 4.3. Photograph of Tomb 7 showing human remains and burial goods, in situ.

was placed 2.3 meters east of Burial 45. We do not know precisely how much time passed between these two burials, but it may have been as little as one or two generations. We are confident that Burial 44 was a direct descendant of the lineage founder and likely to have been a later lineage head. He may have been a son, grandson, or great-grandson of the founder.

Tomb 7 was dug through previous Late Preclassic deposits and into bedrock (Figures 4.3 and 4.4). Judging from the formality of the tomb, the accompanying burial goods, and the later marking of his tomb, Burial 44 was a very important individual. The complete adult male skeleton was recovered oriented north–south and lying on his right side in a partially flexed position. Placed directly above his skull was a Terminal Late Preclassic (Linda Vista complex) red slipped plate with a kill-hole, and a small polychrome bowl was recovered below this plate. A jade pendant (Figure 4.5) in the form of an acrobat glyph was found on his chest, and a triangular jade bead was recovered from within the left portion of the jaw.[18]

This jade bead had either originally been placed in his mouth or was worn around his neck. There is a strong likelihood that the bead was, in fact, placed in the mouth. Michael Coe has linked the Classic Maya burial practice of placing jade in the mouth with a funerary ritual described by Landa in the sixteenth century. Further, Karl Taube indicates that such jade beads were regarded as the breath spirit essence of the deceased.[19]

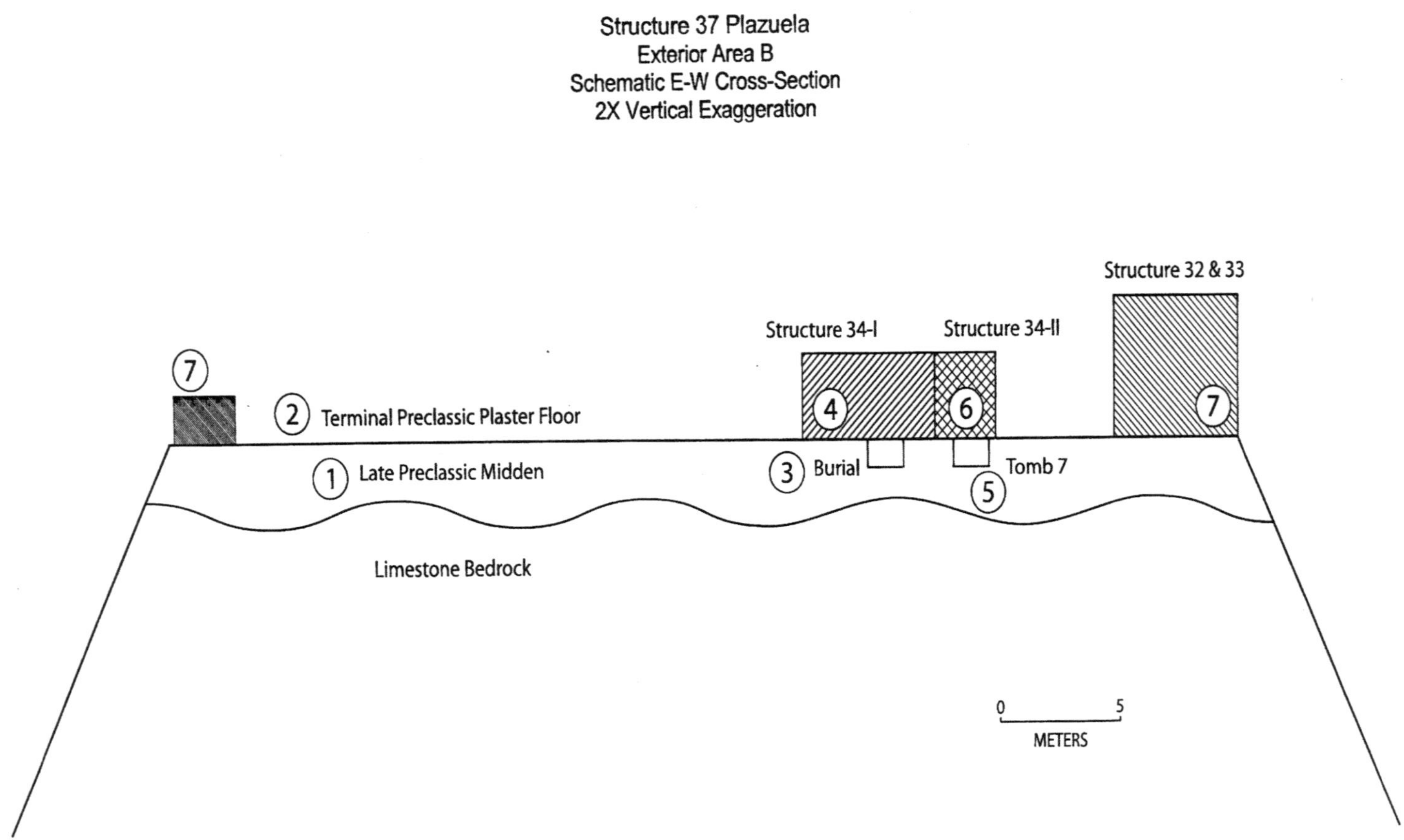

Figure 4.4. Simplified north–south cross-section of Structure 37 Plazuela.

Figure 4.5. Jade acrobat pendant and bead from Tomb 7.

Often in Maya iconography, jade is linked to the concepts of centrality, maize, and rulership. The maize god in an acrobat pose has been found in association with Early Classic burials and caches at Copan and with Late Classic burials at Tikal. Karl Taube has argued that this acrobat position alludes to a growing tree. For instance, Burial 196 at Tikal contained a jade bead portraying the maize god as the world tree.[20]

While the presence of the acrobat is relatively rare in Maya iconography, it is more common in the Olmec world. The acrobat pose in Olmec art signifies "a person in a visionary or ecstatic state who is integrated into the ritual life of the community."[21] This interpretation can also be applied to the occupant of Tomb 7. The presence of the tomb represents a link to the Underworld, and we interpret its occupant, the keeper of the portal to the Underworld, as a shaman.

Phytoliths recovered from beneath the body in Tomb 7 revealed the presence of reeds and grasses that could have been from a reed pillow and grass burial mat.[22] The woven mat or *pop* symbolizes rulership and elite status. For instance, a ruling lord was often referred to as *ah pop*, or "He of the Mat." This was synonymous with *ahau*, or lord. In addition, mats are often portrayed as settings for important ritual events. Among the Yucatec Maya, the *popol na*, or "mat house," was a place for the rulers of the community to meet and perform ritual acts.[23] Clearly, the association of Burial 44 with a woven mat in conjunction with the mode of interment and the burial goods associated with his remains speaks to his prestige and clearly marks his continuing importance within the lineage.

Cache 49 was placed directly above Tomb 7's capstones and consisted of two redware bowls placed lip-to-lip. These date to the transition between the Terminal Late Preclassic (Linda Vista complex) and Early Classic (Río Hondo complex) periods. Recovered from them were the remnants of a smashed jade bead, jade flakes, numerous marine shells, pieces of coral, fish bones, a stingray spine, charcoal, and red ochre. Biosilicate analysis revealed that there were also numerous sponge spicules present, marking this cache as another symbolic re-creation of the cosmos. Finally, large quantities of land snails (jute and *Pomacea*) were deposited in the shaft to Tomb 7 as it was being filled. While this is not unusual in itself, later events make it intriguing. The opening was then sealed with plaster.

Shortly after, the residents of the Structure 37 Plazuela resurfaced the southern exterior space. This thick layer of plaster covered the capped intrusion of Tomb 7. However, Tomb 7 was not to be ignored. Pecked into the surface of the layer of plaster was an outline of the tomb beneath. His memory was so important that his location had to be visually marked. Again, the elapsed time between the interment of Burial 44 and this event cannot be clearly established, but both occurred in the Early Classic period (Río Hondo complex).

The final event was the construction of the second phase of Structure 34. Intriguingly, the location of Tomb 7 was not only marked by a pecked outline in the plaster floor but also by the placement of jute snails and *Pomacea* on the floor above Tomb 7, referring back to the shell previously placed in the tomb shaft.

The fundamental form of the structure remained the same though it was expanded to enclose the sacred space surrounding Tomb 7. While the top of Structure 34 had been damaged by bulldozer activity before excavation, we have no reason to believe that it had a superstructure. Instead, it was a central shrine honoring the lineage founder and the lineage head beneath. Other such shrines have been found elsewhere and they commonly contain burials of the elite. In this case, however, the burials were beneath rather than within the shrine. Again, its centrality in a four-sided space replicates the *axis mundi.*

Structure 34 remained a central shrine to these two important individuals and only to these individuals throughout the Late Classic. During this time the residential buildings surrounding them were expanded as the importance of the lineage grew, while the Structure 34 shrine remained central to the lives of the Structure 37 Plazuela residents for several hundred years.

Ancestor-related shrines in large residential complexes from Copan to Palenque to Uaxactun show variability in form, orientation, and interment of human remains. Nonetheless, from the very beginning, the maintenance of links with the ancestral realm via interment practices within such sacred shrines is a prominent characteristic of Maya society. For instance, residences of the K'anjobal Maya of Huehuetenango have a prominent structure referred to as the *yatut jichman*, or "house of the ancestor." Also, both the Quiche Maya and the Tzotil Maya maintain lineage shrines and venerate ancestors within their residences. These shrines were not constructed merely to house the dead but also to commemorate them and to engage their assistance in the continued prosperity of the family line.[24] Similarly, mortuary practices at Altun Ha[25] have been interpreted as evidence of the use of ancestors to define the *axis mundi* in a new construction event.[26]

The individuals interred beneath Structure 34 had substantive roles in the rise of this lineage in the Blue Creek community. We see Burial 45 as the interment of the founder of this nonroyal lineage at the time of the beginning of Blue Creek's complexity when the first rulers asserted their authority. He was revered at his death and afterward with the construction of Structure 34, a shrine in his honor.

As time passed, the importance of the lineage grew within the political spectrum of Blue Creek. This is reflected at the beginning of the Early Classic period (Río Hondo complex), when another member of the lineage was buried. His interment, compared with that of his predecessor, was marked with increased formality and more valuable and ritually charged artifacts. These included a jade acrobat pendant linking him to the centrality of the lineage and the universe and marking the close relationship between him and his lineage and the royalty of Blue Creek. His lineage honored his life by incorporating his tomb into their daily lives for several hundred years.

In a larger sense, Kín Tan consisted of a multigenerational corporate group that itself consisted of distinct lineages. The power and authority of this multigenerational group grew with the larger fortunes of Blue Creek over time. It seems apparent that they controlled the agricultural resources around them to the degree that they were closely involved with the authority and power of the residents of the core area. Given the scale of their architecture and how they restricted other people from access to their residences, the lineages of Kín Tan had increasing prestige and authority from their founding through the rest of Blue Creek's history.

Sayap Ha

Another situation altogether existed at Sayap Ha (Figures 1.5 and 3.7), directly below the core area at the base of the Bravo Escarpment. Since 1996, field teams have tested 41 of the approximately 80 structures at Sayap Ha and its neighbor, Chan Cahal. The more than 30 structures at Sayap Ha are virtually surrounded by ditched agricultural fields.[27] The earliest occupation of both areas was in the Middle Preclassic period (Cool Shade complex) at Chan Cahal, and extensive settlement is seen throughout the area by the Late Preclassic (Tres Leguas complex). Terminal Late Preclassic (Linda Vista complex) residential structures generally consist of perishable structures at ground level or built in low (20 centimeter) platforms. Most of the visible architecture seems to have been constructed in the Early Classic period, when a public plaza group with two small pyramids was also built. Occupation continued into the early part of the Late Classic, although without any known residential construction. Later in the Late Classic only Chan Cahal and the far northern portions of Sayap Ha show any settlement occupation. There is also an ephemeral Early Postclassic reoccupation of Structure U-5 at Chan Cahal.

A small civic-ceremonial group consisting of Structures L-26 and L-25 was intensively excavated.[28] Structure L-26 was built on a low platform covering approximately 140 square meters. When it was originally built in the Early Classic period, Structure L-26 was a two-room masonry building. Later in the Early Classic, this building was modified into a 3.5-meter-tall tiered pyramid that probably had a small perishable superstructure. Structure L-27, a two-meter-high platform mound facing Structure L-26, was built on the same platform as Structure L-26 (platforms 3E-11 and 3E-12 on Figure 3.7).

The construction dates of Structures L-26 and L-25 correspond well to the general dates of housemounds at Sayap Ha. These housemounds are the low platforms, perhaps only 10–20 centimeters thick, on top of which perishable buildings were constructed. Commonly, they are in the range of 8 × 5 meters in size. Most commonly they were built in the Terminal Late Preclassic period (Linda Vista complex). These very low platforms are often the only surface indicators that a residence existed. So, while earlier deposits are occasionally found underneath housemounds, they may also exist elsewhere. Our excavation locations were chosen because of the existence of the housemounds and only rarely did we test other locations.

Also, burials are often found underneath housemound floors. Most commonly these are the burials of adult males interred with relatively simple grave goods, such as a plate that is ritually killed by a puncture in its center. These are regarded as the remains of important individuals in the history of the households' residents—again, perhaps the lineage founders. The ceramics from these graves are one of our best tools for assessing the age of the housemounds. Consistently, they date to the transition between the Terminal Late Preclassic (Linda Vista complex) and the early part of the Early Classic period (Río Hondo complex).[29]

Eighteen burials or partial burials dating to the Terminal Late Preclassic and Early Classic periods have been recovered from Chan Cahal and Sayap Ha. Most (14) were recovered from residential buildings. However, one was recovered from an unknown/special-function building and three were recovered from what was probably a nonresidential building. Thirteen of the 14 burials in clear residential contexts were intrusive while one may have been interred during construction of the building. These show a consistent pattern of placement under the floors of thatch-roof houses. Of these residential burials, only five (all tightly flexed) included any grave goods. One burial included two pieces of jade in the vicinity of the cranium, three burials had one upturned vessel placed over the head, and one burial had two upturned vessels over the head as well as a jade bead and a jade pendant near the head. In short, the consistent pattern here is of burials with few or no grave goods.

At first glance, the situation at Sayap Ha appears to be that of a group of lowly commoners who built their own central place to imitate the high ritual they saw occur in the much more grand plaza at the top of the escarpment above them. It is reasonable to argue that they were the workers who toiled in the fields around them. Further, it is reasonable to argue that they did not control the large ditched field complexes. Instead, they worked in the fields of the elites and probably had control only over the kitchen gardens that they grew near their homes.

There are two problems with this view. First, our understanding of Classic Maya social organization has become vastly more detailed in recent years. Too often it had formerly been described as a simple dichotomy between elites and commoners. Despite the existence of more complex models, commoners are still often perceived as a homogeneous group without internal social and political stratification and structure.[30]

In general, archaeologists believe that the Classic Maya were organized into lineal descent groups, or lineages.[31] Such descent groups often have acknowledged "founders" as well as other ancestors who were also revered for their contributions to the status of the lineage, such as we see at Kín Tan.[32] Archaeologists have been successful in applying the concept of lineages to the Classic Maya through analysis of residential patterns and mortuary patterns.[33] Ancestor reverence formed the basis for the transmittal of land rights and a lineage's prestige, and patterned expansion of elite residences indicates the linkage between the lineage and its home. Earlier in this chapter, I argued that the growth of prestige and authority of a nonroyal, elite lineage at Blue Creek is traceable through several centuries. Expansion of residential buildings around the shrine, especially during the Late Classic, clearly indicates that the lineage continued to become more and more important in the fabric of Blue Creek's authority structure.[34]

In addition to the growing acceptance of the idea that the Classic Maya were a lineage-based society, there is also a growing perception that there were multiple pathways to authority and prestige for the Classic Maya. Heterarchies or multiple lines of authority within Maya societies are just now being explored.[35] While the scholarship on heterarchies is still young, it is only reasonable to expect that variability of patterns of authority and prestige within individual Maya sites would exist as they do in our society today.

Aside from the complexity now recognized in Maya societies, the second problem with the oversimplistic dichotomy of commoners and elites is that a burial at Sayap Ha offers clear evidence that complexity among commoners existed. Burial SH2 in Structure L-11 is a dramatic exception to the mortuary pattern discussed earlier (labeled Structure 3E-15 on Figure 3.7). To begin with, the Structure L-11 mound is somewhat larger than most of the neighboring housemounds, at approximately 10 meters in diameter and 50 centimeters in height. Unfortunately, modern agriculture has damaged the building to the extent that its form cannot be ascertained. It was built in two construction phases, both dating to the Early Classic period. The earlier is a low (20 centimeter) platform extending at least eight meters east to west. The later phase consisted of raising the western part of the platform another meter.

Burial SH2 was placed in a cist cut into bedrock that intruded through the early phase of the building. A surprising number of lithic flakes (653 chert and 46 obsidian pieces) were recovered immediately above the cist burial. This was a far higher density of flakes than was recovered from the excavation of the rest of the housemound, and it is clear that these were intentionally deposited as part of the interment ritual. It is not unusual that the shafts of elite tombs in monumental architecture were partially filled with chert or obsidian flakes produced for that specific interment. For example, tombs with such flakes associated with them have been found at nearby La Milpa and Kakabish and such deposition was probably the case at Structure 24 at Blue Creek. Usually, these deposits consist of thousands rather than hundreds of artifacts. However, Burial SH2 is the only case that I know of in which a burial in a humble housemound was treated in such a manner. While archaeologists do not fully understand the emic nature of these deposits, the etic nature is that they were part of the public acknowledgment of the status and importance of the interred person during life. So, while the flake deposit on top of Burial SH2 consists of fewer artifacts than are found in the very high status burials, it mimics them and emphasizes the importance and status of the person.

The individual was probably a male, aged 20–30 years; he was buried in a flexed position on his left side with his hands placed beside the face and his head to the northeast. Buried with him was a set of unexpectedly lavish grave goods that included two inlayed shell disks found on either side of the skull and an anthropomorphic head carved of bone. The carved bone head was found along with jade and hematite beads on the neck and upper chest area. Many other carved bone beads were found in the neck area and along the back. These may have been parts of a headdress or a long hair braid. A few were also found at the feet and knees. Four bone beads were found in the mouth, but this could be due to displacement.

The anthropomorphic head is a small bib-head sculpture of a human head carved of bone (Figure 4.6).[36] Bib-head or "helmet-bib" motifs were first identified by Tatania Proskouriakoff and are generally carved of jade and considered to be royal jewels during the Early Classic period. In some cases, they may be depictions of actual kings, whereas in other cases they may be deities whose vestiges have been appropriated by royalty. Hammond has argued that they represent Kinich Ahau, the sun god. Alternatively, the contexts of the bib-heads from Cerros and Nohmul led Schele and Freidel to identify them as the "Jewels of Kingship." Likewise, their contexts at Blue Creek and nearby Chan Chich lead to similar conclusions.[37] In either case, the general consensus is that these are closely associated with royalty.

Seven other Early Classic bib-head pendants—all made of jade, importantly—have been recovered from Blue Creek. In each case, they derived from very high status contexts such as the ritual event at Structure 4 that resulted in the deposition of nearly a thousand jade artifacts at approximately A.D. 500. For the most part, these pendants depict unknown deities or persons. Related images are also seen on the stucco masks on Structure 9-IV that were discussed in Chapter 2. The masks

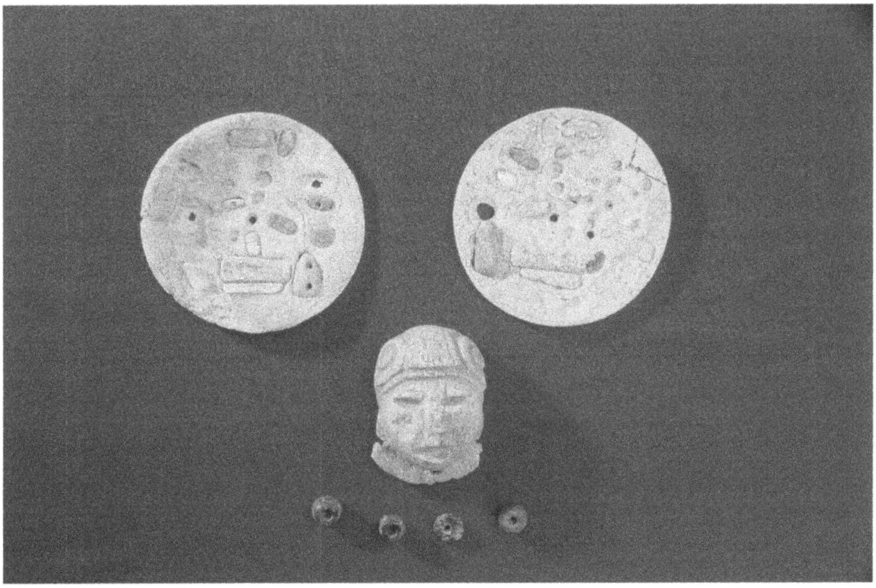

Figure 4.6. Bone anthropomorphic head found in Burial SH2.

may represent at least one actual individual, an Early Classic *ahau* of Blue Creek, or the maize god.

Regardless of the identification of the maize god or *ahau,* it is clear that the bib-head representation is closely associated with royalty and power as well as the economic and political ability to obtain exotic goods such as jade. This does not, though, explain the presence of the carved bone bib-head interred with Burial SH2.

Equally interesting in Burial SH2 is the pair of carved shell ear adornments with clear Teotihuacan style imagery. These were incised and inlaid with stones of various colors (Figure 4.7). Each shell depicts a high-status, elaborately ornamented man seated on a cushion within a larger circular frame. Both men have hunched backs and lean forward, grasping something in their hands. Both are also wearing "backpacks," which are clearly a trait derived from Teotihuacan. While it is no longer surprising to find bib-heads at Blue Creek, Teotihuacan imagery is unexpected. The only other even remotely related artifact is a single Early Classic sherd found in the shaft in Structure 4 that probably derives from Tikal (Manik phase) when it was intensively interacting with Teotihuacan. Further, the jade and coral inlays on the shells are unlikely to be found outside of the elites of Blue Creek.

While it is possible that the presence of the inlaid shell reflects some sort of contact between Blue Creek and Teotihuacan, the only additional evidence of such contact at Blue Creek consists of the single Manik phase sherd from Tikal, and this gives little support to a concept of direct contact. Nevertheless, Teotihuacan

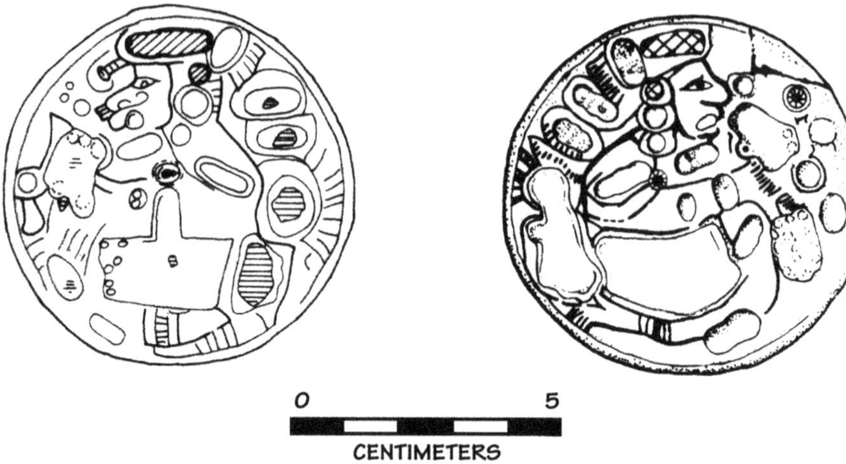

Figure 4.7. Pair of inlaid shells from Burial SH2 showing Teotihuacan imagery.

related imagery is seen throughout the southern lowlands during the Early Classic period, especially in royal contexts, where it would comment on the power structure of Blue Creek. However, its association with the low status level of Burial SH2 is not typical. Furthermore, the acquisition by a resident of Sayap Ha of a shell artifact inlaid with jade is also an unlikely occurrence.

The Social and Political Implications of Burial SH2

It is clear that the individual of Burial SH2 was of higher status than his neighbors and contemporaries. I believe that Burial SH2 represents an individual within the Sayap Ha community who gained prestige and perhaps power through his interaction with the ruling elite residing in the core area of Blue Creek. This is similar to the Big Man model observed by Malinowski in the Trobriand Islands and later examined by Marshall Sahlins.[38] To be clear, I am not imposing a Big Man model on the ancient Maya. Rather, I am simply saying that individual achievement could elevate an individual's status. However, that status might not be inherited by descendants.

Still, it is worthwhile to examine how Big Men operate in New Guinea. Such leaders typically work harder than other individuals and hold larger stores of food, and this often enables them the option of polygyny. They stand out based on their own industriousness. While Big Men clearly achieve internal status within their communities, their status is also acknowledged outside of their communities. Interaction among and exchange between Big Men of different communities marks and reinforces each others' status by the exchange and display of exotic goods, such as jade among the Maya, commonly used as adornments.

This Big Man model has been used effectively to understand other fundamentally egalitarian societies such as the Late Woodland period Hopewell culture of the eastern United States.[39] The Hopewell culture is seen as being a nonstratified society in which individual males achieved high status as a result of their activities as Big Men. Consequently, the exotic goods that came into their possession by exchange with foreign Big Men through a prestige goods economy were interred with them at death. Other than such grave goods, there is a fundamental lack of stratification seen in residential architecture or mortuary practices.

There is no question that Maya societies were much more stratified and complex than these fundamentally egalitarian societies in New Guinea and prehistoric North America.[40] In general, most scholars concur that Maya lineages created, then maintained, power and authority through multiple generations. However, Burial SH2 indicates that there was a role for individually achieved status that did not translate into status for the lineage within Classic Maya society as well. This would have been one route to prestige, and it augments our growing understanding of the multiplicity of routes taken to achieve status within Classic Maya society.

Throughout Blue Creek, each residential area has a unique signature in terms of the dates of its founding, the type of associated natural resources, and the quantity and quality of residential buildings. This heterogeneity appears to be associated with the multiple pathways to power and authority that were available in Classic Maya communities. We know a great deal about the intra-site relations between the core area of Blue Creek and the more elite residential areas, such as the Structure 37 Plazuela at Kín Tan, where we identified the lineage founder for the group. His interment, somewhat earlier than that of Burial SH2, was followed by a sequence of events that included the construction of a shrine over his burial, then construction in front of the shrine of the tomb of a prestigious male, possibly a shaman and probably the founder's descendant. Then the shrine was expanded to cover the descendant's tomb. The shrine remained a central focal point for the lineage for several hundred more years. During this period, the lineage grew in power and prestige within the larger Blue Creek community, as evidenced by the growth in construction during the Late Classic period. It is clear that the long-term power relations between the Kín Tan lineage and the rulers residing in the center of Blue Creek were strong for several centuries.

In contrast, Burial SH2 is very different. To begin with, Sayap Ha and Chan Cahal both appear to be residential areas for fundamentally equalitarian groups. While prestigious grave goods were included in the SH2 burial, there is no evidence for consistent or future power associated with his elite status. Consequently, we must assume that his status was achieved in a manner that would not further the authority of his lineage and descendants. This individual achieved personal status through his relationship with sources of authority outside of the Sayap Ha community but could not transform that relationship into a source of authority for Sayap Ha and its future role within greater Blue Creek.

However, he had access to some of the most rare and valuable materials and iconography that existed. The presence of the jade alone makes that clear. The royal iconography of the bib-head associated with the iconography of distant and exotic power emanating from Teotihuacan indicates that he was a participant in the upper-level political processes of Blue Creek as well as an individual who was an active participant in the religious rituals and principles that integrated the social and political system. At the same time, there is no indication that he shared in the wealth and power of the rulers and other elites of Blue Creek. His rudimentary home makes clear that he was a commoner, not a royal. In fact, the simple fact that the bib-head was made of such a mundane material as bone, rather than, say, jade, makes it clear that he was not in the upper echelon of Blue Creek's politics.

Instead, he probably gained access to the iconography and material of power in a transitory manner. The implications are that the individual in Burial SH2 was given the artifacts that reflected his association with the powerful elements of society. These artifacts reflected his association with the power of the rulers, but they do not reflect any significant power of his own. While he may have become a local leader or at least held local status within Sayap Ha, his power beyond Sayap Ha was limited.

This supports the idea that exotic, status-reinforcing goods such as jade came to such individuals through their individual relationships with more elite members of society. Such materials were probably gifted to non-elites for service or other sorts of relationships with the rulers who resided in the center of the city. In the classic Big Man model, local leaders acquired internal status as a result of their relationships with powerful external leaders. In this case, the external leaders were not remote members of another polity or island community but the rulers only a few kilometers away.

Consequently, this burial event illustrates and underscores the presence of multiple heterarchial structures within Classic Maya society. While he was close to power, the individual who we know as Burial SH2 was never powerful himself, except perhaps within his local community, Sayap Ha.

U Xulil Beh

Kín Tan and Sayap Ha are examples of residential settings that are repeated elsewhere at Blue Creek. The situation at Kín Tan is probably repeated at Rosita, Nukuch Muul, and other elite residences above the escarpment. Likewise, Sayap Ha is closely related to Chan Cahal and probably other non-elite components. Of course, the site core, by its nature, is a unique residential setting. Another unique component is U Xulil Beh.

U Xulil Beh is a small, informally clustered group located 2.5 kilometers southwest of the core area that consists of 22 small, Classic period housemounds (Figure 3.4).[41] Unlike all other known components of Blue Creek, U Xulil Beh has no monumental architecture or larger residential structures. Likewise, test excavations of most of these housemounds resulted in the recovery of no jade or other exotic goods and not even burials under the floors of houses.[42] While U Xulil Beh's initial occupation postdates the Late Preclassic–Early Classic transition when this practice was common, the lack of such activities and goods indicates that the residents of U Xulil Beh were of relatively low social status.

Further, U Xulil Beh is in a resource-poor margin area of Blue Creek. It is located on a largely flat expanse of land bounded by several large drainages and a series of small hills. While agricultural terraces were built at the west end of the group, the large expanses of highly productive agricultural land available to other components did not exist at U Xulil Beh.

Patricia McAnany's first-arrivals view explains a great deal about U Xulil Beh's role in the fabric of greater Blue Creek. The first arrivals "staked claim" to the best and most important resources both above and below the escarpment. While their interaction with each other and the elites of the site core led to their multigenerational success or failure in terms of power, legitimacy, and authority, they controlled the best agricultural resources. By the time that U Xulil Beh was settled, the most valuable resources had been claimed for centuries. So, the residents of U Xulil Beh can be seen as a lateral expansion of Blue Creek and unable to become major players in Blue Creek's authority structures as they had neither the legitimacy acquired through multiple generations nor control over any significant resource. U Xulil Beh probably had the agricultural potential for production for its own food purposes but it did not participate in the large-scale production of other residential areas.

We have no way of knowing whether the residents of U Xulil Beh were immigrants into Blue Creek from other areas or members of Blue Creek who moved from other components to found a new residential area. If either could be demonstrated to be the case, U Xulil Beh could represent a powerful argument for relocation of people as a result of warfare and conflict or local population expansion during the Classic period. Unfortunately, to paraphrase every archaeologist everywhere, more research must be done.

Summary

This examination of four examples of residential components is meant to underscore several points. Residential components at Blue Creek exhibit diversity in terms of social status, internal complexity, and access to exotic goods as well as diversity in terms of power, legitimacy, and authority. The causes for this diversity can be seen in terms of two interacting factors: the control of strategic resources by first arrivals and human agency in regard to how local leaders in residential components interact with each other and the ruling elites of the core area.

In some cases, such as the core area and Kín Tan, control of resources and multigenerational interaction among leaders were mutually beneficial. Each participant grew in power, legitimacy, and authority as a consequence. However, in the case of Sayap Ha, the status acquired by Burial SH2 during his lifetime was not ascribed to future generations. I argue that this was because the ruling elite, rather than Sayap Ha's residents, already controlled the important agricultural resources around Sayap Ha. Consequently, the residents were already relegated into a social status in which their interaction with the ruling elite for mutual gain was limited.

On the far end of the spectrum was U Xulil Beh. Lacking both resources and authority and legitimacy acquired by multigenerational interaction with other components, the residents of U Xulil Beh were permanently marginalized much as Wallerstein argued that the periphery of the modern industrial world was marginalized. Not only did multiple avenues to power exist at Blue Creek, but there were also dead end streets.

5 Agriculture as Blue Creek's Economic Base

Blue Creek, though modestly sized, was a wealthy community that had access to an unusually high degree of exotic goods. The people of the community displayed their wealth through monumental architecture and the many times that they disposed of valuable exotic goods in burials and caches. Underlying this wealth were the local resources that Blue Creek controlled. As I argued in the previous chapter, differential control over these resources was also instrumental in how some lineages acquired and then maintained authority and power within Blue Creek. In this chapter, I will summarize the nature of Blue Creek's most important economic resource, the highly productive agricultural soils of the area.

In the larger context, this discussion is bedded in cultural materialism. While great strides have been made in understanding relationships among ancient Maya polities through structuralist approaches to Maya iconography and political organization, archaeologists working within a framework of cultural materialism have also made progress in explaining these important processes. For example, the nature of Late Classic warfare is seen by many as a consequence of increased competition for agricultural resources as population rose and productivity declined.[1] Consequently, understanding the relationship between population and productivity is crucial in understanding causation of major processes of the Classic Maya. However, it has been difficult under most circumstances to quantify or even reasonably characterize the extent of the agricultural base of a Maya polity, despite recent research that gives us good comprehension of the complexity of Maya agricultural systems.[2] Still restraining our understanding is Mayanists' past focus on the monumental architecture of site core areas. In recent decades, scholars have shifted focus to the study of households and other aspects of the archaeological record. Nevertheless, there remains a general paucity of large-scale projects that analyze the core and settlement zones of Maya sites as integrated units.

I do not claim that we have solved this problem at Blue Creek. However, our intensive surveys and the identification of large systems of ditched fields have been followed by the efforts of a series of investigators who have worked to better understand Maya agriculture at Blue Creek.[3] In this chapter, I summarize what is known about the agricultural systems at Blue Creek, thanks to their efforts.

A Population Estimate for Blue Creek

Before moving on to the issue of agricultural productivity, it is useful to consider how many people lived at Blue Creek.[4] To frame the question in a larger sense, did Blue Creek produce significantly more agricultural goods than were needed by the local population? If so, then they were well situated to become wealthy because of the trade of those products to other polities.

Despite more than a decade of surveys and excavations, we are not yet prepared to offer a truly reliable population estimate for Blue Creek. However, a crude estimate can be calculated. Within the 16 square kilometers now surveyed, there are approximately four hundred residential structures. Test excavations indicate that at least 80 percent were occupied in the Late Classic period,[5] and we can assume that perhaps only 80 percent of those were contemporaneous, giving a total of 256 structures occupied at the population peak. Using the estimate of 5.6 persons per household,[6] there were an estimated 1,330 people living within these 16 square kilometers or approximately a hundred persons per square kilometer. If this is extrapolated over the approximately 125 square kilometers of Blue Creek, then the Late Classic population can be estimated at approximately 12,500.[7]

This population density is quite low compared with other Maya sites. For example, Copan's population is estimated at approximately 20 thousand persons over approximately 24 square kilometers, for a density of more than 850 persons per square kilometer. Seibal's Late Classic population is estimated at 7,577 persons in the central 15.25 square kilometers, for a density of more than six hundred persons per square kilometer. Tikal had a population density of approximately 440 persons per square mile in the central 120 square miles during the Late Classic. Other population estimates range from three to five hundred persons per square kilometer at Maya sites.[8] So, even given the possibility of measurement or computation error, Blue Creek's population density was low by generally accepted standards for the Maya.

Agricultural Systems at Blue Creek

Far from the simplistic view archaeologists once held, we now know that ancient Maya agricultural systems were highly productive, complex, intensive, and varied to take advantage of specific environmental settings. The agricultural systems at Blue Creek reflect that complexity. The Blue Creek Maya employed at least five distinctive agricultural strategies. While some, such as local kitchen gardens associated with residences, were certainly controlled by individual households, others, such as the large-scale ditched and upland dry farming systems, were controlled by elites residing in the core area or other residential complexes such as Kín Tan.

Agricultural products are not necessarily restricted to food. For example, the ethnohistoric record indicates that the Río Hondo area was the source for large quantities of cacao produced for export into the coastal trade network.[9] Further, ongoing biosilicate studies at Blue Creek indicate that numerous other economically important plants were grown. Phytoliths from squash rinds (*Cucurbita*), maize (cob and leaf), cacao, and platanillo (*Heliconia*), the leaves of which were used to wrap foods, were recovered from residues in cache vessels. Significant quantities of phytoliths of maize, cacao, and chico sapote (grown for its fruit and gum) were present in midden deposits. Further, a tall-grass (Panicoid) phytolith was found in such quantities that it was probably used as a roofing material for thatch-roof houses. The phytoliths were fused by heat in such a way that the buildings must have burned at a very high temperature. We have also recovered intact maize kernels and beans from a sealed tomb, and pollen recovered from both the ditched fields and the bottoms of the ditches includes *Zea mays* and other economically useful plants.[10]

Upland Dry Farming

The most extensive agricultural system was probably dry farming of the upland *bajitos.* The landscape west of and above the Bravo Escarpment consists of karstic hill and *bajo* terrain. The limestone hills that often rise 50 meters above the surrounding landscape are covered by virtually no soil but were intensively used for habitation. Further, many of these habitations were of Blue Creek's most affluent and elite residents. Separating these nodes of population are large expanses of low-lying areas, bajitos, which have deep rich soils (black medium loam; Munsell color 2.5Y 2.5/1) and no evidence of prehistoric occupation. For example, Kín Tan is separated from Plaza A by a bajito that covers approximately 100 thousand square meters (Figures 1.5, 2.2, and 3.3). In this bajito, modern commercial farming has made any prehistoric features completely visible to us. Despite this, we have yet to find any indication of prehistoric habitation in this or other bajitos. Contemporary farmers report that these are the second-most productive soils in the region, with the lowest risk factor. Consequently, these extremely deep and rich soils are used today for corn agriculture, normally for two crops annually.

While there is no direct evidence that the bajitos were used prehistorically, it is almost incomprehensible that they were not. They are highly productive, easily farmed, and surrounded by prehistoric populations who also built terraces, check dams, and other features along the bajito margins in order to maximize usable land. Similarly, massive energy was expended to construct the large network of ditches to manage soil moisture and reclaim lands in similar soils east of the escarpment. None of these efforts would have been necessary or even sensible if the upland bajitos were not already under cultivation.

As discussed Chapter 3, these upland bajitos were a major agricultural resource at Blue Creek, covering 40 square kilometers or more. Further, the estimate in that chapter that 50 percent of the bajito terrain is covered by highly productive soils with no occupation was obtained conservatively—as was the 80-square-kilometer estimate of the extent of the terrain itself. A more precise estimate could range considerably higher.

These resources were controlled and most likely farmed by the residential communities on the hills overlooking them. Further, as seen in the previous chapter, these communities had internal stratification so that the elites who controlled the resources had ample local labor forces to farm these lands.

Lowland Ditched Fields

Since the 1970s, archaeologists have recognized that the Maya built intensive agricultural systems in low-lying areas that were composed of networks of ditches surrounding fields in the range of one to three hundred square meters. Since their initial identification, the nature of these systems has been the focus of controversy. The early debates regarding whether these were artificial or natural features have been resolved and contemporary discussion deals with formation processes, hydrology, and productivity. In general, it is safe, but somewhat simplistic, to state that these networks of ditches were built to control water and moisture and provide stable growing surfaces for agriculture. At Blue Creek, the function was clearly to drain areas that were often seasonally inundated (Figure 5.1). Contemporary landowners have converted these lands from corn agriculture, common from 1954 to about 1985, to grasslands for grazing cattle because the low-lying lands are often seasonally inundated, causing complete crop failure. Interestingly, they have also used mechanized ditching to drain the same locations.

While we have found direct evidence for cacao at Blue Creek, it is still uncertain that it was grown there. However, the Río Hondo area was certainly a major source for cacao exported through ancient Chetumal in the colonial period.[11] Further, high phosphate levels in the ditched fields of Blue Creek would have made it unlikely that maize could be grown in them.[12] Consequently, it is very likely that some tree crop such as cacao was grown instead. If so, Blue Creek may have been a major exporter of cacao in the Classic period.

I first identified the network of fields at Blue Creek during a low-elevation airplane reconnaissance, and it has since been the focus of intensive research. We have now positively identified large tracts of ditched fields in the lowlands immediately east of the Bravo Escarpment. Further, significantly more existed prior to the deep plowing for agriculture that occurred between 1954 and 1985. Modern pastures that were not impacted by this plowing show clear networks of ditches (Figures 5.2 and 5.3) while adjacent pastures that were deep plowed do not. Consequently, we can minimally estimate the existence of eight square kilometers of networks of the

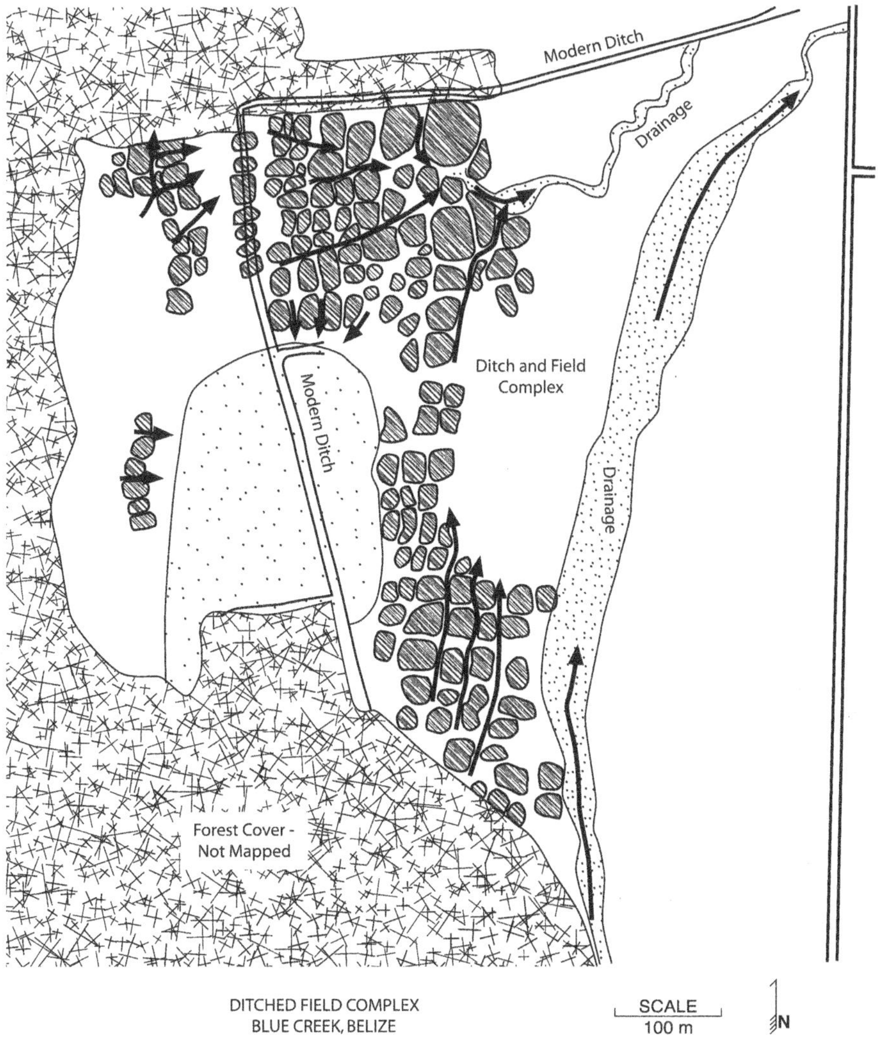

Figure 5.1. Plan view of a sector of ditched agricultural fields (redrawn from drawings by C-Dimensions, Inc.).

ancient field systems from the escarpment to the east. Further, the Río Bravo flows three to five kilometers east of the escarpment and there is a swampy area covering 22–25 square kilometers between the identified fields and the river that has recently been developed for rice agriculture. Ancient field systems may have existed in this zone as well, although recent land modifications make positive identification impossible.

Ditched fields are notoriously difficult to date. However, recent work places the

Figure 5.2. Photograph of ancient and modern ditching. These fields are partially depicted in Figure 5.1.

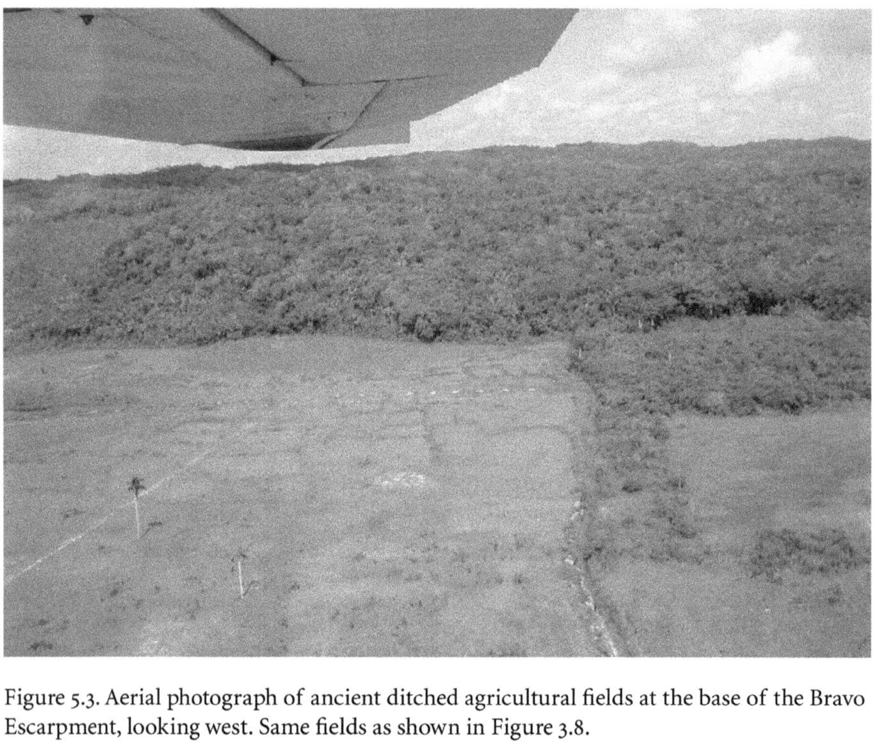

Figure 5.3. Aerial photograph of ancient ditched agricultural fields at the base of the Bravo Escarpment, looking west. Same fields as shown in Figure 3.8.

construction of at least some of the ditches at approximately A.D. 650, or the beginning of the Late Classic period.[13] Debate continues as to whether these ditches were built to expand the agricultural base into new areas or as a risk-management response to rising water tables that threatened the usefulness of existing agricultural lands.

It is almost certain that these fields were controlled by the royal elites who lived in the core area of Blue Creek. The alternative possibility is that corporate groups in areas such as Chan Cahal controlled these resources. However, this is highly unlikely given the status distinction between Chan Cahal and the elites living elsewhere. Further, Chan Cahal households were organized in a manner that suggests that they had local kitchen gardens. These would have been unnecessary if Chan Cahal also controlled the ditched fields.

Terraces, Check Dams, and Other Agricultural Construction

In areas with little easily accessible arable soil and/or significant vertical relief, the ancient Maya used intensive techniques such as terracing to create agricultural lands. The range and complexity of these relatively small, local systems were far greater than originally expected.[14] While the necessity to optimize productivity in marginally productive areas is not surprising, at Blue Creek, given the abundance of soil resources, the presence of such a quantity and range of variability of such features was not expected.

Many of these features have not been systematically recorded, as their visibility is ephemeral. In one case, we discovered a complex system when a landowner burned the grass from a cattle pasture. A week later, when we returned to document the features, rapidly growing grass had already obscured the features and only part of the complex was mapped. This complex on the west back-slope of the escarpment included two cases in which, in drainages formed between two hills, the Maya had built very solid retaining walls and then filled behind them. In addition to managing runoff, these features were designed to provide additional growing surfaces of approximately 25 square meters. At the base of one of the drainages, a 50-meter-long, U-shaped feature had been built, apparently to capture or slow runoff from the hills. Also, on the sides of upland hills, numerous terraces existed that could have resulted from a combination of limestone quarrying for construction and later agriculture. Importantly, while the full nature of these features remains vague, they were built for water management and agriculture and are located adjacent to the highly productive upland soils discussed previously.

Further, large terraces, presumably for agriculture, were built in marginal upland areas. For example, U Xulil Beh had limited agricultural potential. While there was clearly ample space around the residences at U Xulil Beh for kitchen gardens and small growing plots, there was little available land for larger corporate groups to farm. On the west side of the area, the Maya constructed two large terraces by cutting and filling the slope. The resulting terraces were more than 40 and 50 meters wide and covered more than four thousand square meters and six thousand square meters, respectively (Figure 3.4).

At the base of the Bravo Escarpment on the east side, many Classic period growing platforms were built immediately above the flat lowlands.[15] One of these, covering approximately 50 square meters, was excavated under the belief that it was a residential platform with a meter of colluvial deposits on top. However, further survey work and excavation made it clear that this was only one of many such platforms at and near the base of the escarpment that were engineered growing surfaces.

Consequently, despite the immediate availability of vast tracts of highly productive agricultural soils, the Blue Creek Maya built a wide range and large quantity of small-scale, intensive systems designed to expand and optimize their agricultural productivity. These systems were probably controlled by the corporate groups from the residential components located in closest proximity to them.

Specialized Niches: *Rejolladas*

As Blue Creek is located on an ecotone, specialized natural areas exist that held potential for specialized-use farming. Among these, *rejolladas* had the greatest potential for agriculture. Like cenotes, rejolladas are sinkholes in the karstic topography. Cenotes, however, provide access to underground rivers and are important water sources. Rejolladas do not have water at their bottoms and serve as sediment traps and retain moisture well. Elsewhere, rejolladas are highly prized agricultural lands where farmers are able to cultivate two crops a year. In early colonial sources, rejolladas were used for growing fruit, including cacao, and were often controlled by elites.[16] A number of rejolladas are located in the rolling hills of the Bravo Escarpment, including three adjacent to the site core. One is an enormous sediment trap with deposits approximately three meters deep that receives all surface water runoff from the monumental architecture. The Blue Creek royal elite likely controlled these features during the Classic period much like their colonial counterparts in the north, and these features may also indicate why the site core was established at this particular location. So, while such specialized niches were relatively small components of the overall agricultural system, perhaps less than one percent, they were highly productive and important.

Kitchen Gardens and the Houselot Model

The final component of the Blue Creek agricultural production system is the kitchen gardens associated with individual households. Thomas Killion forwarded a simplified model of small gardens owned by individual contemporary and prehistoric households that were located nearby. Today, such gardens are located within the *solares* or walled compounds surrounding residences in traditional villages such as Yaxunah, Yucatán. Prehistorically, these walled compounds did not exist and kitchen gardens would have been placed just beyond the open area around individual houses. The applicability of this model was tested at Chan Cahal, one of the residential components of Blue Creek.[17] Chan Cahal and similarly structured residential components, such as Sayap Ha and U Xulil Beh, certainly had such kitchen gardens associated with individual residences. On the other hand, other residential components, such as Kín Tan, could not have such gardens because of lack of space near the residences, unless they were located on now destroyed hillside terraces. However, since Kín Tan apparently controlled large tracts of agricultural lands, its residents probably did not need such gardens. Equally so, the presence of kitchen gardens at Chan Cahal, despite the fact that Chan Cahal was surrounded by ditched fields, indicates that the residents of Chan Cahal did not control the ditched fields but were probably workers in them. A conservative estimate of the impact of kitchen gardens on the overall agricultural productivity of Blue Creek would be in the range of one percent.

Summary of Agricultural Systems

At least five distinct components of the agricultural production system have been identified at Blue Creek. Each was controlled by a distinct group of people and functioned differently than all others. Collectively, they make up a complex and varied approach to production that minimized risk through diversity and provided far more agricultural products than needed locally. The "macro-systems" of dry upland agriculture and ditched lowland agriculture were probably controlled by the royal elites of the core area and the nonroyal elites of residential components such as Kín Tan. Similarly, rejolladas and other specialized niches were probably controlled by the royal elites. Local elites also probably controlled terraces and check dams built at the bases of hills below their residences. These may have functioned for such larger and more powerful lineages much like household kitchen gardens did for individual, lower-status, households.

A very crude, but quite conservative, estimate of the amount of agricultural land utilized by the Blue Creek Maya would incorporate the 40 square kilometers of known, upland dry farming plus the 8 square kilometers of confirmed lowland ditched fields, with this figure modified upwards by one percent each for the rejolladas, terraces, other constructed agricultural areas, and kitchen gardens. Consequently, a total of at least 50 square kilometers or 40 percent of Blue Creek's approximately 125 square kilometers was being cultivated. Especially remembering that an additional 25 square kilometers between the Río Bravo and the ditched fields at the base of the Bravo Escarpment may have been cultivated, this estimate could easily rise to 75 square kilometers or 60 percent of the land under control of the Blue Creek polity. While the agricultural productivity of these various systems is poorly known, there was certainly far more agricultural output than required to feed a community of the size of Blue Creek. Clearly, agricultural products were exported from Blue Creek in order to support the import of the many exotic goods that we have recovered and to support the relatively opulent lifestyles of the royal and nonroyal elites.

The Role of Centralized Water Control

Control of resources is clearly a means to power and authority. Agricultural lands are, of course, not the only resource that archaeologists have discussed as being important to the ancient Maya. Even in the subtropical moist environments of the southern Maya lowlands, water is not equally available to everyone. Vern Scarborough has shown that systems for controlling water were tied to political economies and central power structures at a number of Maya sites.[18] While we do not believe that Scarborough and his associates regard centralized water-control systems as necessary components to Maya rule, others seem to take this position. In the case of Blue Creek, water control was clearly not a mechanism of political control and power.

Below the Bravo Escarpment, the single largest water-control system is the network of ditched agricultural fields. These are extensive systems—probably much more extensive than we have recorded. While there has been considerable impact from modern land clearing, we do not find the significantly more grand residences at critical junctures as in the system that Scarborough and Gallopin found at Tikal. Instead, we find associated populations in locations such as Chan Cahal, which has some of the least elaborate grand residences of Blue Creek. A better way of viewing Chan Cahal is that it was a resident farming community with its own central places (in a sociopolitical, not geographic sense).

Blue Creek also lacks features such as the large-scale reservoirs and geographically central water-control features found at sites such as Tikal and La Milpa. There is a reservoir at Blue Creek, but it is the relatively small one associated with the Structure 25 Courtyard near the monumental architecture.

At the household level, we find numerous check dams and terraces that are probably for agriculture. However, their scale and association with nearby residences indicate to us that these were "owned" by the local family or corporate group rather than by any sort of central authority.

Why was there no central control of water at Blue Creek? The answer is straightforward. Water is plentiful and broadly distributed throughout the community. Aside from the Río Azul, Río Hondo, and Booth's River watercourses, there are numerous springs, cenotes, and lakes. At the base of the Bravo Escarpment, there are five or six small lakes, and several others exist between the escarpment and the Río Bravo. There are several cenotes and *aguadas* near the site center above the escarpment. There are at least four within a half kilometer from our research station, and there are several springs along the escarpment. There is no lack of water at Blue Creek. Water only becomes a resource for political or economic purposes when it is scarce, or at least seasonally scarce, or when it is heterogeneously distributed (or when a large population is convinced that cold, bottled water is preferable to tap water with ice). At Blue Creek, none of these things were the case.

The environmental adaptations of Maya populations were as variable as the environments to which they adapted. In this case, control over water resources was not a necessary condition for centralized authority. Instead, extant centralized authorities incorporated water control into their realm of authority when they could.

Conclusions

The data from Blue Creek demonstrate that ancient Maya cities had complex agricultural economic bases that incorporated risk-managed intensive agriculture. More important, despite the crudeness of our information, Blue Creek's low population density combined with its vast resources of agricultural productivity indicates that Blue Creek clearly produced agricultural products in excess of local consumption.

So, if resource control is a measure of power and wealth, the resource controlled by Blue Creek was its vast agricultural productivity. To return for a moment to how power, legitimacy, and authority were created, maintained, and cultivated within Blue Creek, it is clear that the lineages that controlled agricultural resources were much better off than those that did not. Once the first arrivals took control of agricultural resources, they maintained that control through many generations.

6 The Importance of Trade and Commerce at Blue Creek

In this chapter, I examine Blue Creek's wealth and how it was obtained. In previous chapters, I have argued that Blue Creek based its economy upon the community's access to high-quality and large-scale agricultural lands. However, the presence of this agricultural resource, alone, is not adequate to explain how Blue Creek acquired material wealth. In order to convert such a resource into wealth, Blue Creek also required access to outside markets, trade, and interaction with other Maya polities.

The focus of this chapter is jade at Blue Creek. Jade is commonly seen as a proxy for ancient Maya wealth and power. While other exotic goods could also be used and are broadly found at Blue Creek, jade is easily recognizable and recoverable in field settings. Further, its source is well understood and it was clearly important to the ancient Maya.

The Maya Coastal and Riverine Trade System

While Blue Creek's agricultural productivity gave it the means to acquire wealth, its location at the headwaters of the Río Hondo enhanced the community's ability to transport products to other markets (Figure 1.6).[1] The Río Hondo is the farthest north of the rivers draining the Maya lowlands. It is a slow-moving stream that also provided canoe access to Chetumal Bay, the Caribbean Sea, and, ultimately, populations in northern Yucatán who had fewer and less reliable agricultural resources. Experimental canoe trips show that a dugout canoe requires approximately three days to reach Chetumal Bay from Blue Creek (Figure 6.1).[2]

Chetumal Bay linked the coast with a series of important accesses into the interior of the Maya lowlands. Not only do the Río Hondo and the New River drain into Chetumal Bay, but also there is an artificial canal that links the large Bacalar Lagoon to the north end of the bay. Further, the Xkalak Peninsula and Ambergris Caye protect the bay from the open sea. As a consequence, it was easily accessible to canoe travel.

Figure 6.1. Construction of a dugout canoe used to navigate the Río Hondo.

Archaeologists have long known that the coastal trade system was operating at the time of contact.[3] However, its complexity and intensity in the Postclassic period was only begun to be understood in the mid-1970s, when research on Cozumel Island was undertaken.[4] Other research has shown that a robust trade in commodities such as salt existed, in addition to the well-known status-reinforcing exotic objects such as jade, obsidian, and ceramics.[5] In the 1980s, intensive field projects established that well-organized coastal trade incorporating specialized port-of-trade and transshipment ports were in place at least as early as the middle of the Classic period.[6] Further, the site of Cerros was established in the Late Preclassic at the mouth of the New River on Chetumal Bay's southern extension, Corozal Bay.[7] Cerros was likely to have also controlled access to the Río Hondo, only a few miles north. From that time on, a succession of polities controlled Chetumal Bay and the linkage between the coastal and riverine trade systems.[8] Further, by A.D. 600, Ambergris Caye had been separated from the Xkalak Peninsula by a narrow channel.[9]

Despite debate as to whether this channel was artificial, it certainly shortened the distance a canoe would need to travel up the northern coast by about a hundred kilometers. Further complexity in the system has been revealed by Heather McKillop's research.[10] She has demonstrated that small-scale salt production on the islands off the coast of Belize augmented the existing long-distance trade from the large northern Yucatecan coastal *salinas*, lagoons where salt can be collected. Importantly, this occurred at the same time inland populations reached their peaks in the Late Classic.

The coastal and riverine trade system was in place by the Late Preclassic period, and by the mid-Classic period its complexity included transshipment ports, probable canals, and small-scale production of coastal goods for inland consumption. Confirming that Blue Creek was directly linked to this system via the Río Hondo, we have identified a dock feature at the terminus of the navigable portion of the river, and several other likely landing locations exist within the Blue Creek polity.[11] Blue Creek, at the terminus of the system on the northernmost river of the system, enjoyed two major advantages because of its location. First, the system increased the efficiency of exporting Blue Creek's agricultural products. Second, all exotic goods moving upstream to the large Petén sites would pass through Blue Creek.

Exotic Goods at Blue Creek

Blue Creek displays a pattern of conspicuous consumption of exotic, status-reinforcing goods and other public displays of wealth. This wealth and the import of such goods was made possible by Blue Creek's setting in the Maya "breadbasket" and its location at the terminus of the riverine trade system.

Beyond Blue Creek, Mayanists debate the degree of community craft specialization. For example, Colha was a large-scale producer of stone tools distributed throughout the region.[12] Yet, it is uncertain how much of Colha's economy was based on stone tool manufacture. While the Blue Creek data indicate that significant specialization could occur, dependent upon resource availability, this question remains murky.

There has also been significant debate regarding whether Maya coastal trade systems carried commodities in large amounts. If Blue Creek, at the headwaters of the Río Hondo, produced as much and had as low a population as seems to have been the case, then it is very likely that products were being shipped down the river, through the bay, and up the coast to populations that had fewer and less secure agricultural resources. Whether this was done with regularity or only in times of stress in the northern lowlands is unclear. However, these data certainly reinforce the thesis that an established, institutionalized system of interpolity trade did exist. Further, this institutionalized trade system bound polities together in important ways.

The rather amazing fact is that Blue Creek has yielded one of the largest collections of exotic materials such as jade in the Maya area.[13] As with most archaeological observations, there may be more than one cause for this situation. Perhaps Blue Creek simply had access to a disproportionate amount of exotic material because of its wealth and location at the terminus of the riverine trade route. However, it must be recognized that our excavations at Blue Creek have been some of the most intensive as well as some of the most extensive in the Maya area. Consequently, we probably have recovered a higher percentage of the exotic goods at Blue Creek than other projects have. Yet, we cannot ignore the fact that looters robbed the site of many jade artifacts before our efforts began.

Regardless of such biasing factors, it is clear that the exotic goods from Blue Creek constitute a valuable database because of their sheer number and the range of contexts from which they were excavated. While the task of documenting this entire database is not yet complete, the database for jade artifacts is. Further, as jade was the most valuable exotic material for the Maya, it is reasonable to use it as a proxy for access to all exotic goods.

We have recovered approximately 1,350 jade artifacts from Blue Creek derived from numerous diverse contexts. While much of the collection comes from the "shaft caches" dug in Structure 4, nearly four hundred artifacts come from other contexts.

An examination of the Blue Creek jade offers insight on three levels. First, it gives us the opportunity to compare the wealth of Blue Creek with that of other Maya sites. Second, and possibly more important, it allows us to examine how jade was distributed within Blue Creek and how different people enjoyed differential access to it and, presumably, other exotic goods. Finally, the Blue Creek database offers some insight into how jade functioned within the political economy of the Maya in general. Was jade available to anyone who could afford it? Or was jade available only to those whose status allowed it?

Mineralogy and Sources of Maya Jade

The colloquial term *jade* has been generally used to describe a group of minerals including jadeite, nephrite, diopside, apatite, amazonite, and other co-occurring, related minerals. The variability of trace elements within these minerals largely determines color variation, and it is often not possible to determine the composition of a specific stone through visual analysis. Consequently, use of the term *jade* throughout this discussion means that I have not discriminated among the minerals. Effectively, this is the same group of minerals that Norman Hammond has referred to as "social jade."[14] I do, however, distinguish between that suite of minerals and "greenstones," which are generally of lower aesthetic quality and include minerals such as schists, shales, and serpentines, which are easily distinguished from "jades" or "social jades" by hardness, density, and friability.

There have been several attempts to characterize the composition of jade and to trace artifacts to their sources.[15] Jade occurs in cobbles and boulders with variations in chemical composition, but, despite this, some groupings based on chemical composition have been established for reference collections from the major source area, the Motagua Valley in Guatemala and Honduras.[16] While reference collections from the Motagua Valley are still incomplete, commercial exploration has revealed materials that visually span the entire range of examined collections of prehistoric artifacts.[17] Not all of these, though, have been characterized chemically. The Motagua Valley with its nearly unique geology is probably the sole source of jade in Mesoamerica. Jadeite, the mineral that composes much of the range of "jade," has been known to co-occur with serpentine in the Motagua Valley since 1954, and the valley is probably the only location in which the high pressures required to form these minerals exist.[18]

A second possible source, particularly for some jade used by the Middle Preclassic Olmecs, has been suggested to be in Guerrero, Mexico.[19] However, such a source has not been positively identified and, if it existed, was probably largely exhausted during Olmec times.[20] As no contemporary jade is known from Guerrero, comparison with prehistoric artifacts is impossible. Further, the range of color variability from the Motagua Valley also includes those used by the Olmecs.

Jade in the Mesoamerican Archaeological Record

Jade appears early in the archaeological record north of the Maya area. Olmec traders imported large quantities of jade and serpentine for use at their Middle Preclassic center of La Venta and for distribution to other centers such as Chalcatzingo. At about the same time, jade enters the record at Copan, probably because Copan serviced the jade needs of La Venta.[21] In the Late Preclassic period, jade becomes an elite, status-reinforcing, exotic material in the Maya area. Jade remains uncommon but not rare in the record and is generally restricted to elite and royal contexts in burials and caches. New depositional patterns also emerge in the Late Preclassic. Jade artifacts were generally deposited in caches in public buildings.[22] However, they also appear in non-elite caches and burials and are found smashed and broken in termination rituals as public buildings were abandoned.[23]

In the southern Maya lowlands during the Late Classic period, the quantities of jade artifacts decline dramatically and jade generally becomes restricted to elite burials and caches.

Forms of Jade Artifacts

As Hammond notes, jade is a raw material well suited for manufacture of a variety of tools. However, the use of jade was almost completely restricted to the manufacture of ornaments. This restriction indicates that jade's social value eclipsed its utility. The vast majority (probably more than 90 percent) of jade artifacts are beads in a wide range of shapes.

Other artifact forms include anthropomorphic pendants such as bib-head pendants or *ahau* heads. These are frontal views of a human head with a bib underneath the chin that may represent an *ahau* or king. In northern Belize, jade bib-head-shaped pendants have been found at Blue Creek, Cerros, Nohmul, Lamanai, Santa Rita, and Chan Chich. These bib-head pendants have also been argued to be parts of royal crowns. Aside from bib-head pendants, anthropomorphic figures posed as acrobats and associated with shamanism occasionally are found.[24] Some jade objects, such as *ahau* pendants, particularly in sets of four, have been viewed as marking royalty.

Earflares are an uncommon form apparently restricted to use by the ruling elite. For example, at Altun Ha, with a very large collection of recovered jades (n = 1,030), earflares only represent 1.3 percent of the collection.[25] These are generally found in paired sets in high-status burials and occasionally singly in caches.

Artifacts formed into plaques are another Classic period artifact form found only rarely in northern Belize. These are low-relief, thick, flat pendants with anthropomorphic figures carved into them. Only one such plaque, apparently looted from the site of Indian Creek, is known from northwestern Belize. However, many are known from high-status burials at Altun Ha.

Maya Political Economy and the Role of Jade

In the Maya area, a view of two parallel systems of political economy and resource control has developed.[26] One system consisted of commodities and utilitarian goods produced and exchanged in a household-oriented mercantile system. The second system consisted of gift exchange of prestige goods that supported and reinforced the authority of kings and other nobles. In particular, the exchange and distribution of exotic, status-reinforcing objects is seen to have been controlled by royalty. For example, Joe Ball argues that Maya ceramic workshops were supported by ruling elites in order to provide sumptuary goods for Maya palaces.[27] Therefore, the inter-site distribution of these goods occurred through gifting among elites. Similarly, Patricia McAnany argues that elite households were created and maintained social power through control of artisans.[28] If true, then control of the distribution and display of jade would have been a central principle in the maintenance of social status.

Still, the role of jade in the Maya political economy remains somewhat ambiguous. Freidel argues that jade functioned as currency and was accessible to anyone with the wealth to own it.[29] This would mean that access to jade was based upon an individual's wealth, and its distribution in the archaeological record should co-vary with status. For example, the distribution of jade would be expected to be higher in elite households than in non-elite households. Alternatively, jade may have been only exchanged and circulated among elites of different polities, perhaps assuming the heirloom qualities associated with Trobriand Islanders' Kula and

Kwakuitl copper plaques.[30] This alternative explanation sees the control of jade removed from the hands of nonroyals. Jade artifacts that did move from the possession of royalty to nonroyalty did so as gifts to individuals. The purpose of such gifting would have been to recognize particular acts of service and/or lifetimes of service to the ruling classes.

The Distribution of Jade Artifacts at Other Sites

While jade artifacts have been recovered from nearly every Maya center, most databases generally have limited applicability because of the research designs of the excavations. For example, 1,030 jade artifacts were recovered from Altun Ha in seven years of excavation. However, the excavations were largely focused on public architecture. Consequently, there are few comparative data about nonelite behavior.

Similarly, large or important single-event deposits of jade artifacts dating to the Early Classic period have been found at Calakmul, Chan Chich, Nohmul, and La Milpa.[31] However, all of these again derive from monumental contexts and little is known of the distribution of jade artifacts throughout those sites.

By contrast, excavations at Colha and Cerros in northern Belize have been extensive enough to clarify broad, multicontextual patterns.[32] However, only data regarding the Preclassic jade from Colha have been published and these cannot be applied to understand Classic period complexity. The Cerros collection (n = 236) is significantly different, as 187 of the artifacts were recovered from ritual termination deposits on top of Late Preclassic and Early Classic buildings. Another 31 artifacts were recovered from dedicatory caches and only 18 came from other contexts. While the jade collection from Cerros is important for a number of reasons, it too offers limited insight into the distribution of jade throughout the entire community.

The most relevant studies to this discussion derive from excavations at Tikal and Uaxactun. While the Tikal materials were described long ago by William Coe, that report only exists in manuscript form. However, Hatula Moholy-Nagy re-examined that collection and used the material culture from Tikal as a basis for her doctoral dissertation. Additionally, David Maxwell examined caches from Uaxactun as a part of his doctoral dissertation.[33] Consequently, all of the Tikal data and a significant part of the Uaxactun data are available. In both cases, excavations were conducted in contexts diverse enough that comparability exists with the Blue Creek database.

Patterns of Jade Disposal at Blue Creek

The pattern of jade disposal through time at Blue Creek (Table 6.1) parallels the general regional pattern discussed by Rathje and is similar to the temporal patterns seen at Tikal and Uaxactun. Though 10 artifacts were deposited prior to

Table 6.1. Occurrence of jade in caches at Blue Creek, Tikal, and Uaxactun by temporal period

Period	Blue Creek		Tikal		Uaxactun	
Middle Preclassic	10	0.7%	3	<0.1%		
Late Preclassic	191	14.2%	205	2%	1	5%
Early Classic	1,120	83.0%	10,260	90%	16	76%
Late Classic	29	2.1%	947	8%	4	19%
Terminal Classic			9	<0.1%		
Early Postclassic			2	<0.1%		
Total	1,350		11,426		21	

Note: From Moholy-Nagy (1994) for Tikal and Maxwell (1996) for Uaxactun.

the Late Preclassic at Blue Creek, the vast majority of the collection derives from ritual contexts in the Late Preclassic and Early Classic periods (Linda Vista complex, A.D. 100/150–250, and Río Hondo complex, A.D. 250–600). Only 29 artifacts, approximately two percent, date to the Late Classic. Importantly, 25 of these 29 artifacts were found in a single cache dating to the early part of the Late Classic (Aguas Turbias complex, A.D. 600–750).

The contexts in which jade artifacts are found are more critical in understanding jade's social role for the ancient Maya of Blue Creek. Three general contextual categories can be discerned for Blue Creek. Monumental contexts include both caches and burials in public buildings and in the associated site center residences. Elite residences include the large masonry buildings not located in the site core such as plazuelas and courtyards in the Kín Tan residential group and others throughout the settlement zone. Finally, non-elite residences generally include those structures with perishable roofs and walls that are today visible as housemounds such as those at the Chan Cahal and Sayap Ha residential groups.

If jade artifacts were fungible and available to anyone who could afford them, their distribution would be expected to follow economic status. Few artifacts would be expected in non-elite residences, more in elite residences, and most in monumental contexts. Conversely, if royalty controlled jade, relatively few artifacts would be expected outside of monumental contexts.

Most jade artifacts occur in caches and burials in monumental architecture (n = 1,114). In Plaza A, jade artifacts were associated with four buildings (Table 6.2). In Structure 1, an Early Classic (Río Hondo) tomb and series of related caches yielded 32 artifacts. In Structure 3, an "early" Late Classic dedicatory cache (Aguas Turbias complex) yielded another 25 jade items. In Structure 4, caches associated with the filling of the shaft in approximately A.D. 500 yielded 966 jade artifacts. Finally, a single fragment was found in the collapse of Structure 6. In the Plaza B

Table 6.2. Jade from Blue Creek

Context	Structure	Provenience	Date	Quantity
Monumental architecture (n = 1,114)	Structure 1	Cache 4A	A.D. 500–550	10
		Cache 6A	A.D. 550–650	6
		Cache 6B	A.D. 550–650	14
		Tomb 4	A.D. 500–550	2
	Structure 3	Cache 45	Late Classic II	25
	Structure 4	Caches with the "jade shaft"	A.D. 500	966[a]
	Structure 6	Collapse debris		1
	Structure 12	Cache 28	A.D. 450–550	7
		Cache 30	A.D. 450–550	78
	Structure 24	Burial 32	Early Classic	2
		Cache 48	Early Classic	2
		Backdirt		1
Elite residences (n = 33)	Structure 25	Burial 20	Middle/Late Preclassic?	1
	Structure 31	Room	Late Classic	1
	Structure 33			1
	Structure 34	Tomb 7	Early Classic	2
		Cache	Early Classic	25
	Structure 36		Terminal Classic?	1
	Structure 45	Tomb 8	Early Classic	1
	Structure 60	Doorway	Late/Terminal Classic?	1
Non-elite residences (n = 148)	U-2	Burial 26	Early Classic	2
	U-5		Late Classic II	1
	U-9	Midden	Early Middle Preclassic to Late Preclassic/ Early Classic	2
	U-14	Below humus	???	3
	U-17	Cache 43	Late Preclassic	2
	U-18	Room fill	???	1

Table 6.2. Jade from Blue Creek

Context	Structure	Provenience	Date	Quantity
	U-19	Burial 34	Late Preclassic/ Early Classic transition	1
	U-49	Cache 31	Late Preclassic	24
		Cache 41	Early Classic	5
		Burial 15		2
		Ceramic concentration	Late Preclassic	46
		Other	???	47
	U-50	Humus	???	2
	U-54	Midden	Early Middle Preclassic to Late Preclassic	1
	Sayap Ha 1	Midden	Early Classic	1
	Sayap Ha 2	Burial	Early Classic	8

[a]Includes a canister of 100+ fragments that was counted as one piece.

complex, Early Classic caches (Río Hondo) include one in Structure 12 that yielded 85 jade artifacts and a cache in Structure 24 that yielded five other jade artifacts. Interestingly, all of these were recovered from public architecture contexts rather than from the major residences associated with Plaza B.

Jade artifacts were also found in Blue Creek's elite residences (n = 33; see Table 6.2). Twenty-seven artifacts were found in a tomb and associated cache in Structure 34. In the same residence, one other jade fragment was found in a terminal deposit and another may have been incorporated into a stucco decoration on the interior of a room. Another fragment was found on the floor of the doorway of Structure 60, apparently deposited upon abandonment. However, it also may be part of a Late Classic architectural composition.

The most surprising discoveries of jade were at Chan Cahal, a non-elite residential area (n = 148; see Table 6.2). Nearly one hundred jade artifacts were recovered from a Terminal Late Preclassic (Linda Vista complex) ceramic concentration at Structure U-49. Additionally, 31 jade artifacts were recovered from three Terminal Late Preclassic–Early Classic (Linda Vista–Río Hondo) caches (Caches 31, 41, and 43) and four artifacts were recovered from Burials 19 and 26, also dating to the Early Classic (Río Hondo complex). Further, eight jade pieces were used as inlays in the shell ear ornaments from Burial SH2 at Sayap Ha.

Tomb 5 is a special case in which significant numbers of jade artifacts were recovered but the context does not fit well into any of the three defined contexts.[34] The burial was placed in a large *chultun* on top of a hill approximately three kilometers northeast of the site center. By all appearances, this was an elite or royal tomb, but many years of quarrying for construction material had destroyed much of the contextual information. This Terminal Late Preclassic tomb included three individuals, 28 ceramic vessels, and 105 finely carved jade beads. Many of the vessels are exotic imports, and the tomb itself is a symbolic re-creation of the Maya cosmos. It is located in a strategic overlook above the agricultural fields and riverine access to Blue Creek. There was an Early Classic masonry structure built on top of a Late Preclassic midden near the tomb, but little else is known of its context and it cannot be securely placed in any of the contextual categories used here.

The relative abundance of jade at Chan Cahal clearly is aberrant. Regardless of which model is used, jade artifacts are perceived to be elite goods and deposition in monumental architecture rather than non-elite residential contexts is expected. While there are biases as a result of excavation strategy, the data from other sites support this. Information from some other sites, though, is helpful in putting the Blue Creek sample into perspective. For example, at Cerros from the Late Preclassic period, 236 pieces of jade were recovered but only three beads from a single cache came from a residential context. At Colha during the Late and Terminal Preclassic periods, the vast majority of jade and other greenstone artifacts are found in burials and caches, although the status of the individuals is unclear. At Salitron Viejo in Honduras, 2,212 carved jade and marble objects were recovered, apparently all from public and elite contexts.[35] However, the excavation did not focus on residential areas, so this perception may be a consequence of the excavation strategy rather than a past reality. Nevertheless, in none of these cases were large quantities of jade recovered from non-elite contexts.

Further, Hirth and Hirth report four common patterns for the deposition of jade at Salitron Viejo. In order of occurrence, these are (1) scattering or caching in construction fill, (2) careful placement behind facades, (3) caches along exterior walls after construction, and (4) breaking and burning prior to abandonment. Importantly, the only one of these patterns replicated at Blue Creek is caching (but not scattering) in construction fill. This contrasts with the Cerros pattern as reported by Garber in which the most common occurrence of jade is in termination rituals.

Blue Creek's pattern is more similar to the burial and caching pattern seen at Colha and Tikal. Palma Buttles reports that for the Late Preclassic at Colha, 44 percent of the ground greenstone artifacts are found in burials and 49 percent are found in caches.[36] A small number are found in middens. For the Terminal Preclassic, a greater percentage (61 percent) are found in burials, but otherwise the pattern remains roughly the same. Moholy-Nagy notes that jade is found at Tikal predominately in burial contexts and far fewer pieces are found in monument and structure caches. Further, jade debitage is found in general excavations, indicating that jade workshops may have existed at Tikal. With the exception of the possible evidence for jade workshops, the pattern at Blue Creek is quite similar. At Blue Creek, most jade is found in (1) Early Classic caches, (2) Late Preclassic and Early Classic burials, and (3) Middle and Late Preclassic middens (Table 6.3).

Distribution of Forms and Symbolic Materials at Blue Creek

For the most part, the Blue Creek jade collection consists of various forms of beads. At the lowest end of the "quality of craftsmanship" scale is the material from Chan Cahal that largely consists of beads and fragments. These artifacts were generally less well carved, had more inclusions, and tended to be broken more often.

Well-made, high-quality round and sub-spherical beads were common in many locations. In particular, the 105 beads found in the Late Preclassic Tomb 5 were consistently round and sub-spherical. Probably most of them were strung together as a single necklace. The high quality of the jade in Tomb 5 strongly supports the idea that the individual interred there was of very high status, despite the fact that the interment was approximately three kilometers from the monumental center of the site.

Interestingly, the distribution of anthropomorphic and zoomorphic pendants, bib-head pendants, and earflares is much more restricted than the general collection and all date to the Early Classic (Table 6.4). By far, most of these objects were found in the Structure 4 caches. However, other important locations yielded these artifacts. In particular, Tomb 7 contained an acrobat pendant and was located under a shrine in the Kín Tan residential area. Tomb 2 in Structure 1, dating to A.D. 500–550, included a pair of jade earflares. One zoomorphic pendant was also recovered from a non-elite burial in Structure X-34 at Chan Cahal. The other earflares and anthropomorphic and zoomorphic pendants all derive from the caches in Structure 4. This event has been well dated to approximately A.D. 500 by two radiocarbon dates.[37]

Symbolic Aspects of Beads and Pendants

Along with quantities and contexts, it is also worthwhile to examine the nature of the symbolism portrayed in the pendants recovered from Blue Creek. This area is distinctly difficult to interpret, but some patterning and meaning are clear. At Blue Creek, all anthropomorphic and zoomorphic beads and pendants, with two notable exceptions, derive from the A.D. 500 caches in Structure 4.

Nine anthropomorphic and zoomorphic beads and pendants were recovered from the Structure 4 caches. These include two tubular beads carved into anthropomorphic figures (BC671, BC857). These have been described previously by Dale Pastrana, and her descriptions are largely repeated here.[38] BC671 is the largest jade

Table 6.3. Contexts of jade at Blue Creek by time period

Period	Representative Deposits	General Contexts
Before Late Preclassic	Midden (8) Burial 20 (1)	Core area middens
Late Preclassic	Tomb 5 (105)	Uncertain
	Dedicatory cache in housemound (24) "Ceramic concentration "(46) Cache 31 (24) Cache 43 (2) Burial 34 (1)	Chan Cahal
Early Classic	Structure 1, Tomb 2 and associated caches (34) Structure 4 caches (966) Structure 12 dedication caches (85) Structure 24, Burial 32 (2) Structure 24 dedication caches (2)	Monumental architecture
	Structure 34, Tomb 7 (2) Structure 34 cache (25) Structure 45, Tomb 8 (1)	Western group
	Burial 26 (2) Cache 41 (5) Burial 23 (1)	Chan Cahal
Late Classic	Structure 3, Cache 45 (25)	Monumental architecture
	Structure U-5 (1)	Chan Cahal
Late/Terminal Classic	Structure 60 doorway (1)	Monumental architecture
	Structures 33 and 36 (2)	Special deposits

Table 6.4. Contexts of pendants and earflares

General Context	Specific Context	Pendants	Earflares	Totals by General Contexts
Public architecture	Structure 1, Tomb 4	0	2	
	Structure 3, Cache 45	0	2	
	Structure 4	20	37	61
Elite residential	Structure 34, Tomb 7	1	0	1
Non-elite residential	Structure X-34	1		1
Totals		22	41	63

artifact from Blue Creek, weighing 407.55 grams, and is 11.35 centimeters long and 4.5 centimeters in diameter (Figure 2.11a). This is a representation of a human face wearing something similar to an Olmec-style skullcap. The eyes and corners of the mouth were formed by drilling and the features were carved between drill holes. A very similar artifact was recovered from the Sacred Cenote at Chichén Itzá.[39] The other Blue Creek example, BC857, is considerably smaller, weighing 7.2 grams, and is 7.2 centimeters long and 1.45 centimeters in diameter. The piece is very similar in style and execution to BC671. However, crude, secondary engraving converted the image into a skull or death's head.

Also from the Structure 4 caches is an especially well-made pendant (BC729) that depicts God K (Figure 2.11b).[40] The figure wears a headpiece or topknot of hair and has a sloping forehead with something, possibly a celt, protruding. Most distinctively, a large scroll begins under the eye and extends to the neck below the jaw. BC674 is also quite distinctive, depicting a human face with a protruding tongue that appears to be laughing (Figure 2.11c). This individual also appears to be wearing a skullcap or a distinctive hairstyle.

Additionally, four other anthropomorphic bib-head figures were recovered (BC505 [Figure 2.11d], BC596, BC984, and BC1013). This artifact form was originally defined by Proskouriakoff as "helmet-bibs" and Hammond has argued that they represent the sun god, Kinich Ahau.[41] While they are generally seen as Late Preclassic expressions, it is clear from the Blue Creek sample that their use continued well into the Early Classic. Their contexts, usually in royal tombs, link them directly to kingship. If so, their presence in the Structure 4 caches connects the event with royalty. Interestingly, all were recovered intact except BC984, which was intentionally broken into pieces that were recovered from significantly different elevations within the shaft. With them was a bib-head representing not a human face but a monkey (BC513). Another zoomorphic found in the Structure 4 caches is BC540, which depicts an alligator head.

The only two anthropomorphic and zoomorphic pendants not found in the Structure 4 caches are BC6753, the acrobat pendant found in Tomb 7 at Kín Tan that was discussed in Chapter 4 (Figures 2.11e and 4.5), and a zoomorphic pendant found in Burial 23 in Structure X-34, a non-elite residence at Chan Cahal.

What Does the Jade from Blue Creek Tell Us about the Maya?

As I said earlier, Blue Creek's jade offers insight on several levels. We can learn about Blue Creek's relationship to the rest of the Maya world at the inter-site level, as well as the relationships among Blue Creek's components at the intra-site level.

At the inter-site level, the sheer quantity of jade artifacts found at Blue Creek is surprising. No other site of Blue Creek's size has yielded nearly as many artifacts; this is a clear marker of the site's wealth. The fact that Blue Creek imported such significant amounts of jade and other valuable exotic materials raises the question of what was exported in return. Blue Creek's two major economic resources were highly fertile agricultural lands and its strategic location at the terminus of a significant riverine trade route. A combination of production of exportable agricultural products and a location that facilitated the export of these products appears to have greatly benefited Blue Creek.

Clearly, in the Late Preclassic and Early Classic periods, Blue Creek was importing large quantities of jade artifacts. At the same time, public construction projects were being commissioned and Blue Creek may have been an independent kingdom.

However, Blue Creek's access to jade diminished greatly in the Late Classic period. Aside from the 25 artifacts from the dedicatory cache at Structure 3, only three small fragments and one jadeite celt date from the Late Classic. Further, the dedicatory cache for Structure 3 dates to very early in the Late Classic period. The vastly diminished access to jade after approximately A.D. 600 may have been due to a political transformation at Blue Creek itself. I have argued that by this time, Blue Creek was probably no longer an independent kingdom. If royalty controlled access to jade and there were no royalty at Blue Creek in the Late Classic, the lack of jade would be clearly understandable. However, there is a regional Late Classic pattern of declining access to jade that equally well explains the decline of jade at Blue Creek.[42] Further, public construction slowed at Blue Creek in the Late Classic. However, many elite residences were greatly expanded, new residential areas were established, and large-scale public works projects in the agricultural systems appear to have occurred. So, it is still uncertain whether this Late Classic decline in access to jade was related to internal or external events.

During the Late Preclassic and Early Classic periods, jade artifacts were highly concentrated in the public architecture of the site, with 1,114 artifacts found in 10 distinct caches and burials. Artifacts of higher-quality material, artifacts of high-quality craftsmanship, and larger artifacts were all also concentrated in the public architecture. Jade disposal at Blue Creek is largely associated with public rituals such as building dedication and burial. While the nature of the ritual associated with the caches in Structure 4 is uncertain, it too was highly public.

While in much lesser quantities, jade artifacts were also recovered from elite residential and non-elite residential contexts. In elite residences, disposal is also associated with ritual activities such as caching behavior and burial. However, a few small jade artifacts also may have been integrated into building ornamentation. Interestingly, only about a third of the 148 artifacts from non-elite residences were associated with caches and burials. Others were found seemingly randomly in excavations. In one case, in the Late Preclassic "ceramic concentration" in Structure U-49, 46 jade artifacts were recovered. The meaning of this feature is still far too ambiguous to discuss. This anomalous pattern for non-elite residences, though, indicates that jade was somehow operating differently than it did for the royalty who dealt with public architecture or the other elites.

The Role of Jade in the Maya Political Economy

The Blue Creek data can be used to examine the two competing views of the role of jade in the Maya political economy. One view is that jade was a fungible currency, the possession of which was limited only by economic means. The other position sees jade as controlled by royalty and only distributed outside of royalty through gifting.

In the case of the "currency" model, jade disposal would be expected to be concentrated in the public district as royalty also controlled the most resources. However, it would be expected that jade would be more common in the elite residences than in the non-elite residences, which is not the case. This is particularly surprising given the extensiveness of excavations in the elite residences of Blue Creek.

The "royalty" view would also anticipate jade's being concentrated in the public district but for other reasons. Ostentatious, public display of jade disposal during ritual events would have reinforced the authority of royal individuals. The "royalty" model would not suppose that there would be more jade in elite than in non-elite residences. In fact, the reverse could be true. While elites already controlled significant economic resources, non-elites may not. Consequently, reward systems that symbolically recognized non-elites but more tangibly reinforced the authority of elites could have existed. This view more completely explains the pattern of disposal seen at Blue Creek.

While the Blue Creek pattern fits the "royalty" model somewhat better that the "currency" model, neither is clearly precluded. The Blue Creek database gives us great information regarding the wealth of the community and the ways in which jade was used by the Maya but no concrete appraisal of who controlled it and how.

Summary

By all standards employed by Maya archaeologists, Blue Creek was a small but wealthy city. Public plazas, monumental architecture, a ballcourt, stelae aggrandizing its rulers, and complex masonry homes of the elite all leave us with the clear impression of wealth and power. That impression is underscored by the jade amassed by Blue Creek's residents, both elite and non-elite.

This wealth came about as a consequence of several factors. Blue Creek's location is the most obvious: it controlled hugely productive agricultural soils at the terminus of the riverine-coastal trade system. However, less than obvious is the role of human agency in exploiting these circumstances.

The construction of the ditched agricultural fields, presumably in the Early Classic, is an example of this agency. If Tim Beach and Sheryl Luzzadder-Beach are correct, this was a response to rising water tables in a successful effort to maintain existing agricultural systems. Further, it is likely that ditched field construction both maintained existing systems and expanded them laterally into previously unusable swampy lands. It is also likely that the Blue Creek Maya would have been self-sufficient without the ditched field agricultural systems. However, their leaders were not satisfied with self-sufficiency. Instead, they invested in the construction of intensive agricultural systems that increased productivity and created wealth.

This wealth was clearly not just limited to the elite members of Blue Creek society. So much wealth existed that it was allowed to "trickle down" into the lower ranks of Blue Creek society. In the Terminal Preclassic and Early Classic, "commoners" of Sayap Ha and Chan Cahal also had access to jade, the most valuable object in the Maya world. Admittedly, their access was limited to small and aesthetically less pleasing and less valuable artifacts that most likely derived from gifting by elites to commoners. However, ownership by non-elites at all was an exception to the general Maya pattern.

Much more obscure to us is the role that human agency played in other aspects of Maya society. How did leaders and/or merchants market Blue Creek's agricultural wealth into the riverine-coastal trade system? If Jeff Baker is correct, these products were also marketed to other polities in the more immediate region, such as the large cities in the central Petén.[43]

Somewhat less obscure is the role of human agency on an intra-site level to create an integrated economic system. The residential components of Blue Creek interacted with each other, probably through their local leadership, to create a community that was fundamentally stable for nearly a millennium and that also created wealth, power, authority, and legitimacy for its leadership.

7 Power and Authority at Blue Creek

In the previous chapters, I have summarized the public, residential, and agricultural components of Blue Creek and have dealt with some issues of trade and wealth. My intent has been to provide a case study of a single Maya city and some insight into its inner workings. However, I have only peripherally addressed one of the central issues in Maya archaeology, namely the nature of power in Maya society.

Where I have addressed this topic, I have framed it in two constructs, control over resources using McAnany's "first-arrivals" concept and how human agency, as viewed through a version of Wallerstein's world systems theory, applies to the situation. I believe that once first arrivals established control over resources, power and authority in Maya polities developed through multigenerational interaction among lineages that controlled resources such as agricultural lands.

This simplistic version is, of course, not entirely correct. For example, the first-arrivals view would imply that wherever we see the earliest occupation of Blue Creek, we would also see that later residents acquired significant multigenerational power, and this is not always the case. The earliest residents at Blue Creek were Middle Preclassic (Cool Shade complex, 1000–800 B.C.) residents of Chan Cahal. Yet, Chan Cahal does not show evidence of having become a major player in Classic period authority. Instead, components such as Kín Tan that were apparently not occupied for another six or seven hundred years assumed such roles. The question can be reexamined by considering which resources are important for the development of power, but that is beyond the scope of this discussion. What is important is that control of resources at the beginning of the Classic period largely defined which lineages would have the opportunity to participate in the Classic period authority structure. Then human agency became critical in how authority structures developed.

I cannot overstate the importance of human agency in the creation of power and authority. Agency is too often overlooked, especially by non-social scientists, in analyses of causation in complex society. For example, Jared Diamond's celebrated book, *Guns, Germs, and Steel,* begins with a description of Francisco Pizarro's fateful and dramatic capture of Atahuallpa in front of an Inca army of 40 to 80 thousand men in 1532. Three hundred pages are then consumed explaining to the reader that this was caused by environmental determinism devoid of human agency.[1] While Diamond's version of environmental determinism does help set the stage for understanding the conquest of the New World, Pizarro had not only swords of steel but also nerves of steel. His action was one of the most dramatic examples of how human agency can change the course of history.

So, while I am about to describe how I believe multigenerational lineages interacted at Blue Creek and elsewhere to create and reinforce their own power and authority, this is simply the social context for the actions of individual human beings.

The Nature of the Maya City and Its Internal Political Economies: Integrating the Residential Components to the Core Area

The scholars who object to the notion that Maya cities ever existed argue that the Maya were not an urban society. The problem with this approach remains that we cannot use models and definitions that were developed to be applied to other societies when examining the Maya. It does not matter whether we are trying to determine whether there were Maya cities or whether the Maya were a state or whether commoners or hinterlands were heterogeneous. Whenever we use definitions that simply do not fit the circumstances, these terms become impediments to understanding rather than tools for understanding. So, instead of trying to jam Blue Creek or the Maya in general into the nomothetic boxes of preexisting typologies, it is better and more useful to describe the Maya in their own terms.

For example, earlier views of Maya sociopolitical organization held that a large, undifferentiated mass of "commoners," usually stated to be more than 90 percent of the population, was ruled by a small group of royalty or elites, often as little as one percent of the population. At Blue Creek, as elsewhere, it is very clear that this simplistic situation never existed.

Instead, Blue Creek consists of numerous residential components, each with its own distinct nature. While not all of these components have been identified yet, we have identified 8 to 10 of them and intensively investigated several. These residential components exhibit vastly more diversity and complexity than would be expected of an undifferentiated mass of commoners. Most important, the internal stratification and differential access to exotic goods within each component indicate that each had its own internal mode of local leadership and that those modes were not identical in each component.

In some cases, such as Kín Tan, local leadership consisted of the authority of multigenerational lineages that appear to have controlled large holdings of agricultural lands. Similar power structures probably existed in other components such as Nukuch Muul, Rosita, and others. However, such multigenerational lineages do not seem to have existed at Chan Cahal and Sayap Ha, where local central places such as Structure L-25 indicate that these were integrated communities with their own public places and leadership. Instead of multigenerational lineages leading these communities, leadership and authority seem to have been achieved by individuals in their lifetimes rather than ascribed to a lineage from its ancestors.

So, there were multiple modes of local leadership among the residential components of Blue Creek. Further, there was a group of elites who controlled the large, grand public places of the core area and who also most likely controlled the large agricultural resources available below the Bravo Escarpment. How can the existence of both of these apparently conflicting structures of power, legitimacy, and authority be reconciled?

I believe that Wallerstein has pointed us in the right direction. His initial evaluation of core-periphery relations was an argument that there would be a permanency in the nature of the relationship between the core and the periphery as a result of their economic interaction. In our world this has proven to be somewhat less than true as the variables involved, such as markets for energy, have dramatically shifted. In the Maya world, relationships between groups of people were also dynamic; for example, the relationship between Kín Tan and the core area. But Wallerstein and world systems theory in general direct us to examine the relationships and interaction among people and institutions. Institutionalized structures of power, legitimacy, and authority, such as the core area and Kín Tan, simply could not coexist unless they were mutually supportive of each other.

In this framework, the relationship among components of Blue Creek can be seen as the interaction among lineage heads of varying authority. These multigenerational lineages legitimized each other's authority by public acknowledgment of that authority. They also certainly facilitated each other's access to resources. Clever players in this prestige-building interaction system can become very powerful.

This certainly continues today. I know of many instances in which generous North Americans have given money, books, computers, or other useful materials to a community only to find they have given it to the "wrong" person. Typically in these cases, the people in existing positions of authority, such as the town council, then chastise the donor for not giving the gift to the community through them. The donor had, unwittingly, undercut the authority of existing power and acknowledged another individual's importance—perhaps creating competing authority structures within the community.

Theoretical frameworks as diverse as Durkheimian structuralism, general systems theory, and evolutionary biology all tell us the same thing about the coexistence of multiple structures of authority at Blue Creek. If they in fact existed, then the larger system must have somehow worked. Wallerstein's general systems theory leads us to understand that the larger system worked because of the interactions among these multiple structures of authority.

For example, when the individual in Burial SH2 at Sayap Ha was living, a member of the ruling elite likely gave him the goods that accompanied his grave. This, as in the case of the Trobriand trading partner, increased his authority. It also certainly enhanced his loyalty. But, the enhanced status did not have multigenerational impact—at least there was no discernable multigenerational impact in any archaeologically visible manner. On the other hand, there were multigenerational impacts at Kín Tan, which most likely consisted of numerous interactions between the lineages of Kín Tan and the core area.

Another point of interest is that polities such as Blue Creek were strategically organized to maximize their access to resources. Blue Creek is located at the top of the Bravo Escarpment in a setting that allows for access to the many resources on this ecotonal area. It is no accident that stone resources from the Dumbbell Bajo on the western side of the Blue Creek polity were used for centuries to manufacture tools. As Jason Barrett has demonstrated, the elite of Blue Creek either had control over or unfettered access to the stone resources in that area.[2]

So, it was not simply the authority of the rulers over the commoners that explains the integrity of Blue Creek or the power, legitimacy, and authority of the ruling elite of the core area. Instead, power and authority derived from the interaction among the local leadership within each residential component and the ruling elites of the core area.

The archaeological markers of these structures are easily seen. We find complex residences and public sacred spaces within residential components. Further, we see connectivity between residential components and the core area.

Causeways, or *sacbeob*, are incorporated into many Maya sites. At Blue Creek, two small sacbeob are located at the base of the escarpment immediately below the core area. They cross a low-lying area that is seasonally inundated and extend to Sayap Ha.[3] Causeways are relatively uncommon in the region. The only others that I am aware of are at Chan Chich, where a major causeway connects settlement on the upper Río Bravo (also known as Chan Chich Creek) to the core area, approximately three kilometers away; another connects an outlying elite residential group to the core; and a third connects Ekenha to Chan Chich.[4] In the case of the first causeway at Chan Chich, there is no known evidence of the causeway continuing beyond the Río Bravo. However, this broad sacbe is running directly toward Chan Chich's nearest large neighbor, Punta de Cacao (see Figures 1.1 and 1.6 for the locations of many of the sites discussed in this chapter).

In the northern Yucatán, causeways are much more common and connect important areas within polities, and in some cases they connect sites that are clearly politically aligned but not part of the same polity. The most apparent example of this is the hundred-kilometer-long causeway between Chichén Itzá and Yaxunah.

Like contemporary roads, Maya causeways connected and facilitated interaction between groups of people who already had close interaction. They also symbolically reinforced existing political relationships. While the Chan Chich causeway may not have extended all the way to Punta de Cacao, whenever people from Punta de Cacao came to Chan Chich, they certainly walked that causeway and understood clearly that it had been built to publicly acknowledge the importance of the relationship of the two polities and to reinforce continued interaction between them.

If these complex residences, public sacred spaces, and evidence, such as causeways, of connectivity are archaeological signatures of integration at Blue Creek, then they should be present at other sites as well. Unfortunately, field research at most other Maya sites has not been organized in a manner to easily test these propositions. Nevertheless, there are some locations where data exist that reinforce my arguments.

I argue that residential communities at Blue Creek were tethered to the ruling lineages of the core area through complexities of political economy and interaction among leaders. If this is true, then they should also exhibit archaeological signatures of this sort of interaction. Despite the general lack of relevant data, several sites do in fact display these similar patterns.

For example, outlying central places that are probably surrounded by unrecorded residential components are architecturally linked to the core area. At the Belize Valley site of Baking Pot, causeways extend approximately a kilometer east and west of the core area, then terminate at ritual buildings.[5] Similarly, at other sites in the Belize Valley such as Cahal Pech, causeways sometimes, but not always, connect such terminus groups to the site core.[6] It is not clear whether these ritual buildings are central places for residential components as seen at Blue Creek, but they probably are.

In addition, similar patterns exist at sites north of Blue Creek. The core area of the large Classic site of Dzibanche in southern Quintana Roo, Mexico, is situated on an erosional remnant "island" surrounded by a very large *bajo* and its high-quality soils. A causeway leads north from Dzibanche approximately two kilometers to a small site, Kinich Na, which consists of a single very large temple complex surrounded by a group of relatively small elite residences. It is clear that Kinich Na was the home of an important lineage that was part of the Dzibanche polity. Kinich Na probably functioned to consolidate Dzibanche's authority over the northern sector of the bajo.

A related pattern is seen at the Becán-Xpuhuil-Chicanna complex, another Classic period site in southern Quintana Roo, less than a hundred kilometers north of Blue Creek. The core area of Becán is surrounded by a large moat with five crossings. Only a kilometer to the south is Chicanna, a small center with elite residential compounds and its own temples and ritual space, none of which are as large as those of Becán. Even more clearly connected to Becán is Xpuhuil, approximately four kilometers east. Xpuhuil also has compounds of elite residences and on its west side, a three-towered pyramid. Two towers face east, the direction of the Xpuhuil elite residences, defining the ritual space for Xpuhuil. However, the third tower faces west and has an ornate facade designed to mark the large terminus of the causeway from Becán. While incorporated into larger polities, Kinich Na, Chicanna, and Xpuhuil all have the political authority and economic bases to build large, complex masonry residences and large public monumental architecture. These, like the causeway terminus buildings at Baking Pot, represent central places for components of larger polities and the homes for the lineages that control them. Further, the ruling lineages of the core area are connected to the people of the outlying residential components through social and political ties to the local elite lineages.

Gair Tourtellot and his colleagues argue that La Milpa was similarly organized, with four outlying minor centers at roughly the cardinal directions from the site center serving to integrate the population into the royal center.[7] In the case of La Milpa, causeways have not been found that connect these minor centers to the site center. In addition, the nature of the survey work conducted at La Milpa does not allow us to know whether these minor centers were surrounded by population aggregates. However, I strongly suspect that they were and that La Milpa was organized much like Blue Creek. This is supported by Laura Levi's recent reports of a settlement structure much like Blue Creek at the center of Wari Camp approximately halfway between Blue Creek and La Milpa.[8]

At Blue Creek, the same structure and functional interrelationships are seen. With the exception of U Xulil Beh, each residential component had its own central place and, often, its most complex residence housed a lineage that was more prestigious than all others. In the cases of Kín Tan, Nukuch Muul, Rosita, Chan Cahal, and Sayap Ha, lineages in each component, or community, formed relationships through political economies with the ruling lineages of the core area. In the case of U Xulil Beh, it appears that the community was settled late in Blue Creek's history, possibly to exploit additional agricultural resources. Further, it appears that the community never developed internal stratification or a central place or a lineage that regularly articulated with the lineages of the core area.

Religion as an Integrative Device in the Early Classic

The role that religion plays in society has been debated by scholars from many fields. One of the most influential of these was Emile Durkheim, the founder of French structuralism, who viewed religion as an integrative mechanism. A shared religion means shared values and worldview. Further, those who do not share religion are often in conflict, as the Judeo-Christian and Islamic traditions have been for centuries.

An alternative view held by past Mayanists is that religion was controlled by the ruling elite and used as a means of subjugating and controlling the commoners.

In this view, most essential religious information was not shared among all members of society, and control over information by the elite supported their control over commoners.

I ascribe to the first, Durkheimian, view. Leaders have certainly used religion to motivate people into a wide range of action. However, this can only occur if the central precepts and beliefs are shared by all, or at least most, members of a society.

The question then is raised as to how religion was shared, or not, among Maya society. Mayanists have now assembled much information about Maya religion, and I do not pretend to be one of those scholars who know it well. But, the point has been raised that most of what we know about Maya religion derives from royal elites in Maya society. Certainly, much material was publicly displayed and, therefore, must have been understood by the public. However, some argue that control over religious concepts separated the elite from the commoners.

An almost accidental discovery at Blue Creek sheds some light on this question. When Steve Bozarth of the University of Kansas joined the Blue Creek team, we were most interested in looking into issues of agriculture. We had recently located the ditched agricultural fields east of the Bravo Escarpment and were excavating into prehistoric middens in locations such as Chan Cahal. Steve's work with phytolith analysis fit well into the evolving research domain of understanding agriculture at Blue Creek. At some point, though, Steve suggested that we should consider looking into the contents of ceramic vessels in primary contexts such as dedicatory caches in public buildings. As it turned out, we had already excavated many such caches and had curated the residue of the materials found within them. Generally, this amounted to a tablespoon or so of residue from the interior of a vessel that had been closed and sealed at burial. It also happened that we excavated an important cache from Structure 3 while Steve was present, and he was able to collect samples of the contents himself. With Steve, I entered our collections and found that we had seven other well-preserved samples from other caches.

To our surprise, all of the caches contained microscopic glassine structures, called spicules, produced by sponges.[9] There were truly huge quantities of these spicules—what was to be made of this? It can be understood by referring back to the story of the fourth creation related in the Popul Vuh. As I discussed in Chapter 2, we now understand these dedicatory caches to be symbolic cosmograms that recreate the landscape of the fourth creation, which featured the Witz Mountain rising from the primordial sea. The creators used the maize that grew on the mountain to mold the first four humans, and the water became their blood. So, the large quantities of sponges in many of these vessels represent the primordial sea, the jade and other terrestrial components represent the earth, and the dome of the upper vessel represents the sky—all of the components of the Popul Vuh story.

Most important, though, is that this was shared by all people at Blue Creek. We have examined all eight such caches that we have found and this pattern is consistent and occurs in every case. Four of the caches came from public architecture in Plaza A, two came from public architecture in Structure 12 before it was converted to a residence, another came from an elite nonroyal residence in Kín Tan, and the final derived from a non-elite residence in Chan Cahal. So, it is clear that this cosmological concept was incorporated into very public rituals as well as private rituals held by both the elite and non-elite. This is a clear case of religion being a mechanism to bind together the community of Blue Creek and not being a mechanism to divide it.

Was Blue Creek an Independent Kingdom?

The nature of Classic Maya political organization is one of the truly "BIG" issues in Maya archaeology. It is clear that there were many kingdoms and that some powerful kingdoms had influence over others at various times. It is also clear that familial machinations among rulers involved complex power plays in at least some cases. Most of our data related to this issue come from epigraphy. Stelae at Tikal and Uaxactun deal with their relationship. The hieroglyphic staircase recently discovered at Dos Pilas confirms the long-suspected relationship between that city and Tikal. However, Blue Creek is essentially in a "glyph-free" zone. Since we have no written records to assess this question at Blue Creek, we need to rely on non-written archaeological data.

At issue here is nothing less than whether Maya polities were hierarchically arranged into regional states or whether they were all fundamentally independent. Of course, it is obvious that neither the "regional states" nor the "forest of kings" model completely describes the nature of Maya geopolitics. Since archaeological models are simplified depictions of the past, it is inherently impossible for them to ever completely describe anything. Even so, Blue Creek represents a case study in understanding more about the relationships among Maya polities. Our most complete data come from Blue Creek's Terminal Preclassic and Early Classic periods. Was Blue Creek fundamentally independent at this time, when the great regional power of Calakmul, a little more than a hundred kilometers to the northwest, was at its strongest? If so, then we must recognize that other polities probably were as well.

The evidence for Blue Creek's independence comes from the excavations of the monumental architecture in the site core. In the Early Classic, Blue Creek had two large public plazas surrounded by buildings that almost certainly had civic, administrative, and religious functions. There were at least two stelae in front of Structures 4 and 6. There was also a ballcourt immediately north of Plaza A. What was the point of these buildings whatsoever if they did not represent local power and authority? In particular, the existence of the ballcourt is unusual in Early Classic northwestern Belize and marks some sort of special status for Blue Creek. Further, the construction of these public works was commissioned by someone. It seems unlikely that this would be a king of Calakmul a hundred kilometers away. So, I have to admit that I am skeptical of any model that does not allow for some sort of local independence.

Additionally, there are other data that support the idea of independence at Blue Creek. The Terminal Preclassic Cache 21 at the base of Structure 4 is an example. Dating to approximately A.D. 100, this consists of 425 obsidian blades that could have been used for ritual bloodletting, along with other exotic items. If, as I suggested in Chapter 2, this cache is the material remains of a large, public bloodletting ritual, it was a ritual such as those described by Schele and Freidel for the installation of a king while dedicating a public building in his honor. It was what Prudence Rice has argued was "the passing of the way."[10]

The general view of the stucco masks on the front of Structure 9 is that they represent an actual person, possibly someone relating himself to the maize god. With few exceptions, such as at Nakbé, it was not until the Classic period that images of actual persons were displayed on public architecture and monuments. Further, it is clear from the foliated *ahau* headdress that the individual was publicly acknowledged to be the king. Admittedly, he may have resided elsewhere. However, the model that I have developed in the preceding chapters would indicate that the central authority for Blue Creek must have resided in the elaborate residences of the core area.

The architecture of Structure 1 also lends credence to the idea of independence. Structure 1 was one of the earliest buildings with a columned superstructure in the Maya area. It represents a public display of architectural innovation. Such innovations do not always reflect political independence; however, it is more likely that such innovation would occur in a politically independent setting than not. Further, the individual buried in Structure 1 was almost certainly a royal personage. The tomb's presence in the largest building at the site and the razing of the previous columned superstructure certainly suggest that this was a royal tomb.

The temporal patterns seen in the distribution of jade at Blue Creek clearly indicate that it was a wealthy community. While others regard jade as a medium of currency, I see it as a medium that was controlled by royalty. Clearly, if I am correct, then Blue Creek housed a royal lineage. However, even if I am not correct, the distribution of jade at Blue Creek during the Terminal Preclassic and Early Classic periods indicates that powerful lineages had access to surprisingly large quantities of the Maya world's most valuable material. Again, even supposing that I am wrong about control of jade by royalty, the sheer volume at Blue Creek seems more likely to have occurred in the presence of a royal lineage than not.

Finally, the shaft caches in Structure 4 also represent an important cosmogram in the form of the World Tree. Again, this seems more likely to occur in the presence of independent local leaders than not.

No one of these pieces of information makes for an absolute case that Blue Creek was independent. However, collectively, the preponderance of the evidence strongly suggests that Blue Creek was a fundamentally independent polity during the Terminal Preclassic and Early Classic periods. Whether that independence extended into the Late Classic period, though, is another debate with an uncertain answer.

If Blue Creek was independent, the larger implications for understanding Maya political organization are far reaching. As I noted earlier, quite powerful arguments have been developed based upon epigraphy and iconography that Maya kingdoms fought each other throughout their history. However, the Early Classic version of this warfare seems to yet be restricted to "star wars," in which a polity would defeat another in battle, capture its ruler, and publicly denigrate him. While this would leave the losing polity in disarray, it would not be a war of conquest such as those documented for the Late and Terminal Classic periods.

The implication here is that Early Classic warfare was conducted among preexisting kingdoms. Consequently, all participants already had developed into what I will call "fundamentally independent" polities. If so, all Maya centers with monumental architecture were probably independent at one time or another in their histories. Certainly, this would apply to Blue Creek from roughly A.D. 100 to A.D. 500 or 600.

Whether Blue Creek was independent in the Late Classic is much more difficult to assess, though it seems unlikely. First, there was a new environment in which wars of conquest were becoming more common. Second, there is less data from Blue Creek to apply to the question. Clearly, the site's population continued to expand. Even more clearly, residents of places such as Kín Tan continued to thrive and elaborate on their already enviable residences. There continued to be more construction in the core area. Most especially, Structure 9 was expanded in the early part of the Late Classic in what was perhaps the largest public construction project in Blue Creek's history.

However, there were some important changes. The Structure 13 Courtyard was transformed from public to residential space. This may have been to house an outside authority while leaving the previous authority, the residents of the Structure 19 Courtyard, in place. Additionally, the Petén style structures of the Early Classic, such as Structure 9-IV, were replaced with flat-topped buildings more related to those found at such sites as Altun Ha on the coastal plain. Architecturally, Blue Creek was looking east not west. And, there was an inherent motivation for the possibility of outsiders' interest in taking over Blue Creek. Blue Creek controlled large-scale agricultural production and the headwaters of the Río Hondo. Further, it had a relatively low population, meaning that there was much to gain with the potential of relatively little resistance.

But none of this builds a compelling case either way. I *feel* that Blue Creek lost its independence in the Late Classic because it was taken over by a polity to the east, perhaps Kakabish. Further, I feel that this is related to the jade cached in the shaft in Structure 4 and the paucity of jade in the tomb in Structure 3. Admittedly, though, this cannot be demonstrated.

8 Addressing Some Large and Small Issues

When I introduce my students to Maya archaeology, I like to frame my course around the "BIG issues." What are our debates within the field and how can we design research to address these issues? The model that I have developed for understanding the Maya of Blue Creek is based upon the paradigms or principles that I believe must have operated in the past. So, if my interpretations and understandings of Blue Creek are accurate, there are implications for our understanding of the Maya on a larger scale. In this final chapter, I discuss some of those implications. Additionally, I examine some of the important questions that we still face at Blue Creek as a step toward building the research designs of the future.

Addressing Some Big Questions

"Blue Creek was a wealthy city whose wealth was based upon agriculture and trade." Such a simple statement carries huge connotations. If it is true, then the economic interaction among Classic Maya polities was far more robust than is often credited. For Blue Creek to have been an exporter of commodities with any regularity, there must have been well-developed trade routes, markets, and ready "buyers." In short, there was an institutionalized framework for trade. Only a few Mayanists would argue that significant commodities export ever occurred. However, I cannot see how Blue Creek could have acquired so much highly valued exotic material without having something to reciprocate with. Further, when I look at the larger cities of the north, I see large populations with limited agricultural resources and highly variable weather patterns and growing conditions. The idea that they did not import food is improbable. This may or may not have been a consistent practice. However, a well-developed structure for trade could have been in place so that food could be transported in years when large-scale crop failures occurred. Such crop failures have been caused by tropical storms, hurricanes, and drought several times in the past 15 years. In each case, however, only a part of the Maya lowlands was affected. During the Classic period, these problems could be resolved by using trade as a risk-management mechanism.

Even more compelling than the implications of the Blue Creek data are the data from Ambergris Caye and elsewhere that indicate that the well-documented traders of the Postclassic grew out of a well-developed, preexisting trade system that existed in the Classic period. Data from Cerros indicate that these activities were already under way in the Late Preclassic period. It only makes sense that trade, the process of acquisition of exotic goods, became institutionalized with the beginning of great kingdoms. The rulers required exotic goods to symbolically and tangibly reinforce their authority.

Viewed through world systems theory, rulers of polities could establish alliances that would be marked by the exchange of elite status-reinforcing objects. These alliances could then be operationalized to build trade partnerships.

Wealth, power, and authority were created and maintained by control over resources. In this case, the resources were agricultural. However, other resources were important in other places. Mayanists have debated whether individual communities and polities provided the essentials for their own lives and whether individual polities ever organized single-industry production. Certainly Colha, for example, produced many more stone tools than they used and people who lived at considerable distances from Colha used their products. The question is whether this production was incidental or focal in the life of the community. We can actually evaluate this question at Blue Creek, at least to a degree. It appears that Blue Creek's relatively low population was organized around agricultural productivity far in excess of their needs. So, the Blue Creek example shows us that at least some Maya cities were focally organized around the export of their resources.

Blue Creek also offers an unusually clear view of how Maya cities were organized. Pragmatic issues elsewhere have hampered our ability to understand this at other sites. Sites covered with forest present huge complications to adequate survey work. The sites that have been well surveyed, such as Tikal, demonstrate such complexity and high population density that it is difficult to distinguish the boundaries of corporate groups' residences. However, at Blue Creek, residential components are clearly bounded, with large tracts of unoccupied agricultural lands separating them. This, combined with the high visibility of the site, allows us to distinguish components and compare and contrast their attributes.

As a result, the nature of power, legitimacy, and authority can be examined in a new light. I have described a setting in which each residential component has unique characteristics but also shares the need for a local central place. The existence of these central places indicates that each community had its own internal structures of authority and legitimacy. As Canuto and Yaeger note, such communities have shared experiences and resources, as well as shared interaction with higher-level authorities.[1] I argue that the interaction among these higher-level authorities, in this case the ruling elites of the core area, is what created and maintained power structures that persisted and grew over many generations. It was the human agency involved in these interactions over many generations that created and maintained the power of the rulers as well as that of the local leaders.

There is no evidence from Blue Creek that would support the notion of external rule during the period A.D. 100 to A.D. 600. There is actually little evidence to support the idea in the Late Classic either. Consequently, we cannot accept a model of Maya states that does not allow for Blue Creek to be fundamentally independent. It appears that every center at which a ruler had the authority to commission the construction of large-scale public architecture was, at least at one time, independent. Further, public architecture, stelae, masks adorning building facades, and probably ballcourts all had a single purpose. They were built as public displays of power and reinforced the legitimacy of those who commissioned them. Those leaders are described by the Maya as *ahau* and by us as lords or kings.

Remaining Issues about the Archaeology of Blue Creek

The research conducted by myself and by my colleagues at Blue Creek is a case in point of what may be accomplished by a long-term, intensive field project. Blue Creek stands as one of the few projects in the Maya area that have investigated so many aspects of a Maya city so intensively. Yet, there are many things about Blue Creek that have not been resolved. Future work will be aimed at these questions because they now are our avenues to broader understanding about some of the BIG questions.

The first BIG question has to do with the creation of Classic Maya political structures—the beginning of kingship. At Blue Creek, we have documented the Middle Preclassic ancestors of the later complex polity. Further, we have found some evidence in Structure 4 that may be related to the installation of Blue Creek's first king. However, a thick veil still separates us from understanding the processes that led to kingship and complex society at Blue Creek. Some of the first arrivals seem to have become some of the least powerful lineages in the Classic period. Further, we really do not know very much about the coming of kings. Were they members of lineages such as those at Kín Tan? Or were they residents of the locations that later became the public plazas? Either or both could be true. For us to gain better understanding of this process, we will need to revisit the core area and look for better evidence of the antecedents of monumental architecture.

Another issue of intense interest is the Early Classic to Late Classic transition. We do know of some things that occurred. For one, architectural styles changed. Buildings that were Petén style pyramids were renovated to resemble those of the Belize coastal plain. Masonry superstructures were replaced with flat-topped summits. These may have supported perishable buildings, but they were quite unlike their predecessors. Some public buildings were completely redesigned. Structure 9 was reoriented, as was Structure 12. The small plaza flanked by Structures 12 and 13 was reorganized into a private living space. There were now two major residences of equal prestige in the core area. Access to jade dramatically dropped as well. While we know this was a regional pattern, what does it tell us about change at Blue Creek?

If we had ended the project in the late 1990s, we would have seen the Late Classic at Blue Creek as a pretty dismal time. But we did not end the project and our view of what happened after A.D. 600 is quite different from what it would have been if we had. Elite lineages residing outside of the core area, such as at Kín Tan, built substantial new masonry structures in the Late Classic. They were truly prospering. The population of Blue Creek continued to grow and some communities, such as U Xulil Beh, were founded at the margin of the site. So, the Late Classic at Blue Creek was anything but dismal. It was, however, different from the Early Classic.

What was the nature of this transformation? Were the dynamics of Blue Creek such that there was no dramatic cause for these shifts? Did an outside polity take control of Blue Creek and its substantial economic resources? I am still unsure how to devise future research to address this question.

The underlying economics of Blue Creek and its role in larger economic interaction and trade will not be fully understood until we know several more important pieces of information about the ditched agricultural fields. First, we must know when these ditched field complexes were built. Currently, our best information indicates that they were built sometime after about A.D. 1 and probably before A.D. 600. Why were they built? Was land that was previously not used being converted into usable land? Or did rising water tables necessitate ditching to control soil moisture in existing agricultural lands? And, possibly most important, what was grown on these fields? We know that high phosphate levels made maize agriculture problematic. Were crops such as cacao and other products that were grown only for export the focus of these agricultural endeavors? I suspect this was the case and, if so, the implications are enormous. If we can demonstrate that Early Classic Blue Creek was a "commercial" producer of agricultural materials for export, then we will also know that economic interaction, trade, among Maya polities was much more intensive and organized than most investigators believe.

Finally, and there must be a "finally" when we deal with an ancient city that no longer exists, what were the processes of abandonment at Blue Creek? This is a subject of great debate among scholars involved with this project. We have found large deposits of ceramics at various places as the terminal deposits at Blue Creek. I argue that these are the results of termination rituals. Others argue that these are simply postoccupational debris. This debate is certainly not unique to Blue Creek, but it is pivotal in understanding the processes of abandonment of the city. We have only the slightest evidence of occupation anywhere at Blue Creek after approximately A.D. 850. And we have little idea of why this city, like most in the southern lowlands, was so dramatically depopulated. We can know more, however. This will require concerted searches for more terminal deposits throughout the site and excavations aimed at clarifying the abandonment of Blue Creek.

As my final point, I want to return to the importance of a long-term, intensive field project. This volume is a partial result of 14 summer field seasons. If we had stopped research at Blue Creek at any time during those years, this volume would not have been possible. Or, worse, I would have written it without nearly as complete information as exists now. Yet, as the last few pages have pointed out, what seems to be a "complete" picture of Blue Creek today will seem very antiquated in a few more years.

Notes

Chapter 1

1. In particular, David Webster and William Sanders have argued that the Maya were not an urban society or a civilization in anthropological terms. While they are certainly correct that the Maya were not like the densely packed, pre-Columbian urban cities of central Mexico and Peru, that fact alone does little to help understand the Maya themselves. So, in this volume I do not intend to debate the issue. Instead, I will both refer to the Maya as a civilization and refer to their large population agglomerates as cities. While I am in fact taking a stance on the issue, my terminology is largely for the convenience of the reader.

2. The literature on the subject of archaeological epistemology is vast. However, two recent contrasting positions are taken by Binford (2001) and Hodder (1986), both based upon decades of work in opposing theoretical camps.

3. Elsewhere, I have argued that the Blue Creek project is a good example of the dynamism of this process. For a more in-depth discussion, see Guderjan (2004a).

4. See Guderjan (1991), Guderjan and Garber (1995), Guderjan, Garber, and Smith (1989), and Glassman and Garber (1999) for some of the results of the Ambergris Caye project.

5. Guderjan (1991).

6. Harry Shafer (personal communication 1994).

7. Barrett and Guderjan (2006).

8. The literature on population size is vast, but perhaps the most comprehensive treatment is a volume edited by Culbert and Rice (1990).

9. Happily, our work for several years was assisted by Lauren Sullivan and Lorraine Williams-Beck. While their assistance was on a part-time basis, it was very real. See Kosakowksy and Lohse (2003) for a discussion of the ceramic complexes at Blue Creek.

10. See Garber et al. (2003); Clark and Hansen (2001).

11. The belief that these attributes did not exist into the Classic period derives from Richard Adams's (1971) analysis of the ceramics of Altar de Sacrificios. Despite much discussion and verbal consensus that they in fact did and that dates as well as population estimates were being badly skewed, it was not until Kerry Sagebiel's doctoral dissertation (2005) that this situation was corrected.

12. Hammond et al. (1998).

13. Padilla, Morgan, and Lohse (2006).

14. Xnoha is named after Xnoha Creek, which drains into the Río Hondo from the north. It has also been spelled "Ixnoha" by Gonzalez (2005a, 2005b).

15. De Perigny (1908); Guderjan, Bedford, and Preston (2002).

16. Guderjan, Haines, et al. (1994).

17. Gonzalez (2005a, 2005b).

18. The first modern work at La Milpa was our mapping project in 1990. Since then, Norman Hammond and his colleagues have conducted a decade of fieldwork at the site. Their reports include Hammond et al. (1996, 1998) and Tourtellot, Everson, and Hammond (2003).

19. Bey et al. (1998); A. Chase and D. Chase (1987); Puleston (1983); Tourtellot, Everson, and Hammond (2003).

20. Durst (1995); Guderjan (1996); Renaud and Popson (1997); Lohse and Sagebiel (2005).

21. There are numerous publications relating to Lamanai: some key publications are Pendergast 1981, 1986, 1991, and 1992.

Chapter 2

1. This chapter is significantly rewritten from an article published in *Ancient Mesoamerica* (Guderjan 2004b).

2. Freidel et al. (1993:63).

3. Reilly (1994).

4. Mathews and Garber (2004).

5. Ashmore (1991, 1992).

6. Houk (1996).

7. Roys (1954).

8. Freidel (1986).

9. See Scarborough and Wilcox (1991) for a discussion of the importance of ballcourts and ballgames throughout Middle America.

10. Guderjan (1991).

11. Driver argues that there is also a third plaza at Blue Creek, "Plaza C," located a hundred meters or so south of Plaza A (Clayton et al. 2005). In this, we simply disagree. I interpret his Plaza C as one of many such elite residences located south of the core area along the top of the escarpment. I have seen several of these and do not believe that Driver has seen any of the others.

12. This discussion of Structure 1 derives largely from previous discussions by David Driver (1995, 1996, 2002).

13. In the system employed at Blue Creek, construction episodes are first numbered in the order encountered, meaning the latest episode has the lowest number. So, Structure 1-1st is the most recent and Structure 1-6th is the earliest episode. However, once excavation is complete, these are renumbered so that the earliest construction has the lowest number; Roman numerals are employed to distinguish between the two systems. So, Structure 1-I is the earliest construction while Structure 1-VI is the latest.

14. The architecture of Structure 1 at Aké has never been penetrated by excavation, so its construction date is not absolutely certain. However, its context in an otherwise Early Classic site supports the argument for early construction (Mathews 1998; Roys and Shook 1966).

15. This date is based on dated ceramics from Altun Ha that are virtually identical to those in Tomb 4.

16. All discussions regarding human remains in this volume are based on analyses by David Glassman and James Tyler.

17. All biosilicate analysis at Blue Creek has been conducted by Steve Bozarth at the University of Kansas. The single most surprising consequence of this effort has been the identification of sponges in a series of caches. This is mentioned throughout this volume but specifically reported in Bozarth and Guderjan (2004).

18. An understanding of the variability and votive nature of Maya caching activities has long existed (see Chase 1988; Coe 1959). However, a major step in our understanding comes from a Society for American Archaeology symposium on Maya rituals (Mock 1998). This is best exemplified by a paper by Garber et al. (1998) in which Garber and his colleagues demonstrate that an early Classic cache in a residential patio group at the site of Blackman Eddy in the Belize Valley is a re-creation of the Maya cosmos. In this cache, which consisted of two blackware bowls placed lip-to-lip, the lowest level of materials consisted of a white marl with chert flakes representing the underworld and its nine lords. The second level consisted of burned twigs and a rodent skeleton, representing the earth. The upper part of the cache represented the sky and the heavens by capping the materials with the inverted upper bowl.

Garber's assertion only makes sense in light of the placement of dedicatory caches into the symbolic Witz Mountain that is a Maya temple. However, there was a critical problem with empirical data and replicability of the idea. We have long known the enormous variability involved in such dedication caches. In some cases, there were elements of both the land and sea in these lip-to-lip placements. However, more commonly than not, there was no evidence of materials from either the land or the sea or both. Archaeologists have commonly assumed that these caches may have contained perishable materials and that their absence was a matter of preservation rather than presence.

More recently, Steve Bozarth has been analyzing plant use at Blue Creek through their biosilicate remains. We have been able to demonstrate that all eight caches analyzed included large quantities of sponges, representing the primordial sea. Further, all of these caches included materials from the sea, materials from the land, and the domed ceiling of the sky, and all were symbolic re-creations of the cosmos (Bozarth and Guderjan 2004; Guderjan 2004a).

This work is part of an ongoing collaboration between Steve Bozarth and myself dealing with plant use at Blue Creek in agricultural, household, and ritual contexts (Bozarth and Guderjan 2004; Guderjan 2004a). This has been funded by the Foundation for the Advancement of Mesoamerican Studies, the American Philosophical Society, and private donors.

19. E-groups have fascinated archaeologists since Group E at Uaxactun was first recognized to have astronomical alignments during the equinoxes and solstice (Ricketson 1928; Ricketson and Ricketson 1937). Many archaeologists have discussed them in terms of their astronomical alignments (Aveni and Hartung 1989) and their role in social integration (Aimers 1993; Rice 2004). Recently, I built the argument that I repeat in this chapter, that dual buildings on the east side of plazas in the Late Classic, especially in the eastern Petén, were later variants of these earlier complexes and were integral in ritual, public displays of authority and as part of the Maya identity (Aimers 1993; Aimers and Rice 2006; Guderjan 2006). Other known Pseudo-E-groups are found at Chan Chich, Quam Hill, and San Jose (Thompson 1939).

20. Rice (2004).

21. The last Maya act at Structure 3 was to deposit a large quantity of ceramics. This has been interpreted alternatively as a termination ritual (Guderjan 2004b) or as post-occupational debris (Clayton et al. 2005). I hold that this deposit, like those in Kín Tan and the Structure 13 Courtyard represent the intentional smashing of pots during a termination ritual. However, the debate is outside the scope of this volume.

22. Driver and Wanyerka (2002).

23. Excavations at Structure 4 were conducted under the supervision of Pam Weiss (1995, 1996) and later excavations were supervised by David Driver (1999). The obsidian analysis was conducted by Helen Haines (2000). Initial documentation of the jade and other materials by Pam Weiss was supported by the Foundation for the Advancement of Mesoamerican Studies. More complete analysis was done by Dale Pastrana, and overall the most complete published reports are mine (Guderjan 1998, 2004b). Pam Weiss, Lorraine Williams-Beck, and Laura Kosakowsky conducted the ceramic analyses.

24. Schele and Freidel (1990).

25. Ceramics from these caches were analyzed by Lorraine Williams-Beck (1998).

26. These materials are more fully discussed in a paper on the Structure 4 caches (Guderjan 1998).

27. Garber (1989).

28. Guderjan (1996, 1998).

29. Structure 5 was excavated in 1993–1994 by Dale Pastrana (1995), and this summary derives from her work.

30. Structure 6 was excavated by Dale Pastrana (1995).

31. See Ashmore (1991), Santley, Berman, and Alexander (1991), and Scarborough and Wilcox (1991) among others for extensive discussions of the meaning of ballcourts in Maya sites.

32. The workshop at Chan Chich was originally located by us in 1990 (Guderjan 1991). Similar chert debitage deposits were analyzed by Rick Meadows (2000).

33. Several years of excavation, supervised by Helen Haines, were invested in Structure 9. This discussion is largely derived from her work (Haines 1995, 1996) and a discussion of the masks by Grube, Guderjan, and Haines (1995). The analysis of the iconography of the masks is by Nikolai Grube.

34. Grube (1990); Stuart (1991).

35. Wagner (2000).

36. The discussion of the Structure 13 Courtyard is based upon the efforts of several investigators over several field seasons (Driver et al. 2002; Gilgan 1996, 1997; Guderjan, Haines, et al. 1993; Guderjan, Haines, et al. 1994).

37. Excavations at the Structure 19 Courtyard in 1995 and 1996 were supervised by Bob Lichtenstein and reported in Guderjan, Lichtenstein, and Hanratty (2003) and Lichtenstein (1996, 1997).

38. Mary Neivens's initial description of Blue Creek was published in the report from our 1988 and 1990 field seasons (Neivens 1991). Subsequent work at the building was done in 1999 and 2000 (Driver et al. 2002).

39. The enigmatic Tomb 5 is located on top of a hill overlooking the agricultural fields east of the escarpment. Unfortunately, modern quarry activity has all but destroyed the evidence of residential activity on the hilltop. Nevertheless, Tomb 5 is important for a

number of reasons not directly related to this volume (Guderjan 2000; Guderjan, Bozarth, et al. 2006; Lichtenstein 2000a).

Chapter 3

1. A recent work on this topic is a volume edited by Jon Lohse and Fred Valdez (2004).

2. In archaeological literature, this area is often termed the "hinterland." However, geographers long ago abandoned the term, as it tends to obscure the variability seen across the landscape. Interestingly, archaeologists who object to the term *commoner* because that term obscures variability have recently used *hinterland* as a replacement, despite the fact that the same variability is lost.

3. Well-mapped Maya cities include Cerros, Edzna, Sayil, and Tikal.

4. The Maya coastal trade system has been recognized as the mechanism for moving exotic goods for decades (Thompson 1954). However, it has been intensely studied for the past three decades (i.e., Sabloff and Rathje 1975a, 1975b) and is now understood to have involved large-scale commercial transport of commodities (Andrews 1983) and to have been highly structured (Andrews 1991) and well-developed on the Belizean coast (McKillop 2003; McKillop and Healy 1989) including Ambergris Caye, which protects the mouth of the Río Hondo from the open Caribbean Sea (Guderjan 1995; Guderjan and Garber 1995).

5. Studies of the settlement zone of La Milpa have been directed by Gair Tourtellot (Everson 2003; Tourtellot, Estrada-Bella, et al. 2003).

6. Thompson (1954).

7. Sanders and Webster (1988).

8. Marcus (1983).

9. Ashmore (1991, 1992).

10. Ashmore and Sabloff (2002).

11. Adams (1983); Hammond (1983); Haviland (1983).

12. Puleston (1973, 1974, 1983).

13. Matheny et al. (1980; Edzna); Tourtellot (1988; Seibal); Scarborough (1991; Cerros).

14. Scarborough (1992).

15. See Ed Barnhart's (1998, 1999, 2000) reports of the Palenque mapping project.

16. Pyburn (1988).

17. Kín Tan was originally termed "Group C" by Neivens (1991) and later termed the "Western Group" in our earlier publications.

18. Unfortunately, base topographic maps that were available prior to 2004 were published by the British Department of Overseas Surveys (DOS) with 20-meter contour intervals. These are now being replaced by satellite imagery with three-meter intervals.

19. Lichtenstein (2000b).

20. Numerous reports pertain to the excavations in these areas (Clayton 2004; Currid 2002; Driver 2004; Ek 2002; Farr 2002; Giacometti 2002; Guderjan, Bozarth, et al. 2006; Hanratty 2002a, 2002b; Lichtenstein 2000b; Popson 2000; Popson and Baker 1999).

21. Excavations at Kín Tan were largely directed by Colleen Hanratty, who is writing her doctoral dissertation on these elite residences. Additional information about Kín Tan can be found in the following publications: Currid (2002), Ek (2002), Guderjan and Hanratty (2006), Guderjan, Lichtenstein, and Hanratty (2003), Hanratty (2002a, 2002b), and Lichtenstein (2000b). Our use of terms such as *patio group, courtyard,* and *plazuela* follow

generally accepted usage. However, they are also specifically defined in Guderjan, Lichtenstein, and Hanratty (2003) and Lichtenstein (2002).

22. See Guderjan and Hanratty (2006) for a full discussion of these burials and their importance.

23. The information from Nukuch Muul derives from Bob Lichtenstein's (2000b) work.

24. The information from Rosita derives from our original mapping and surface collection in 1990 (Guderjan 1991:85) and excavations in 1998 that dated major construction to the Late Classic period (Lichtenstein 2000b:29). Excavations at one structure confirm that significant amounts of Late Preclassic construction are present there (Clayton 2004).

25. The information from U Xulil Beh derives from Bob Lichtenstein's (2000b) mapping and testing of the area.

26. Clayton et al. (2005).

27. Excavations at Chan Cahal were conducted during several field seasons and by several investigators (Clagett 1997; Giacometti and Lalonde 2002; Lichtenstein 2000b; Popson 2000; Popson et al. 2000). Currently, Sarah Skinner is completing a master's thesis at San Francisco State University summarizing the excavations at Chan Cahal and Sayap Ha. Skinner argues that these are actually a single, large, residential area. She is completely correct in this analysis. However, I will continue to treat them separately in this volume as they have somewhat distinct characteristics that can be more readily distinguished when treated separately.

28. Initial excavations at Sayap Ha were conducted by Bob Lichtenstein (2000b) and later by Antoine Giacometti (2002). Additionally, the information from the burial discussed here is also reported in Guderjan, Diel, et al. (2007).

29. See Guderjan, Diel, et al. (2007) for more details regarding this burial.

30. Bob Lichtenstein (2000b) first excavated one of these platforms believing it to be residential. Jeff Baker later excavated another and identified its agricultural function.

31. Killion (1992) forwards a simplified model of contemporary and prehistoric households with small gardens that are owned by and located near the individual households. Grace Bascopé reports that these are in common use in Yaxunah as they also are in the nearby villages of La Union and San Felipe.

32. Heather Clagett (1997) tested Killion's houselot model at Chan Cahal with positive results.

33. Barnhart (1998, 1999, 2000).

34. See Beach, Luzzadder-Beach, Dunning, et al. (2002) and Hughbanks (1998) for discussions of terracing and similar features in northwestern Belize.

35. See Scarborough and Valdez (2003) for discussions of the relationships between land tenure, resources, and power.

Chapter 4

1. One of the best treatments of power and authority among the ancient Maya is the volume *Mesoamerican Elites,* edited by Diane and Arlen Chase (1992). In particular, they deal with the value of the segmentary state model developed by Robert Carmack (1973, 1981) and John Fox (1978, 1987). The major criticism of the model is that lineage structure is not a powerful principle among the Quiche Maya. However, archaeological data from Blue Creek are more powerfully supportive of the role of lineages in the structure of

power. More recent treatments of ancient Maya power and authority include *Ancient Maya Political Economies*, edited by Marylin Masson and David Freidel (2002).

2. Jason Yaeger's work at San Lorenzo, a residential component of Xunantunich, is particularly useful as a frame of reference for studies of how communities in the archaeological record can be examined to gain insight into their shared experiences and interrelations (Canuto and Yaeger 2000; Yaeger 2000a, 2000b).

3. Wallerstein's early work was published in 1954 and perhaps his capstone effort was world systems theory (Wallerstein 1974). Today, an entire academic journal is devoted to world systems theory.

4. See, among many other examples, Chase-Dunn and Hall (1991), Frankenstein and Rowlands (1978), Friedman and Rowlands (1978), Hall (1987, 1988), Peregrine (1991), and Peregrine and Feinman (1996).

5. Rathje (1972), which interestingly, has no reference to Wallerstein's work.

6. Masson and Freidel (2002).

7. Examples include Andrews (1983), Garber (1989), Guderjan (1995), Guderjan and Garber (1995), and McKillop (1996).

8. See Masson (2002).

9. Bourdieu (1977).

10. See Barrett (2004) and Dobres and Robb (2000) for discussions of the concept of agency applied to archaeology.

11. Hirth (1996) summarizes the literature on "Exchange/Distribution oriented" models and Jason Barrett (2004) has applied such a framework to his dissertation on the use and distribution of stone tools at Blue Creek.

12. This follows the theme of heterarchy in ancient societies established by Carole Crumley and recently applied to the Maya by Vernon Scarborough and his associates. This is a research theme that we at Blue Creek have participated in and find applicable (Crumley 2003; Guderjan, Baker, and Lichtenstein 2003; Guderjan, Diel, et al. 2007; Scarborough et al. 1995; Scarborough et al. 2003).

13. McAnany (1995).

14. See Anne Pyburn's doctoral dissertation on Nohmul (Pyburn 1988) and our Chan Chich report (Guderjan 1991).

15. See Chapter 2 for a more complete discussion of this bench.

16. Excavations at Kín Tan are discussed in the following reports: Currid (2002), Ek (2002), Guderjan and Hanratty (2006), Guderjan, Lichtenstein, and Hanratty (2003), Hanratty (2002a, 2002b), Lichtenstein (2002), and Lichtenstein and Hanratty (2002).

17. Guderjan and Hanratty (2006); Hanratty (2002a, 2002b).

18. Many thanks to David Freidel, Nikolai Grube, and others who examined the acrobat pendant. This was initially a confusing artifact that we believed was a variant of an *ahua* pendant. However, Freidel's identification of it as an acrobat pendant was then confirmed by Grube and others.

19. Landa (1978); Taube (2005).

20. Taube (2005).

21. Tate (1995:64).

22. Steven Bozarth (personal communication 2001).

23. Miller and Taube (1993:110–111).

24. McAnany (1995).

25. Pendergast (1979, 1982).

26. McAnany (1995).

27. Defining the geographic limits of Sayap Ha is a complex task. Most of the structures were first identified by Bob Baker's 1996 survey, although the civic-ceremonial buildings were already known to us. Test excavations were conducted there and in neighboring areas by Bob Lichtenstein (2000b), who identified the neighboring area as a distinct component, Chan Cahal. Intensive excavations at Sayap Ha and Chan Cahal, particularly by Colleen Popson (2000) and Antoine Giacometti (2002), have led Giacometti and then Sarah Skinner to conclude that Sayap Ha and Chan Cahal are in fact a single corporate group. However, Giacometti also divides the collective complex into sub-complexes that correspond to what I am here terming "Sayap Ha" and "Chan Cahal." I believe, at least for the current purposes, that using the smaller analytical units is helpful.

28. Giacometti (2002).

29. There are several issues with dating ceramic vessels from this time period as several Preclassic attributes continue well into the Early Classic period. Consequently, it is often easier to assess the date of a collection of sherds than it is to assess the date of a single complete vessel. This Late Preclassic–Early Classic transition is the subject of ongoing research and debate by ceramicists working in the region.

30. See Lohse (2001), Lohse and Valdez (2004), and Marcus (2004) for important discussions of the complexity of the group formerly only known as commoners.

31. See Hendon (1991), Lohse (2001), McAnany (1995), Schele and Freidel (1990), and Webster (1989) for discussions of Maya lineages and social organization.

32. Founders in the Maya archaeological record were identified by Schele and Freidel (1990).

33. See work by Hendon (1991), Lohse (2001), McAnany (1995), and Yaeger (2000b) for discussions of Maya lineages and how they relate to residential and mortuary practices.

34. This argument was originally made by Guderjan and Hanratty (2006).

35. In particular, see works by Crumley (1987) and a recent volume on northwestern Belize (Scarborough et al. 2003) for the application of heterarchy to the Maya.

36. This discussion of the artifacts from Burial SH2 derives from a paper currently in press (Guderjan, Diel, et al. 2007) and also benefits greatly from discussion and input from Lori Diel, David Freidel, Jim Garber, and Kent Reilly.

37. Proskouriakoff (1974). See Freidel and Schele (1988), Guderjan (2003), Hammond (1987), Houk (1998), Proskouriakoff (1974), Schele and Freidel (1990:102).

38. Malinowski (1920, 1922, 1978); Sahlins (1972).

39. Young and Fowler (1999).

40. The literature on power, legitimacy, and authority among the Maya is vast. For example, Chase and Chase (1992) and their co-authors dealt intensively and extensively with the nature of elites and power.

41. U Xulil Beh was identified and named by Bob Lichtenstein (2000b).

42. Lichtenstein (2000b), among others.

Chapter 5

1. See Demarest et al. (2004) for a discussion of competition for resources, Culbert and Rice (1990) for a recent appraisal of Maya populations, and Deevey et al. (1979) for a major empirical study of declining productivity in the central Petén.

2. See, among other examples, Baker (2001), Beach, Luzzadder-Beach, Dunning, et al. (2002), Fedick (1996), Kunen (2003), and Scarborough et al. (1995).

3. These individuals include Jeff Baker, Tim Beach, Sheryl Luzzadder-Beach, Steve Bozarth, Kim Cox, John Jones, and Jon Lohse. My apologies to them in advance for the shortcomings of this chapter, as any of them could supply a better summary than I do here. The following publications represent some of their efforts to date: Baker (1999, 2001), Beach and Luzzadder-Beach (2004), Beach, Luzzadder-Beach, Dunning, et al. (2002), Bozarth and Guderjan (2004).

4. See Culbert and Rice (1990) for more detailed methodological discussions of how estimates of Classic Maya population can be made and the inherent assumptions.

5. Lichtenstein (2000b).

6. The estimate of 5.6 persons per household derives from twentieth-century information from Chan Kom (Redfield and Villa Rojas 1934). While numerous methodological issues and assumptions are inherent in the use of this figure, it still allows for comparison of data among sites.

7. Hugh Robichaux has pointed out that populations at La Milpa (Robichaux 1995) do decline dramatically at about six kilometers from the core area and that a similar decline occurs at Punta de Cacao at less than three kilometers from the core area. His estimate at La Milpa is based on survey lines that radiate from the core area. This presents methodological issues, as the sample size declines rapidly farther from the core zone. Nevertheless, Robichaux's point may be well taken. If we see the Maya landscape consisting of "towns" and "rural areas" as he does, then extrapolating the density of the central 16 square kilometers to the larger area may be problematic and may artificially elevate the population estimate. On the other hand, it seems likely that populations along the Río Hondo or the north boundary of Blue Creek were exceptionally high. While we have not conducted formal surveys of the area, dozens of informal visits lead to this conclusion.

8. See Webster and Freter (1990), Tourtellot (1990), Culbert et al. (1990), and Turner (1990) for respective population estimates for these sites. See Culbert and Rice (1990) for discussions of the basis and validity of the estimate of persons per household.

9. See Roys (1965) for a discussion of the products grown along the Río Hondo and traded through the ancient coastal city of Chetumal.

10. These have been reported in Beach and Luzzadder-Beach (2004), Bozarth (2002), and Bozarth and Guderjan (2004).

11. Roys (1965).

12. Sheryl Luzzadder-Beach (personal communication 2006).

13. Beach and Luzzadder-Beach (2004).

14. Maya agricultural terraces were first identified by Paul Healy et al. (1983) in the Vaca Plateau of Belize. Since then, a diverse range of such features has been documented, especially in northwestern Belize (i.e., Beach, Luzzadder-Beach, Dunning, et al. 2002; Dunning and Beach 1994; Fedick 1996; Hansen et al. 2002; Hughbanks 1998; Kunen 2003; Scarborough et al. 1995).

15. Jeffrey Baker (personal communication 2003); Guderjan, Baker, and Lichtenstein (2003); Lichtenstein (2000b:54).

16. The colonial use of *rejolladas* is reported by Nancy Fariss (1984:180) while Susan Kepecs and Sylviane Boucher (1996) report use by modern farmers. The modern use is also confirmed by observations by Grace Bascopé (personal communication 2003).

17. See Clagett 1997; Killion 1992. The Yaxunah data come from numerous personal communications with Grace Bascopé.

18. See Scarborough (1991, 1992), Scarborough and Gallopin (1991), and Scarborough et al. (1995).

Chapter 6

1. In this volume, I do not address the important aspect of interregional, overland trade that has been recently the focus of work by Jason Barrett. Barrett (2006a, 2006b) has identified a nonlocal type of chert that appears to be traded into northwestern Belize, probably from southwestern Campeche. This is, of course, in addition to the Colha-based chert trade. Barrett's work holds the possibility of significant revision of our understanding of interaction outside of the immediate region.

2. In July 2002, Henry Lingenfelder, Bob Hibschman, Gerry Emannuelson, and Terri Fonseca canoed from Blue Creek downstream for three days using a traditional Maya dugout canoe, built in the village of San Felipe for the trip, and two modern commercial canoes. They reached the approximate halfway point between Blue Creek and Corozal Bay. However, not knowing the route, they began looking for campsites each day in mid-afternoon, typically stopping early, as they did not know what possible campsites lay ahead. Their assessment was that there would be no problem in making the entire trip in three days for experienced paddlers who knew where to stop in advance, especially if such locations were previously prepared. Also, interestingly, the dugout canoe far outperformed the modern aluminum and fiberglass canoes. It had very little freeboard—only a few inches—but maximized the effort of paddling far better and was much less affected by wind than the modern canoes with little draft and high freeboard. Equally important is that the canoe built for use on the calm waters of the sluggish Río Hondo would be completely unsuitable for use on the coast, even in Chetumal Bay. Even a small wave of 50 centimeters could capsize the canoe.

3. Roys (1965); Thompson (1954).

4. Rathje and Sabloff (1973); Sabloff (1977); Sabloff and Rathje (1975a, 1975b).

5. Tony Andrews's (1983) research on pre-Columbian salt trade was initially somewhat controversial. However, confirming evidence, including the development of secondary sources of salt production along the Belize coast (Andrews and Mock 2003; McKillop 2002; MacKinnon and Kepecs 1989) strongly support his initial argument of the trade of salt as a commodity.

6. Andrews (1991); Guderjan (1995); Guderjan and Garber (1995); McKillop (1996, 2003).

7. Freidel (1978); Garber (1989); Robertson and Freidel (1986).

8. I discuss the shifting centers of power in Chetumal Bay in Guderjan 2005. My fundamental argument is that large populations existed along the bay as early as the Late Preclassic and that power shifted geographically and among lineages for more than a millennium.

9. Garber (1989); Robertson and Freidel (1986).

10. McKillop (2002).

11. Barrett and Guderjan (2006).

12. Shafer and Hester (1983).

13. Dale Pastrana has been examining the exotic materials and jade from Blue Creek, and her work is still in progress. However, parts of this material have been published in our interim reports and elsewhere. See Guderjan (1996) and Pastrana (1999).

14. Hammond (1991).

15. Bishop and Lange (1993); Gendron et al. (2002); Hammond et al. (1977); Harlow (1993).

16. Hammond (1991); Hammond et al. (1977).

17. The jade collection from Structure 4 at Blue Creek was examined by Mary Lou Ridinger of Jades, S.A., in 1998. The vast majority of the artifacts she examined were determined to be jadeite or nephrite on the basis of heavy liquid density tests, and all were visually within the range of variability exhibited by the Motagua Valley sources.

18. Fossag (1957); Johnson and Harlow (1999).

19. Bishop and Lange (1993); Griffin (1993).

20. Garber et al. (1993).

21. Garber et al. (1993).

22. Kresjci and Culbert (1995).

23. Garber (1983, 1989, 1993); Rathje (1970).

24. For information regarding bib-heads in northern Belize see Chase and Chase (1986), Clancy et al. (1985), Garber (1983), Guderjan (1998), Hammond (1987), and Robichaux (1998). Discussions of bib-head-shaped pendants as parts of royal crowns include Freidel and Schele (1988) and Hammond (1987).

25. These figures are my count derived from David Pendergast's (1979, 1982) publications on Altun Ha.

26. See various chapters in a recent volume edited by Masson and Freidel (2002) but especially Marilyn Masson's introductory chapter on political economy (Masson 2002).

27. Ball (1993).

28. McAnany (1993).

29. Freidel (1993); Freidel et al. (2002); Schele and Freidel (1990).

30. Malinowski (1920); Rathje (1970); Sahlins (1972).

31. Folan et al. (1995); Hammond (1987); Hammond et al. (1996); Robichaux (1998).

32. See Buttles (1992) and Garber (1983, 1993) for information about jade from Colha and Cerros, respectively.

33. See Moholy-Nagy (1994) and David Maxwell (1996) for information about jade from Tikal and Uaxactun.

34. Guderjan, Bozarth, et al. (2006).

35. Hirth and Hirth (1993).

36. Buttles (2002).

37. The A.D. 500 date is based upon two radiocarbon assays from the interior of the shaft: Beta-75432, 1440 ± 110 B.P., and Beta-76278, 1450 ± 110 B.P. (Driver 2002:83; Guderjan 2002:15).

38. Pastrana (1999).

39. Schmidt, de la Garza, and Nalda (1998:Plate 163).

40. Kent Reilly (personal communication 2000).

41. Hammond (1987); Proskouriakoff (1974).

42. Maxwell (1996); Moholy-Nagy (1994); Rathje (1970).

43. Jeffrey Baker (personal communication 2002).

Chapter 7

1. Diamond (1997).

2. Barrett (2004, 2006a, 2006b).

3. The existence of these *sacbeob* was confirmed by excavations by Antoine Giacometti (1999).

4. The causeways at Chan Chich are documented in Guderjan (1991).

5. Audet and Awe (2004).

6. Cheetham (2004).

7. Tourtellot, Estrada-Bella, et al. (2003); Tourtellot, Everson, and Hammond (2003).

8. Levi (2006).

9. Bozarth and Guderjan (2004); Guderjan (2004a).

10. P. Rice (2004).

Chapter 8

1. Canuto and Yaeger (2000).

References Cited

Adams, Richard E. W.

1971 *The Ceramics of Altar de Sacrificios.* Papers of the Peabody Museum of Archaeology and Ethnology, Vol. 63, No. 1. Harvard University, Cambridge, Massachusetts.

1983 Settlement Patterns of the Central Yucatan and Southern Campeche Regions. In *Lowland Maya Settlement Patterns,* edited by Wendy Ashmore, pp. 211–248. University of New Mexico Press, Albuquerque.

Aimers, James J.

1993 Messages from the Gods: A Hermeneutic Analysis of the Maya E-Group Complex. M.A. thesis, Department of Anthropology, Trent University, Peterborough, Ontario.

Aimers, James J., and Prudence M. Rice

2006 Astronomy, Ritual, and the Interpretation of Maya "E-Group" Architectural Assemblages. *Ancient Mesoamerica* 17(1):79–98.

Andrews, Anthony P.

1983 *Maya Salt Production and Trade.* University of Arizona Press, Tucson.

1991 The Role of Trading Ports in Maya Civilization. In *Vision and Revision in Maya Studies,* edited by Flora S. Clancy and Peter D. Harrison, pp. 148–159. University of New Mexico Press, Albuquerque.

Andrews, Anthony P., and Shirley B. Mock

2003 New Perspectives on the Prehispanic Salt Trade. In *Ancient Maya Political Economies,* edited by Marilyn A. Masson and David A. Freidel, pp. 307–335. AltaMira, Walnut Creek, California.

Ashmore, Wendy

1991 Site-Planning Principles and Concepts of Directionality among the Ancient Maya. *Latin American Antiquity* 2:3:199–226.

1992 Deciphering Maya Architectural Plans. In *New Theories on the Ancient Maya,* edited by Elin C. Danien and Robert M. Sharer, pp. 173–184. University Museum, University of Pennsylvania, Philadelphia.

Ashmore, Wendy, and Jeremy A. Sabloff

2002 Spatial Orders in Maya Civic Plans. *Latin American Antiquity* 13:201–216.

Audet, Claudia, and Jaime Awe

2004 The Functions of Terminus Groups at Baking Pot. Paper presented at the Annual Meeting of the Society for American Archaeology, Montreal.

Aveni, Anthony F., and Horst Hartung

1989 Uaxactun, Guatemala, Group E and Similar Assemblages: An Archaeoastronomical Reconsideration. In *World Archaeoastronomy,* edited by Anthony F. Aveni, pp. 441–461. Cambridge University Press, Cambridge.

Baker, Jeffrey

1997 Investigations in the Ditched Agricultural Fields. In *The Blue Creek Project: Working Papers from the 1996 Field Season,* edited by W. David Driver, Heather L. Clagett, and Helen R. Haines, pp. 71–78. Maya Research Program, St. Mary's University, San Antonio, Texas.

1999 The Wet and the Dry? Agricultural Intensification in the Maya Lowlands. Paper presented at the Annual Meeting of the Society for American Archaeology, Nashville.

2001 Maya Wetlands: Ecology and Prehispanic Utilization of Wetlands in Northwestern Belize. Ph.D. dissertation, Department of Anthropology, University of Arizona, Tucson.

Baker, Robert

1996 Status Report on the Settlement Survey. *Archaeological Research at Blue Creek, Belize. Progress Report of the Fourth (1995) Field Season,* edited by Thomas H. Guderjan, W. David Driver, and Helen R. Haines, pp. 109–116. Maya Research Program, St. Mary's University, San Antonio, Texas.

Ball, Joseph W.

1993 Potters, Palaces, and Polities: Some Socioeconomic and Political Interpretations of Late Classic Maya Ceramic Industries. In *Lowland Maya Civilization in the Eighth Century A.D.,* edited by Jeremy Sabloff and John Henderson, pp. 243–272. Dumbarton Oaks, Washington, D.C.

Barnhart, Edwin

1998 The Palenque Mapping Project. Report to the Foundation for the Advancement of Mesoamerican Studies. www.famsi.org/reports/97024/index.html, accessed January 2006.

1999 The Palenque Mapping Project. Report to the Foundation for the Advancement of Mesoamerican Studies. www.famsi.org/reports/98063/index.html, accessed January 2006.

2000 The Palenque Mapping Project—Final Report. Report to the Foundation for the Advancement of Mesoamerican Studies. www.famsi.org/reports/99101/index.html, accessed January 2006.

Barrett, Jason W.

2004 Creating Hierarchy through Entitlements: Inequality in Lithic Resource Access among the Ancient Maya of Blue Creek, Belize. Ph.D. dissertation, Department of Anthropology, Texas A & M University, College Station.

2006a Rethinking Long-Distance Exchange and the Economic Interdependence of Maya Sites during the Late Preclassic Period: The View from Northwestern Belize. In *Archaeological Investigations in the Eastern Maya Lowlands: Papers of the 2005 Belize Archaeology Symposium,* edited by John Morris, Sherlyne Jones, Jaime Awe, and Christopher Helmke, pp. 113–128. National Institute of Culture and History, Belize.

2006b Stone Age Economics Revisited: An Examination of Lithic Resource Use in Northwestern Belize. Paper presented at the Annual Meeting of the Society for American Archaeology, San Juan, Puerto Rico.

Barrett, Jason W., and Thomas H. Guderjan

2006 A River Docking Feature at Blue Creek, Belize. *Latin American Antiquity* 17(2):227–239.

Beach, Timothy, and Sheryl Luzzadder-Beach

2004 Patterned Ground in Wetlands of the Maya Lowlands: Anthropogenic and Natural Causes. Poster presented at the Annual Meeting of the American Geophysical Union, San Francisco.

Beach, Timothy, Sheryl Luzzadder-Beach, Nicholas Dunning, John Hageman, and Jon Lohse

2002 Upland Agriculture in the Maya Lowlands: Ancient Maya Soil Conservation in Northwestern Belize. *Geographic Review* 92(3):372–397.

Beach, Timothy, Sheryl Luzzadder-Beach, and Jon Lohse

2002 Maya Wetland Agriculture and Environmental Change at Blue Creek. Paper presented at the Annual Meeting of the Society for American Archaeology, Denver.

Bey, George J. III, Tara Bond, William M. Ringle, C. A. Hansen, C. W. Houck, and C. Peraza Lupe

1998 The Ceramic Chronology of Ek Balam, Yucatan, Mexico. *Ancient Mesoamerica* 9:101–120.

Binford, Lewis R.

2001 *Constructing Frames of Reference: An Analytical Method for Archaeological Theory Building Using Ethnographic and Environmental Data Sets.* University of California Press, Berkeley.

Bishop, Ronald L., and Fredrick W. Lange

1993 Sources of Maya and Central American Jadeites: Data Bases and Interpretations—A Summary. In *Precolumbian Jade: New Geological and Cultural Interpretations,* edited by Fredrick W. Lange, pp. 125–131. University of Utah Press, Salt Lake City.

Bourdieu, Pierre

1977 *An Outline of a Theory of Practice.* Cambridge University Press, Cambridge.

Bozarth, Steven, and Thomas H. Guderjan

2004 Results of Biosilicate Analysis of Residue in Maya Dedicatory Cache Vessels. *Journal of Archaeological Science* 31(2):205–215.

Buttles, Palma

1992 Small Finds in Context: The Preclassic Artifacts of Colha, Belize. Unpublished M.A. thesis, Department of Anthropology, University of Texas, Austin.

2002 Material and Meaning: A Contextual Examination of Select Portable Material Culture from Colha, Belize. Unpublished Ph.D. dissertation, Department of Anthropology, University of Texas at Austin.

Canuto, Marcella A., and Jason Yaeger (editors)

2000 *The Archaeology of Communities: A New World Perspective.* Routledge, London.

Carmack, Robert

1973 *Quichean Civilization: The Ethnohistoric, Ethnographic, and Archaeological Sources.* University of California Press, Berkeley.

1981 *The Quiche Mayas of Utatlan.* University of Oklahoma Press, Norman.

Chase, Arlen F., and Diane Z. Chase

1986 *Offerings to the Gods: Maya Archaeology at Santa Rita Corozal.* Pre-Columbian Research Institute, San Francisco.

1987 *Investigations at the Classic Maya City of Caracol, Belize: 1983–1987.* Monograph 3. Pre-Columbian Art Research Institute, San Francisco.

Chase, Arlen F., and Diane Z. Chase (editors)

1992 *Mesoamerican Elites: An Archaeological Perspective.* University of Oklahoma Press, Norman.

Chase, Diane

1988 Caches and Censorware: Meaning from Maya Pottery. In *A Pot for All Reasons: Ceramic Ecology Revisited,* edited by Charles C. Kolb and Louanna M. Lackey, pp. 81–104. Ceramica de Cultura Maya, Temple University, Philadelphia.

Chase-Dunn, Christopher, and Thomas Hall

1991 *Core/Periphery Relations in Precapitalist Worlds.* Westview Press, Boulder, Colorado.

Cheetham, David

2004 The Role of Terminus Groups in Lowland Maya Site Planning: An Example from Cahal Pech. In *The Ancient Maya of the Belize Valley: Half a Century of Archaeological Research,* edited by James F. Garber, pp. 125–148. University Press of Florida, Gainesville.

Clagett, Heather L.

1997 Household Archaeology at Chan Cahal: A Step Beyond Functionalism. In *The Blue Creek Project: Working Papers from the 1996 Field Season,* edited by W. David Driver, Heather L. Clagett, and Helen R. Haines. Maya Research Program, St. Mary's University, San Antonio, Texas.

Clancy, Flora, Clemency Coggins, T. Patrick Culbert, Charles Gallencamp, Peter D. Harrison, and Jeremy A. Sabloff

1985 *Maya: Treasures of an Ancient Civilization.* Harry S. Abrams, New York.

Clark, John, and Richard Hansen

2002 The Architecture of Early Kingship: Comparative Perspectives on the Origins of the Maya Royal Court. In *Royal Courts of the Ancient Maya,* Vol. 2, edited by Takeshi Inomata and Stephen D. Houston, pp. 1–45. Westview Press, Boulder, Colorado.

Clayton, Sarah

2004 Investigations at Rosita, 2003: Toward Understanding the Socio-Political Landscape of the Blue Creek Region, Northwestern Belize. In *2003 Season Summaries of the Blue Creek Regional Political Ecology Project, Upper Northwestern Belize,* edited by Jon C. Lohse, pp. 81–88. Maya Research Program, Fort Worth, Texas.

Clayton, Sarah, W. David Driver, and Laura J. Kosakowsky

2005 Rubbish or Ritual? Contextualizing a Terminal Classic Problematical Deposit at Blue Creek, Belize. *Ancient Mesoamerica* 16:119–130.

Coe, William R.

1959 *Piedras Negras Archaeology: Artifacts, Caches and Burials.* University Museum, University of Pennsylvania, Philadelphia.

Crumley, Carol

1987 A Dialectic Treatment of Hierarchy. In *Power Relations and State Formation,* edited by Thomas C. Patterson and Christine Ward Gaily, pp. 155–169. American Anthropological Association, Washington, D.C.

2003 Alternative Forms of Social Order. In *Heterarchy, Political Economy, and the Ancient Maya: The Three Rivers Region of the East-Central Yucatán Peninsula,* edited by Vernon L. Scarborough, Fred Valdez, Jr., and Nicholas P. Dunning, pp. 136–146. University of Arizona Press, Tucson.

Culbert, T. Patrick, Laura J. Kosakowsky, Robert E. Fry, and William A. Haviland
1990 The Population of Tikal, Guatemala. In *Precolumbian Population History in the Maya Lowlands,* edited by T. Patrick Culbert and Don S. Rice, pp. 103–122. University of New Mexico Press, Albuquerque.

Culbert, T. Patrick, and Don S. Rice (editors)
1990 *Precolumbian Population History in the Maya Lowlands.* University of New Mexico Press, Albuquerque.

Currid, Demori
2002 Excavations in the Structure 60 Courtyard. In *The Blue Creek Project: Working Papers from the 1998 and 1999 Field Seasons,* edited by Thomas H. Guderjan and Robert J. Lichtenstein, pp. 95–100. Maya Research Program, Texas Christian University, Fort Worth.

Deevey, Edward S., Don S. Rice, Prudence M. Rice, H. H. Vaughn, M. Brenner, and M. S. Flannery
1979 Maya Urbanism: Impact on a Tropical Karst Environment. *Science* 206:298–306.

Demarest, Arthur A., Prudence M. Rice, and Don S. Rice (editors)
2004 *The Terminal Classic in the Maya Lowlands.* University of Colorado Press, Boulder.

De Perigny, Maurice
1908 Yucatan Inconnu. *Journal de la Sociéte des Américanistes de Paris,* n.s., 5:67–90.

Diamond, Jared
1997 *Guns, Germs, and Steel: The Fates of Human Societies.* W. W. Norton, New York.

Dobres, M.-A., and J. E. Robb (editors)
2000 *Agency in Archaeology.* Routledge, London.

Driver, W. David
1995 Architecture and Ritual at Structure 1. In *Archaeological Research at Blue Creek, Belize. Progress Report of the Third (1994) Field Season,* edited by Thomas H. Guderjan and W. David Driver, pp. 27–36. Maya Research Program, St. Mary's University, San Antonio, Texas.

1996 Continuing Excavations at Structure 1. In *Archaeological Research at Blue Creek, Belize. Progress Report of the Fourth (1995) Field Season,* edited by Thomas H. Guderjan, W. David Driver, and Helen R. Haines, pp. 27–36. Maya Research Program, St. Mary's University, San Antonio, Texas.

1999 Excavations in Plaza A. In *The Blue Creek Project: Working Papers from the 1997 Field Season,* edited by W. David Driver, Helen R. Haines, and Thomas H. Guderjan, pp. 12–38. Maya Research Program, St. Mary's University, San Antonio, Texas.

2002 An Early Classic Columned Temple at Blue Creek, Belize. *Latin American Antiquity* 13:63–85.

2004 Intercommunity Architectural Variations: Excavations Conducted in the Blue Creek Settlement Zone. In *2003 Season Summaries of the Blue Creek Regional Political Ecology Project, Upper Northwestern Belize,* edited by Jon C. Lohse, pp. 53–80. Maya Research Program, Texas Christian University, Fort Worth.

Driver, W. David, Elizabeth Boyd, and Stephen Pilcher
2002 Excavations in the Core Zone. In *The Blue Creek Project: Working Papers from the*

1998 and 1999 Field Seasons, edited by Thomas H. Guderjan and Robert J. Lichtenstein, pp. 49–58. Maya Research Program, Texas Christian University, Fort Worth.

Driver, W. David, and Phil Wanyerka

2002 Creation Symbolism in the Architecture and Ritual at Structure 3, Blue Creek, Belize. *Mexicon* 24(1):6–8.

Dunning, Nicolas, and Timothy Beach

1994 Soil Erosion, Slope Management, and Ancient Terracing in the Maya Lowlands. *Latin American Antiquity* 5(1):51–69.

Durst, Jeffrey

1995 Excavations at RB-43 (Gran Cacao) 1994 Field Season. In *Programme for Belize Archaeological Project: 1994 Interim Report,* edited by Fred Valdez, Jr., and Richard E. W. Adams, pp. 45–58. University of Texas, San Antonio.

Ek, Gerald

2002 Excavations in the Structure 46 Courtyard. In *The Blue Creek Project: Working Papers from the 1998 and 1999 Field Seasons,* edited by Thomas H. Guderjan and Robert J. Lichtenstein, pp. 85–94. Maya Research Program, Texas Christian University, Fort Worth.

Everson, Gloria E.

2003 Terminal Classic Settlement Patterns at La Milpa, Belize. Unpublished Ph.D. dissertation, Department of Anthropology, Tulane University.

Fariss, Nancy

1984 *Maya Society under Colonial Rule: The Collective Enterprise of Survival.* Princeton University Press, Princeton, New Jersey.

Farr, Olivia N.

2002 Excavations at Structure 78. In *The Blue Creek Project: Working Papers from the 1998 and 1999 Field Seasons,* edited by Thomas H. Guderjan and Robert J. Lichtenstein, pp. 65–68. Maya Research Program, Texas Christian University, Fort Worth.

Fedick, Scott L. (editor)

1996 *The Managed Mosaic: Ancient Maya Agriculture and Resource Use.* University of Utah Press, Salt Lake City.

Folan, William J., Joyce Marcus, Sophia Pincemin, Maria del Rosario Dominguez Carrasco, Laraine Fletcher, and Abel Morales López

1995 Calakmul: New Data from an Ancient Maya Capital in Campeche, Mexico. *Latin American Antiquity* 6(4):310–334.

Fossag, W. F.

1957 *Mineralogical Studies on Guatemalan Jade.* Smithsonian Miscellaneous Collections, Vol. 135, No. 5. U.S. Government Printing Office, Washington, D.C.

Fox, John W.

1978 *Quiche Conquest.* University of New Mexico Press, Albuquerque.

1987 *Maya Postclassic State Formation: Segmentary Lineage Migration in Advancing Frontiers.* Cambridge University Press, Cambridge.

Frankenstein, D., and M. D. Rowlands

1978 Notes toward an Epigenetic Model of the Evolution of Civilization. In *The Evolution of Social Systems,* edited by J. Freidman and M. Rowlands, pp. 201–275. University of Pittsburgh Press, Pittsburgh.

Freidel, David A.

1978 Maritime Adaptation and the Rise of Maya Civilization: The View from Cerros, Belize. In *Prehispanic Coastal Adaptations: Economy and Ecology of Maritime Middle America,* edited by Barbara Stark and Barbara Voorhies, pp. 235–269. Academic Press, New York.

1986 The Monumental Architecture. In *Archaeology at Cerros, Belize, Central America,* Vol. 1: *An Interim Report,* edited by Robin A. Robertson and David A. Freidel, pp. 1–22. Southern Methodist University Press, Dallas.

1993 The Jade Ahau: Toward a Theory of Commodity Value in the Maya Civilization. In *Precolumbian Jade: New Geological and Cultural Interpretations,* edited by Fredrick W. Lange, pp. 149–165. University of Utah Press, Salt Lake City.

Freidel, David A., Kathryn Reese-Taylor, and David Mora-Marín

2002 The Origins of Maya Civilization: The Old Shell Game, Commodity, Treasure and Kingship. In *Ancient Maya Political Economies,* edited by Marilyn A. Masson and David A. Freidel, pp. 41–86. AltaMira Press, Walnut Creek, California.

Freidel, David A., and Linda Schele

1988 Kingship in the Late Preclassic Lowlands: The Instruments and Places of Ritual Power. *American Anthropologist* 90(3):547–567.

Freidel, David A., Linda Schele, and Joy Parker

1993 *Maya Cosmos: Three Thousand Years on the Shaman's Path.* William Morrow, New York.

Freidman, J., and M. Rowlands

1978 *The Evolution of Social Systems.* University of Pittsburgh Press, Pittsburgh.

Garber, James F.

1983 Patterns of Jade Consumption and Disposal at Cerros, Northern Belize. *American Antiquity* 48(4):400–407.

1989 *Archaeology at Cerros, Belize, Central America,* Vol. II: *The Artifacts.* Southern Methodist University Press, Dallas.

1993 The Cultural Context of Jade Artifacts from the Maya Site of Cerros, Belize. In *Precolumbian Jade: New Geological and Cultural Interpretations,* edited by Fredrick W. Lange, pp. 166–172. University of Utah Press, Salt Lake City.

Garber, James F., Jaime J. Awe, M. Kathryn Brown, and Christopher J. Hartman

2003 Middle Formative Prehistory of the Central Belize Valley: An Examination of Architecture, Material Culture, and Sociopolitical Change at Blackman Eddy. In *The Ancient Maya of the Belize Valley: Half a Century of Archaeological Research,* edited by James F. Garber, pp. 25–47. University Press of Florida, Gainesville.

Garber, James F., W. David Driver, Lauren A. Sullivan, and David M. Glassman

1998 Bloody Bowls and Broken Pots: The Life, Death, and Rebirth of a Maya House. In *The Sowing and the Dawning: Termination, Dedication and Transformation in the Archaeological and Ethnographic Record of Mesoamerica,* edited by Shirley Boteler Mock, pp. 125–132. University of New Mexico Press, Albuquerque.

Garber, James F., David C. Grove, Kenneth Hirth, and John W. Hoopes

1993 Jade Use in Portions of Mexico and Central America. In *Precolumbian Jade: New Geological and Cultural Interpretations,* edited by Fredrick W. Lange, pp. 211–231. University of Utah Press, Salt Lake City.

Gendron, Francois, David C. Smith, and Aicha Gendron-Badou

2002 Discovery of Jadeite-Jade in Guatemala Confirmed by Non-Destructive Raman Microscopy. *Journal of Archaeological Science* 29:837–851.

Giacometti, Antoine
1999 Excavations of Two Causeways at Blue Creek. Manuscript on file, Maya Research Program, Fort Worth, Texas.
2002 The Role of Plaza Complexes in Hinterland Settlements at the Maya Site of Blue Creek, Belize. Unpublished M.A. thesis, Institute of Archaeology, University College, London.
Giacometti, Antoine, and Dane Lalonde
2002 Excavations at Structure U-5. Manuscript on file. Maya Research Program, Texas Christian University, Fort Worth.
Gilgan, Elizabeth
1996 Excavations in the Structure 13 Courtyard Complex. In *Archaeological Research at Blue Creek, Belize. Progress Report of the Fourth (1995) Field Season,* edited by Thomas H. Guderjan, W. David Driver, and Helen R. Haines, pp. 69–77. Maya Research Program, St. Mary's University, San Antonio, Texas.
1997 Excavations in the Structure 13 Courtyard Group. In *The Blue Creek Project: Working Papers from the 1996 Field Season,* edited by W. David Driver, Heather L. Clagett, and Helen R. Haines, pp. 33–38. Maya Research Program, St. Mary's University, San Antonio, Texas.
Glassman, David, and James Garber
1999 Land Use, Diet, and Their Effects on the Biology of the Prehistoric Maya of Northern Ambergris Cay, Belize. In *Reconstructing Ancient Maya Diet,* edited by Christine D. White, pp. 119–132. University of Utah Press, Salt Lake.
Gonzalez, Jason J.
2005a Cultural Landscape Study of Influence and Domesticity: Comparing Classic Maya Communities in the Three Rivers Region of Northwestern Belize (C.E. 550–1000). Unpublished Ph.D. dissertation, Department of Anthropology, Southern Illinois University, Carbondale.
2005b 2004 Ixno'ha Excavation Report. In *2004 Season Summaries of the Blue Creek Regional Political Ecology Project, Upper Northwestern Belize,* edited by Jon C. Lohse and Kerry Sagebiel, pp. 33–52. Maya Research Program, Texas Christian University, Fort Worth.
Griffin, Gillett
1993 Formative Guerrero and Its Jade. In *Precolumbian Jade: New Geological and Cultural Interpretations,* edited by Fredrick W. Lange, pp. 203–210. University of Utah Press, Salt Lake City.
Grube, Nikolai
1990 The Ahau Sign as *Nik,* "Flower." Manuscript on file, University of Bonn.
Grube, Nikolai, Thomas H. Guderjan, and Helen R. Haines
1995 Late Classic Architecture and Iconography at the Blue Creek Ruin, Belize. *Mexicon* 17(3):51–66.
Guderjan, Thomas H.
1995 Maya Settlement and Trade on Ambergris Caye, Belize. *Ancient Mesoamerica* 6:147–159.
1996 Investigations at the Blue Creek Ruin, Belize. *Los investigadores de la cultura Maya* 4:330–334. Universidad Autonoma de Campeche, Mexico.
1998 The Blue Creek Jade Cache: Early Classic Ritual in Northwest Belize. In *The Sowing and the Dawning: Termination, Dedication and Transformation in the Archaeo-*

logical and Ethnographic Record of Mesoamerica, edited by Shirley Boteler Mock, pp. 101–112. University of New Mexico Press, Albuquerque.

2000 The Discovery of Tomb 5 at Blue Creek, Northern Belize. *Precolumbian Art Research Institute Journal* 1(1):1–3.

2002 A Summary of Research at Blue Creek. In *The Blue Creek Project: Working Papers from the 1998 and 1999 Field Seasons*, edited by Thomas H. Guderjan and Robert J. Lichtenstein, pp. 3–36. Maya Research Program, Texas Christian University, Fort Worth.

2003 Spatial Arrangement of a Maya City. Manuscript on file. Maya Research Program, Texas Christian University, Fort Worth.

2004a Recreating the Maya Cosmos: Early Classic Caches from Blue Creek, Belize. In *Continuity and Change: Maya Religious Practices in Temporal Perspective*, edited by Daniel Grana-Behrens, Nikolai Grube, Christian M. Prager, Frauke Sachse, Stefanie Teufel, and Elisabeth Wagner, pp. 33–39. Acta Mesoamericana 14. Verlag Anton Saurwein, Markt Schwaben, Germany.

2004b Architecture, Ritual and Temporal Dynamics at the Maya Center of Blue Creek, Belize. *Ancient Mesoamerica* 15(2):1–17.

2005 Shifting Centers of Authority in Chetumal Bay. In *New Approaches to Archaeological Research in Quintana Roo*, edited by Justine Shaw and Jennifer Mathews, pp. 183–196. University of Arizona Press, Tucson.

2006 E-Groups, Pseudo E-Groups, and the Development of the Classic Maya Identity in the Eastern Petén. *Ancient Mesoamerica* 17:1–8.

Guderjan, Thomas H. (editor)

1991 *Maya Settlement in Northwestern Belize: The 1988 and 1990 Seasons of the Rio Bravo Archaeological Project*. Labyrinthos, Culver City, California.

Guderjan, Thomas H., Jeffery Baker, and Robert J. Lichtenstein

2003 Environmental and Cultural Diversity at Blue Creek. In *Heterarchy, Political Economy, and the Ancient Maya: The Three Rivers Region of the East-Central Yucatán Peninsula*, edited by Vernon L. Scarborough, Fred Valdez, Jr., and Nicholas P. Dunning, pp. 77–91. University of Arizona Press, Tucson.

Guderjan, Thomas H., William Bedford, and Tim Preston

2002 Relocating Chocoha. *Mexicon* 24(5):88–89.

Guderjan, Thomas H., Steve Bozarth, David Glassman, Robert Lichtenstein, and Norbert Stanchley

2006 Mortuary Ritual in the Terminal Preclassic: Evidence from the Maya Site of Blue Creek, Belize. Manuscript on file. Maya Research Program, Texas Christian University, Fort Worth.

Guderjan, Thomas H., Lori B. Diel, Antoine Giacometti, and Elizabeth Andrews

2007 Maya Social Organization and the Implications of a Non-elite Burial at Blue Creek. *Ancient Mesoamerica*, in press.

Guderjan, Thomas H., and James F. Garber

1995 *Maya Maritime Trade, Settlement and Populations on Ambergris Caye, Belize*. Labyrinthos, Culver City, California.

Guderjan, Thomas, James F. Garber, and Herman A. Smith

1989 Maritime Trade on Ambergris Cay, Belize. In *Coastal Maya Trade and Exchange*, edited by Heather McKillop and Paul Healy, pp. 123–134. Occasional Papers in Archaeology 8. Trent University, Peterborough, Ontario.

Guderjan, Thomas H., Helen R. Haines, Michael Lindeman, Shirley Mock, Ellen Ruble, Froyla Salam, and Lea Worchester

1993 *Excavations at the Blue Creek Ruin, Northwestern Belize: 1992 Interim Report.* Maya Research Program, St. Mary's University, San Antonio, Texas.

Guderjan, Thomas, Helen R. Haines, Michael Lindeman, Ellen Ruble, Dale Pastrana, and Pam Weiss

1994 *Excavations at the Blue Creek Ruin, Northwestern Belize: 1993 Interim Report.* Maya Research Program, St. Mary's University, San Antonio, Texas.

Guderjan, Thomas H., and C. Colleen Hanratty

2006 A Thriving Non-Royal Lineage at Blue Creek: Evidence from a Sequence of Burials, Caches and Architecture. In *Jaws of the Underworld: Life, Death and Rebirth among the Ancient Maya,* edited by Pierre Colas, Geneviéve Le Fort, and Bodil Liljefors Persson, pp. 95–110. Acta Mesoamericana 16. Verlag Anton Saurwein, Markt Schwaben, Germany.

Guderjan, Thomas H., Robert J. Lichtenstein, and C. Colleen Hanratty

2003 Elite Residences at Blue Creek, Belize. In *Maya Palaces and Elite Residences,* edited by Jessica Christie, pp. 13–35. University of Texas Press, Austin.

Haines, Helen R.

1995 Summary of Excavations at the Temple of the Masks. In *Archaeological Research at Blue Creek, Belize. Progress Report of the Third (1994) Field Season,* edited by Thomas H. Guderjan and W. David Driver, pp. 73–95. Maya Research Program, St. Mary's University, San Antonio, Texas.

1996 1995 Season Excavations at Structure 9. In *Archaeological Research at Blue Creek, Belize. Progress Report of the Fourth (1995) Field Season,* edited by Thomas H. Guderjan, W. David Driver, and Helen R. Haines, pp. 59–68. Maya Research Program, St. Mary's University, San Antonio, Texas.

2000 Intra-Site Obsidian Distribution and Consumption Patterns in Northern Belize and the North-Eastern Petén. Unpublished Ph.D. dissertation, Institute of Archaeology, University College, London.

Hall, Grant D.

1987 The Discovery of Tomb 23 and Results of Two Other Tomb Investigations at Rio Azul, Season of 1985. In *Rio Azul Reports Number 3,* edited by Richard E. W. Adams, pp. 107–151. University of Texas, San Antonio.

1988 Realm of Death: Royal Mortuary Customs and Polity Interaction in the Classic Maya Lowlands. Unpublished Ph.D. dissertation, Department of Anthropology, Harvard University, Cambridge, Massachusetts.

Hammond, Norman

1983 Settlement Patterns in Belize. In *Lowland Maya Settlement Patterns,* edited by Wendy Ashmore, pp. 157–186. University of New Mexico Press, Albuquerque.

1987 *The Sun Also Rises: Iconographic Syntax of the Pomona Flare.* Research Report 7. Center for Maya Research, Washington, D.C.

1991 Jade and Greenstone Trade. In *Cuello: An Early Maya Community in Belize,* edited by Norman Hammond, pp. 199–203. Cambridge University Press, Cambridge.

Hammond, Norman, Arnold Aspinall, Stuart Feather, John Hazelden, Trevor Gazard, and Stuart Agrell

1977 Maya Jade: Source Location and Analysis. In *Exchange Systems in Prehistory,* edited by Timothy Earle and Jonathon Ericson, pp. 35–70. Academic Press, New York.

Hammond, Norman, Gair Tourtellot III, Sara Donaghey, and Amanda Clarke

1996 Survey and Excavation at La Milpa, Belize, 1996. *Mexicon* 18(5):86–90.

1998 No Slow Dusk: Urban Development and Decline at La Milpa, Belize. *Antiquity* 72:831–837.

Hanratty, C. Colleen

2002a Excavations in the Structure 37 Plazuela. In *The Blue Creek Project: Working Papers from the 1998 and 1999 Field Seasons,* edited by Thomas H. Guderjan and Robert J. Lichtenstein, pp. 73–80. Maya Research Program, Texas Christian University, Fort Worth.

2002b Kín Tan: Excavations in the Western Group at Blue Creek. Paper presented at the Annual Meeting of the Society for American Archaeology, Denver.

Hansen, Richard D., Steven R. Bozarth, John Jacob, David Wahl, and Thomas Schreiner

2002 Climate and Environmental Variability in the Rise of Maya Civilization: A Preliminary Perspective from Northern Peten. *Ancient Mesoamerica* 13(2):273–296.

Harlow, George E.

1993 Middle American Jade: Geologic and Petrologic Perspectives on Variability and Source. In *Precolumbian Jade: New Geological and Cultural Interpretations,* edited by Fredrick W. Lange, pp. 9–29. University of Utah Press, Salt Lake City.

Haviland, William A.

1983 Dower Houses and Minor Centers at Tikal, Guatemala: An Investigation into the Identification of Valid Units in Settlement Hierarchies. In *Lowland Maya Settlement Patterns,* edited by Wendy Ashmore, pp. 89–120. University of New Mexico Press, Albuquerque.

Healy, Paul L., John Lambert, J. T. Arnason, and Richard Hebda

1983 Caracol, Belize: Evidence of Ancient Maya Agricultural Terraces. *Journal of Field Archaeology* 10(4):397–410.

Hendon, Julia

1991 Status and Power in Maya Society: An Archaeological Study. *American Anthropologist* 93:894–919.

Hirth Kenneth G.

1996 Political Economy and Archaeology: Perspectives on Exchange and Production. *Journal of Archaeological Research* 4(3):203–239.

Hirth, Kenneth G., and Susan Grant Hirth

1993 Ancient Currency: The Style and Use of Jade and Marble Carvings in Central Honduras. In *Precolumbian Jade: New Geological and Cultural Interpretations,* edited by Fredrick W. Lange, pp. 173–190. University of Utah Press, Salt Lake City.

Hodder, Ian

1986 *Reading the Past: Current Approaches to Interpretation in Archaeology.* Cambridge University Press, Cambridge.

Houk, Brett

1996 The Archaeology of Site Planning: An Example from the Maya Site of Dos Hombres, Belize. Unpublished Ph.D. dissertation, Department of Anthropology, University of Texas, Austin.

Houk, Brett (editor)

1998 *The 1997 Season of the Chan Chich Archaeological Project.* Center for Maya Studies, San Antonio, Texas.

Hughbanks, Paul
1998 Settlement and Agriculture at Guijeral, Northwest Belize. *Culture and Agriculture* 20(2/3):107–120.
Johnson, C. A., and George E. Harlow
1999 Guatemalan Jadeites and Albites Were Formed by Deuterium-Rich Serpentizing Fluids Deep within a Sub-duction Zone. *Geology* 27(7):629–632.
Kepecs, Susan, and Sylviane Boucher
1996 The Pre-Hispanic Cultivation of Rejolladas and Stonelands: New Evidence from Northeast Yucatan. In *The Managed Mosaic: Ancient Maya Agriculture and Resource Use,* edited by Scott Fedick, pp. 69–91. University of Utah Press, Salt Lake City.
Killion, Thomas W.
1992 The Archaeology of Settlement Agriculture. In *Gardens of Prehistory,* edited by Thomas W. Killion, pp. 1–13. University of Alabama Press, Tuscaloosa.
Kosakowsky, Laura J., and Jon C. Lohse
2003 Investigating Multivariate Ceramic Attributes as Clues to Ancient Maya Social, Economic, and Political Organization in Blue Creek, Northwestern Belize. Report submitted to the Ahau Foundation, Albuquerque.
Kresjci, Estella, and T. Patrick Culbert
1995 Preclassic and Classic Burials and Caches in the Maya Area. In *The Emergence of Lowland Maya Civilization,* edited by Nikolai Grube, pp. 103–116. Acta Mesoamericana 8. Verlag Anton Saurwein, Mockmuhl, Germany.
Kunen, Julie
2003 *Ancient Maya Life in the Far West Bajo: Social and Environmental Change in the Wetlands of Belize.* Anthropological Paper 69. University of Arizona Press, Tucson.
Landa, Bishop Diego de
1978 *Yucatan before and after the Conquest.* Dover Publications, New York. Originally published 1938, The Maya Society, Baltimore.
Levi, Laura
2006 Houses and Society in the Maya Lowlands. Paper presented at the Annual Meeting of the Society for American Archaeology, San Juan, Puerto Rico.
Lichtenstein, Robert J.
1996 Preliminary Report of the Excavation of the Structure 19 Courtyard. In *Archaeological Research at Blue Creek, Belize. Progress Report of the Fourth (1995) Field Season,* edited by Thomas H. Guderjan, W. David Driver, and Helen R. Haines, pp. 78–84. Maya Research Program, St. Mary's University, San Antonio, Texas.
1997 Structure 19 Courtyard. In *The Blue Creek Project: Working Papers from the 1996 Field Season,* edited by W. David Driver, Heather L. Clagett, and Helen R. Haines, pp. 39–50. Maya Research Program, St. Mary's University, San Antonio, Texas.
2000a Tomb 5, A Late Preclassic Elite Burial at the Blue Creek Ruin. Paper presented at the Annual Meeting of the Society for American Archaeology, Philadelphia.
2000b *Settlement Zone Communities of the Greater Blue Creek Area.* Occasional Paper 2. Maya Research Program, Texas Christian University, Fort Worth.
2002 The Blue Creek Project Classification System. In *The Blue Creek Project: Working Papers from the 1998 and 1999 Field Seasons,* edited by Thomas H. Guderjan and Robert Lichtenstein, pp. 37–48. Maya Research Program, Texas Christian University, Fort Worth, Texas.

Lichtenstein, Robert J., and C. Colleen Hanratty
2002 An Introduction to the Western Group. In *The Blue Creek Project: Working Papers from the 1998 and 1999 Field Seasons,* edited by Thomas H. Guderjan and Robert J. Lichtenstein, pp. 69–72. Maya Research Program, Texas Christian University, Fort Worth.

Lohse, Jon C.
2001 The Social Organization of a Late Classic Maya Community: Dos Hombres, Belize. Unpublished Ph.D. dissertation, Department of Anthropology, University of Texas, Austin.

Lohse, Jon C., and Kerry Sagebiel (editors)
2005 *2004 Season Summaries of the Blue Creek Regional Political Ecology Project, Upper Northwestern Belize.* Maya Research Program, Texas Christian University, Fort Worth.

Lohse, Jon C., and Fred Valdez, Jr. (editors)
2004 *Ancient Maya Commoners.* University of Texas Press, Austin.

McAnany, Patricia
1993 The Economics of Social Power and Wealth among Eighth Century Maya Households. In *Lowland Maya Civilization in the Eighth Century A.D.,* edited by Jeremy Sabloff and John Henderson, pp. 65–90. Dumbarton Oaks, Washington, D.C.
1995 *Living with the Ancestors: Kinship and Kingship in Ancient Maya Society.* University of Texas Press, Austin.

McKillop, Heather I.
1996 Ancient Maya Trading Ports and the Integration of Long-Distance and Regional Economies: Wild Cane Cay in South-Coastal Belize. *Ancient Mesoamerica* 7:49–62.
2002 *Salt: White Gold of the Maya.* University Press of Florida, Gainesville.
2003 The Classic Maya Trading Port of Moho Cay. In *The Ancient Maya of the Belize Valley: Half a Century of Archaeological Research,* edited by James F. Garber, pp. 257–272. University Press of Florida, Gainesville.

McKillop, Heather I., and Paul Healy
1989 *Coastal Maya Trade.* Occasional Papers in Anthropology 8. Trent University, Petersboro, Ontario.

MacKinnon, Jefferson, and Susan Kepecs
1989 Prehispanic Salt-Making in Belize: New Evidence. *American Antiquity* 54:522–533.

Malinowski, Bronslaw
1920 Kula: The Circulating Exchange of Valuables in the Archipelagos of Eastern New Guinea. *Man* 51:97–105.
1922 *Argonauts of the Western Pacific.* Routledge and Kegan Paul, London.
1978 Melanesian and Australian Exchange Systems: A View from Mesoamerica. *Mankind* 11:165–174.

Marcus, Joyce
1983 On the Nature of the Mesoamerican City. In *Prehistoric Settlement Patterns: Essays in Honor of Gordon R. Willey,* edited by E. Z. Vogt and R. Levanthal, pp. 195–242. University of New Mexico Press, Albuquerque.
2004 Maya Commoners: The Stereotype and the Reality. In *Ancient Maya Commoners,* edited by Jon C. Lohse and Fred Valdez, Jr., pp. 255–284. University of Texas Press, Austin.

Masson, Marilyn A.
2002 Introduction. In *Ancient Maya Political Economies,* edited by Marilyn A. Masson and David A. Freidel, pp. 1–30. AltaMira Press, Walnut Creek, California.

Masson, Marilyn A., and David A. Freidel (editors)
2002 *Ancient Maya Political Economies.* AltaMira Press, Walnut Creek, California.

Matheny, Raymond T., D. E. Gurr, Donald W. Forsyth, and F. R. Hauck
1980 *Investigations at Edzna, Campeche, Mexico,* Vol. 1, Pt. 2: *Maps.* New World Archaeological Foundation, Brigham Young University, Provo, Utah.

Mathews, Jennifer P.
1998 The Ties That Bind: The Ancient Maya Interaction Spheres of the Late Preclassic and Early Classic Periods in the Northern Yucatan Peninsula. Unpublished Ph.D. dissertation, Department of Anthropology, University of California, Riverside.

Mathews, Jennifer, and James F. Garber
2004 Models of Cosmic Order: Physical Expression of Sacred Space among the Ancient Maya. *Ancient Mesoamerica* 15(1):49–59.

Maxwell, David
1996 An Analysis of Caches from Four Sites in the Maya Lowlands. Unpublished Ph.D. dissertation, University of Arizona, Tucson.

Meadows, Richard
2000 Archaeological Excavations at Group H: Investigating Craft Production and Domestic Architecture at Chan Chich, Belize. In *The 1998 and 1999 Season of the Chan Chich Archaeological Project,* edited by Brett A. Houk, pp. 15–39. Middle American Archaeological Research Laboratory, University of Texas, Austin.

Miller, Mary Ellen, and Karl Taube
1993 *The Gods and Symbols of Ancient Mexico and the Maya.* Thames and Hudson, New York.

Mock, Shirley Boteler (editor)
1998 *The Sowing and the Dawning: Termination, Dedication and Transformation in the Archaeological and Ethnographic Record of Mesoamerica.* University of New Mexico Press, Albuquerque.

Moholy-Nagy, Hatula
1994 Tikal Material Culture: Artifacts and Social Structure at a Classic Lowland Maya City. Unpublished Ph.D. dissertation, University of Michigan, Ann Arbor.

Neivens, Mary
1991 Operations at Blue Creek. In *Maya Settlement in Northwestern Belize: The 1988 and 1990 Seasons of the Rio Bravo Archaeological Project,* edited by Thomas H. Guderjan, pp. 51–54. Labyrinthos, Culver City, California.

Padilla, Antonio, Molly Morgan, and Jon Lohse
2006 2005 Season Excavations at Akab Muclil, Northwestern Belize. In *Final Season Summaries of the Blue Creek Political Ecology Project: 2005 Investigations in Upper Northwestern Belize,* edited by Jon C. Lohse, pp. 12–39. Maya Research Program, Texas Christian University, Fort Worth, and the University of Texas, Austin.

Pastrana, Dale Victoria
1995 Excavations at Structures 5 and 6. In *Archaeological Research at Blue Creek, Belize. Progress Report of the Third (1994) Field Season,* edited by Thomas H. Guderjan and W. David Driver, pp. 63–72. Maya Research Program, St. Mary's University, San Antonio, Texas.

1999 An Analysis of Jades from the Structure 4 Shaft Cache. *The Blue Creek Project: Working Papers from the 1997 Field Season,* edited by W. David Driver, Helen R. Haines, and Thomas H. Guderjan, pp. 43–59. Maya Research Program, St. Mary's University, San Antonio, Texas.

Pendergast, David M.

1979 *Excavations at Altun Ha, Belize, 1964–1970,* Vol. 1. Royal Ontario Museum, Toronto.

1981 Lamanai, Belize: Summary of Excavation Results, 1974–1980. *Journal of Field Archaeology* 8(1):29–53.

1982 *Excavations at Altun Ha, Belize, 1964–1970,* Vol. 2. Royal Ontario Museum, Toronto.

1986 Stability through Change: Lamanai, Belize from the Ninth to the Seventeenth Century. In *Late Lowland Maya Civilization,* edited by Jeremy A. Sabloff and E. Wyllis Andrews, pp. 223–250. University of New Mexico Press, Albuquerque.

1991 Up from the Dust: The Central Lowlands Postclassic as Seen from Lamanai and Marco Gonzalez, Belize. In *Vision and Revision in Maya Studies,* edited by Flora S. Clancy and Peter D. Harrison. University of New Mexico Press, Albuquerque.

1992 Noblesse Oblige: The Elites of Altun Ha and Lamanai, Belize. In *Mesoamerican Elites: An Archaeological Perspective,* edited by Diane Z. Chase and Arlen D. Chase, pp. 61–79. University of Oklahoma Press, Norman.

Peregrine, Peter

1991 Prehistoric Chiefdoms on the American Mid-Continent: A World System Based on Prestige Goods. In *Core/Periphery Relations in Precapitalist Worlds,* edited by C. Chase-Dunn and T. Hall, pp. 193–211. Westview Press, Boulder, Colorado.

Peregrine, Peter, and Gary Feinman

1996 *Pre-columbian World Systems.* Prehistory Press, Madison, Wisconsin.

Popson, Colleen

2000 Political Economy of the Community of Chan Cahal at the Maya Center of Blue Creek, Belize. Unpublished M.A. thesis, State University of New York, Albany.

Popson, Colleen, and Jeffrey Baker

1999 Beneath the Escarpment: Settlement and Subsistence on the Rio Bravo Floodplain. Paper presented at the Annual Meeting of the Society for American Archaeology, Chicago.

Popson, Colleen, James Mower, and Demori Currid

2000 Excavations at Chan Cahal. Manuscript on file. Maya Research Program, Texas Christian University, Fort Worth.

Proskouriakoff, Tatania

1974 *Jades from the Cenote of Sacrifice, Chichen Itza, Yucatan.* Memoirs of the Peabody Museum of Archaeology and Ethnology, Vol. 10, No. 1. Harvard University, Cambridge.

Puleston, Dennis

1973 Ancient Maya Settlement Patterns at Tikal. Unpublished Ph.D. dissertation, Department of Anthropology, University of Pennsylvania, Philadelphia.

1974 Intersite Areas in the Vicinity of Tikal and Uaxactun. In *Mesoamerican Archaeology: New Approaches,* edited by Norman Hammond, pp. 303–310. University of Texas Press, Austin.

1983 *The Settlement Survey of Tikal.* Tikal Report 13. University Museum, University of Pennsylvania, Philadelphia.

Pyburn, Anne K.
1988 The Settlement of Nohmul: Development of a Prehispanic Community in Northern Belize. Unpublished Ph.D. dissertation, Department of Anthropology, University of Arizona, Tucson.

Rathje, William L.
1970 Socio-political Implications of Lowland Maya Burials: Methodology and Tentative Hypotheses. *World Archaeology* 1:359–374.
1972 Praise the Gods and Pass the Metates. In *Contemporary Archaeology: A Guide to Theory and Contributions,* edited by Mark P. Leone, pp. 365–392. Southern Illinois University Press, Carbondale.

Rathje, William L., and Jeremy A. Sabloff
1973 Ancient Maya Commercial Systems: A Research Design for the Island of Cozumel, Mexico. *World Archaeology* 5(2):221–231.

Redfield, Robert, and Alfonso Villa Rojas
1934 *Chan Kom: A Maya Village.* Carnegie Institute of Washington, Washington, D.C.

Reilly, F. Kent III
1994 La Venta and the Olmec: The Function of Sacred Geography in the Formative Period Ceremonial Complex. Unpublished Ph.D. dissertation, Department of Latin American Studies, University of Texas, Austin.

Renaud, Jason, and Colleen Popson
1997 Initial Investigations at the Indian Creek Site. In *The Blue Creek Project: Working Papers from the 1996 Field Season,* edited by W. David Driver, Heather L. Clagett, and Helen R. Haines, pp. 87–88. Maya Research Program, St. Mary's University, San Antonio, Texas.

Rice, Prudence M.
2004 *Maya Political Science: Time, Astronomy and the Cosmos.* University of Texas Press, Austin.

Ricketson, Oliver G.
1928 Astronomical Observatories in the Maya Area. *The Geographic Review* 18(2): 215–229.

Ricketson, Oliver G., and E. B. Ricketson
1937 *Uaxactun, Guatemala, Group E, 1926–1937.* Publication 477. Carnegie Institute of Washington, Washington, D.C.

Robertson, Robin A., and David A. Freidel
1986 *Archaeology at Cerros, Volume I: An Interim Report.* Southern Methodist University Press, Dallas.

Robichaux, Hubert C.
1995 Ancient Maya Community Patterns in Northwestern Belize: Peripheral Zone Survey of La Milpa and Dos Hombres. Unpublished Ph.D. dissertation, Department of Anthropology, University of Texas, Austin.
1998 Excavations in the Upper Plaza. In *The 1997 Season of the Chan Chich Archaeological Project,* edited by Brett A. Houk, pp. 31–52. Center for Maya Studies, San Antonio, Texas.

Roys, Lawrence, and Edwin M. Shook
1966 *Preliminary Report on the Ruins of Aké, Yucatan.* Memoir 20. Society for American Archaeology, Kenosha, Wisconsin.

Roys, Ralph L.
1954 *Political Geography of the Yucatec Maya.* Carnegie Institute of Washington, Washington, D.C.
1965 Lowland Maya Native Society at Contact. In *Handbook of Middle American Indians,* Vol. 3, edited by Gordon R. Willey, pp. 659–678. University of Texas Press, Austin.
Sabloff, Jeremy A.
1977 Old Myths, New Myths: The Role of Sea Traders in the Development of the Maya Civilization. In *The Sea and the Precolumbian World,* edited by Elizabeth Benson. Dumbarton Oaks, Washington, D.C.
Sabloff, Jeremy A., and William L. Rathje
1975a The Rise of a Maya Merchant Class. *Scientific American* 233(4):73–82.
1975b *A Study of Changing Pre-Columbian Commercial Systems: The 1972–1973 Seasons at Cozumel, Mexico.* Peabody Museum, Harvard University, Cambridge.
Sagebiel, Kerry
2005 Shifting Allegiances at La Milpa, Belize: A Typological, Chronological and Formal Analysis of the Ceramics. Unpublished Ph.D. dissertation, Department of Anthropology, University of Arizona, Tucson.
Sahlins, Marshall
1972 *Stone Age Economics.* Aldine de Gruyter, New York.
Sanders, William T., and David Webster
1988 The Mesoamerican Urban Tradition. *American Anthropologist* 90(3):521–546.
Santley, Robert S., Michael J. Berman, and Rani Alexander
1991 The Politicization of the Mesoamerican Ballgame and Its Implications for the Interpretation of the Distribution of Ballcourts in Central Mexico. In *The Mesoamerican Ballgame,* edited by Vernon L. Scarborough and David R. Wilcox, pp. 3–24. University of Arizona Press, Tucson.
Scarborough, Vernon L.
1991 *Archaeology at Cerros, Belize, Central America,* Vol. III: *The Settlement System in a Late Preclassic Maya Community.* Southern Methodist University Press, Dallas.
1992 Flow of Power: Water Reservoirs Controlled the Rise and Fall of the Ancient Maya. *Science* 32(2):38–43.
Scarborough, Vernon L., Matthew E. Becher, Jeffrey L. Baker, Garry Harris, and Fred Valdez, Jr.
1995 Water and Land at the Ancient Maya Community of La Milpa. *Latin American Antiquity* 6(2):98–119.
Scarborough, Vernon L., and G. Gallopin
1991 A Water Storage Adaptation in the Maya Lowlands. *Science* 251:658–662.
Scarborough, Vernon L., and Fred Valdez, Jr.
2003 The Engineered Environment and Political Economy of the Three Rivers Region. In *Heterarchy, Political Economy, and the Ancient Maya: The Three Rivers Region of the East-Central Yucatán Peninsula,* edited by Vernon L. Scarborough, Fred Valdez, Jr., and Nicholas P. Dunning, pp. 3–13. University of Arizona Press, Tucson.
Scarborough, Vernon L., Fred Valdez, Jr., and Nicholas P. Dunning (editors)
2003 *Heterarchy, Political Economy, and the Ancient Maya: The Three Rivers Region of the East-Central Yucatán Peninsula.* University of Arizona Press, Tucson.

Scarborough, Vernon L., and David R. Wilcox (editors)
1991 *The Mesoamerican Ballgame.* University of Arizona Press, Tucson.

Schele, Linda, and David Freidel
1990 *A Forest of Kings.* Morrow, New York.

Schmidt, Peter, Mercedes de la Garza, and Enrique Nalda
1998 *Maya.* Rizzola International, New York.

Shafer, Harry, and Thomas Hester
1983 Ancient Maya Chert Workshops on Northern Belize, Central America. *American Antiquity* 48:519–543.

Stuart, David
1991 The Iconography of Flowers among the Classic Maya. Manuscript on file. Vanderbilt University, Nashville.

Tate, Carolyn
1995 Art in Olmec Culture. In *The Olmec World: Ritual and Rulership.* The Art Museum, Princeton University, Princeton, New Jersey.

Taube, Karl
2005 The Symbolism of Jade among the Classic Maya. *Ancient Mesoamerica* 16(1):23–50.

Thompson, J. Eric S.
1939 *Excavations at San Jose, British Honduras.* Carnegie Institute of Washington, Washington, D.C.
1954 *The Rise and Fall of Maya Civilization.* University of Oklahoma Press, Norman.

Tourtellot, Gair
1988 *Excavations at Seibal, Department of Petén, Guatemala. Peripheral Survey and Excavation: Settlement Patterns and Community Patterns.* Peabody Museum of Archaeology and Ethnology, Harvard University, Cambridge.
1990 Population Estimates for Preclassic and Classic Seibal, Peten. In *Precolumbian Population History in the Maya Lowlands,* edited by T. Patrick Culbert and Don S. Rice, pp. 83–102. University of New Mexico Press, Albuquerque.

Tourtellot, Gair, Francisco Estrada-Bella, John J. Rose, and Norman Hammond
2003 Late Classic Maya Heterarchy, Hierarchy, and Landscape at La Milpa, Belize. In *Heterarchy, Political Economy, and the Ancient Maya: The Three Rivers Region of the East-Central Yucatán Peninsula,* edited by Vernon L. Scarborough, Fred Valdez, Jr., and Nicholas P. Dunning, pp. 37–51. University of Arizona Press, Tucson.

Tourtellot, Gair, Gloria Everson, and Norman Hammond
2003 Suburban Organization: Minor Centers at La Milpa, Belize. In *Perspectives on Ancient Maya Rural Complexity,* edited by Gylles Iannone and Samuel V. Connell, pp. 94–107. Monograph 49. Cotsen Institute of Archaeology, University of California, Los Angeles.

Turner, B. L. II
1990 Population Reconstruction for the Central Maya Lowlands: 1000 B.C. to A.D. 1500. In *Precolumbian Population History in the Maya Lowlands,* edited by T. Patrick Culbert and Don S. Rice, pp. 301–324. University of New Mexico Press, Albuquerque.

Wagner, Elisabeth
2000 An Alternative View on the Meaning and Function of Structure 22A, Copan, Honduras. In *The Sacred and the Profane: Architecture and Identity in the Maya Low-*

lands, edited by P. R. Colas, Kai Delvendahl, Marcus Kuhnert, and Annette Schubart, pp. 25–50. Acta Mesoamericana 10. Verlag Anton Saurwein, Markt Schwaben, Germany.

Wallerstein, Immanuel
1974 *The Modern World System.* Academic Press, New York.

Webster, David L.
1989 *The House of the Bacabs, Copan, Honduras.* Dumbarton Oaks, Washington, D.C.

Webster, David, and AnnCorrine Freter
1990 The Demography of Late Classic Copan. In *Precolumbian Population History in the Maya Lowlands,* edited by T. Patrick Culbert and Don S. Rice, pp. 37–62. University of New Mexico Press, Albuquerque.

Weiss, Pamela
1995 Architecture and Ritual at Structure 4. In *Archaeological Research at Blue Creek, Belize. Progress Report of the Third (1994) Field Season,* edited by Thomas H. Guderjan and W. David Driver, pp. 45–62. Maya Research Program, St. Mary's University, San Antonio, Texas.
1996 The Continuation of Excavations at Structure 4. In *Archaeological Research at Blue Creek, Belize. Progress Report of the Fourth (1995) Field Season,* edited by Thomas H. Guderjan, W. David Driver, and Helen R. Haines, pp. 37–42. Maya Research Program, St. Mary's University, San Antonio, Texas.

Williams-Beck, Lorraine A.
1998 Whole Vessels from Blue Creek. Manuscript on file. Maya Research Program, Texas Christian University, Fort Worth.

Yaeger, Jason
2000a Changing Patterns of Social Organization: The Late and Terminal Classic Communities of San Lorenzo, Cayo District, Belize. Unpublished Ph.D. dissertation, Department of Anthropology, University of Pennsylvania, Philadelphia.
2000b The Social Construction of Communities in the Maya Countryside: Strategies of Affiliation in Western Belize. In *The Archaeology of Communities: A New World Perspective,* edited by Marcella A. Canuto and Jason Yaeger, pp. 123–142. Routledge, London.

Young, Biloine Whiting, and Melvin L. Fowler
1999 *Cahokia, The Great American Metropolis.* University of Illinois Press, Urbana.

Index

www.ingramcontent.com/pod-product-compliance
Lightning Source LLC
LaVergne TN
LVHW051421090926
847619LV00027B/250
9780817354268